THE EVOLUTION OF THE TANK

ASSYRIAN ARMED CAR

As shown on the bronze bands taken from gates of Shalmaneser II, King of Assyria, 860–825 B.C.

British Museum

THE EVOLUTION OF THE TANK

A RECORD OF ROYAL NAVAL AIR SERVICE CATERPILLAR EXPERIMENTS

By

Rear-Admiral SIR MURRAY SUETER,
C.B., M.P.

Hon. Mentioned R.U.S.I. Prize Essay 1904, Technical Papers on Air Subjects; Formerly Inspecting Captain of Airships, 1909–1912; Delegate to International Conference on Aerial Navigation held at Paris, 1910; Director of Admiralty Air Department, 1912–1915; Member of First War Air Committee; Superintendent of Aircraft Construction, 1915–1917; In Command of R.N.A.S. Units, Southern Italy, 1917–1918.

With 61 *Illustrations*

The Naval & Military Press Ltd

Published by

The Naval & Military Press Ltd
Unit 5 Riverside, Brambleside
Bellbrook Industrial Estate
Uckfield, East Sussex
TN22 1QQ England

Tel: +44 (0)1825 749494

www.naval-military-press.com
www.nmarchive.com

In reprinting in facsimile from the original, any imperfections are inevitably reproduced and the quality may fall short of modern type and cartographic standards.

DEDICATION

The TANK, as employed in the Great War and the forerunner of present Mechanized Armament, was developed from the Armoured Car Experiments of the Royal Naval Air Service.

To the Air and Armoured Car Officers associated with me in the great struggle we had in bringing our caterpillar landship ideas to fruition I dedicate this book.

> "I speak bare truth,
> as if to thee in private talk."
>
> WORDSWORTH.

PREFACE

FROM those in the best position to judge I was informed that my book—*Airmen or Noahs*—had considerable useful propaganda value at a time when it was much needed and may have caused some discomfiture to Noahs, with whom we are too well supplied in this country.

Since the War, autobiographical inquests have been many and I have had no desire to add further to the number, but my friends have pressed me hard on many occasions to write a simple record of the evolution of the Tank.

Yielding to this pressure and in the interests of historical truth, I offer this book as a small contribution to Tank literature.

ACKNOWLEDGMENT

The Author's grateful thanks are due to Major Beak, late Royal Tank Corps, and Mr. H. Gray for their great kindness in reading through the first draft of this book and offering valuable suggestions. Also the Admiralty and War Office are cordially thanked for giving permission to publish some of the Official papers and plates.

CONTENTS

	PAGE
PREFACE	7
INTRODUCTION	13

PART I

CHAPTER I

PRELIMINARY RESEARCHES AND IDEAS 27
  (1) The first Royal Naval Air Service armoured cars and shields.
  (2) The first landship proposals.
  (3) Flight-Commander Hetherington's giant land battleship idea.
  (4) Mr. Winston Churchill's steam-roller suggestions.

CHAPTER II

THE FIRST CATERPILLAR EXPERIMENTS 59
  (1) The creation of confidence in caterpillar machines for war purposes.
  (2) The first Royal Naval Air Service caterpillar landship.

CHAPTER III

THE TANK TAKES FORM 85
  (1) Mr. Tritton's and Lieutenant Wilson's fine success.
  (2) Colonel Crompton's and Mr. le Gros' contribution.
  (3) Lieutenant Macfie's and Mr. Nesfield's angularized caterpillar track invention.
  (4) Colonel Swinton's specification.

CHAPTER IV

TANKS IN ACTION 118
  (1) British opinion on value of Tanks.
  (2) French opinion on value of Tanks.
  (3) German opinion on value of Tanks.

CHAPTER V

TANKS OF TO-DAY 148
   (1) Modern Tanks revert to Royal Naval Air Service type.
   (2) Foreign Nations annex the Tank invention.

PART II

CHAPTER I

TO WHOM THE CREDIT? 177

CHAPTER II

THE CLAIMS OF THE ROYAL NAVAL AIR SERVICE . . . 217

CHAPTER III

MAINLY PERSONAL 239

CHAPTER IV

TANKS OF THE FUTURE 287

CHAPTER V

CONCLUSION 302

APPENDIX I

SPEECHES WHEN INTRODUCING MINISTRY OF DEFENCE CREATION BILL . 321
   The need for forging the right weapons of war—Tanks for working with Artillery—Heavy Tanks and light Tanks.

APPENDIX II

MINISTRY OF DEFENCE CREATION BILL 334

APPENDIX III

SOME PRESS OPINIONS ON DEFENCE DEBATE 340

INDEX 347

LIST OF ILLUSTRATIONS

	Assyrian Armed Car . . . . . *Frontispiece*	
PLATE		FACING PAGE
I.	Experiment with Steel Plate to resist Patent Bullet	30
II.	Experiment with Special Steel Plate to resist British Service Bullet	30
III.	Experiment with Special Steel Plate to resist British and German Bullets.	31
IV.	Experiment with Special Steel Plate to resist German Bullet-point First and Reversed . .	31
V.	First Royal Naval Air Service Armoured Car (Open Type).	32
VI.	Rolls-Royce Armoured Car (Revolving Turret Type)	32
VII.	Royal Naval Air Service Heavy Armoured Car (Closed)	33
VIII.	Heavy Armoured Car with Side Armour Down .	33
IX.	Royal Air Force Machine giving Information to Armoured Car Section	44
X.	Royal Naval Air Service Infantry Shield . .	45
XI.	Captain Robert Scott's Antarctic Sleigh . .	66
XII.	Lanchester Armoured Car	66
XIII.	The Diplock Caterpillar Truck	66
XIV.	Experiments with Killen Strait Machine . .	74
XV.	Killen Strait over Railway Metals . . .	74
XVI.	Killen Strait over Railway Sleepers . . .	74
XVII.	Demonstration of the Killen Strait before Mr. Lloyd George when Minister of Munitions . . .	75
XVIII.	Killen Strait cutting through Barbed Wire . .	75
XIX.	Experiments with Bullock Creeping Grip Caterpillar Tractors	78
XX.	Bullock Tractors crossing a Trench . . .	78
XXI.	Bullock Tractors. Front Wheels off Ground .	79
XXII.	Showing Sag of Caterpillar Track . . .	79
XXIII.	Two Bullock Creeping Grip Tractors coupled together	79
XXIV.	Captain F. M. Boothby, C.B.E., R.N. . . .	82
XXV.	The First Royal Naval Air Service Caterpillar Landship	82
XXVI.	Another View of First Royal Naval Air Service Caterpillar Landship mounted on the Bullock Tracks .	82

LIST OF ILLUSTRATIONS

PLATE		FACING PAGE
XXVII.	Experiments with First Royal Naval Air Service Caterpillar Landship	83
XXVIII.	Experiments with Second Design of Caterpillar Landship	88
XXIX.	The First Royal Naval Air Service Caterpillar Landship nicknamed "Big Willie"	88
XXX.	The First Rhomboidal Tank	89
XXXI.	Tank Experiments at Hatfield Park	89
XXXII.	The Angularised Caterpillar Track Model	120
XXXIII.	Tank in Action. Bow On	121
XXXIV.	Tank in Action negotiating Rough Terrain	121
XXXV.	The Aldershot Review. Salute of Tanks	152
XXXVI.	British Light Tank Mark V	153
XXXVII.	French Tanks	158
XXXVIII.	Medium Tanks, United States	159
XXXIX.	Light Tanks, United States	159
XL.	Italian Tanks	166
XLI.	German Tanks climbing	167
XLII.	German Tank, showing Angularized Track	167
XLIII.	Belgium, New Light Tank	168
XLIV.	Russian Tanks	169
XLV.	Japanese Tanks	170
XLVI.	Poland, 6-ton Tank; Smoke-screen Tank	171
XLVII.	Czechoslovakia, 6-ton Tank	172
XLVIII.	Sweden, 11-ton Tank	172
XLIX.	Austrian Light Tank	173
L.	Afghanistan Tanks	173
LI.	Admiral Bacon's Trench Bridging Machine	186
LII.	Squadron of Royal Naval Air Service Armoured Cars	186
LIII.	French Anti-Tank Gun	187
LIV.	British 12-ton Tank	294
LV.	Five 12-ton Tanks firing at Lulworth	295

DIAGRAMS

I. The First Conception of the Royal Naval Air Service Caterpillar Landship . . . 67
This drawing was laid before the Admiralty Landship Committee on 4th March, 1915, and is the first authentic drawing of a Caterpillar Landship laid before Authority in the Great War.

II. The Body of a Revolving Turret Armoured Car was placed upon the Killen Strait Caterpillar Machine, July, 1915 . . . *page* 238

INTRODUCTION

HISTORY teaches us that, generally speaking, fighting men throughout the ages have been equally courageous, and the success one side or the other has achieved was in part due to a small body of men, or sometimes a single man, who adapted the science of the period to produce a flint axe, a spear, sword or some new weapon of war.

In the early Assyrian days, the protective quilted coats, wicker-work and wooden shields were no doubt most useful in the conflicts of that period in keeping out a thrust with a spear or a cut with a sword; the body-armour of the Spartans was similarly useful.

One of the earliest armed chariots to be invented is shown on the Bronze Bands taken from the gates of Shalmaneser II, King of Assyria, 860 B.C. to 825 B.C. These, on close examination at the British Museum, show quite clearly a wheeled vehicle with archers standing up in it, the chariot being provided with a heavy ram probably made of wood sheathed with sheet metal (frontispiece). This specially constructed armoured ram was no doubt used for breaking through a door, the side of a citadel or stockade, and presented at that period a formidable weapon of war against defences of no great fighting strength. In the Old Testament, the first chapter of Judges, verse 19, we find "a chariot of iron" is mentioned. This must have been a very powerful weapon for the verse runs:

> And the Lord was with Judah and He drove out the inhabitants of the mountains, but could not drive out the inhabitants of the valley because they had chariots of iron.

At a later date, the chariot of Britain's Warrior Queen, Boadicea, was developed for war purposes.

The invention of the scythe fixed to the axle made this chariot a formidable weapon when drawn by fiery horses, and we are told it played a very important part against Nero's legions when our celebrated War Queen burnt Roman London and in so doing secured better treatment for the tribes she then ruled in Britain. A statue to Queen Boadicea's memory, showing her war chariot ever rushing forward to battle, is erected beneath the shadow of Big Ben Clock Tower on the Thames Embankment, and upon it is inscribed these inspiring words:

> " Regions Cæsar never knew
> Thy posterity shall sway."

From a study of more recent wars in many Countries, whenever the attackers were held up by great fortifications from which the defenders made themselves exceedingly unpleasant to their enemy, various siege devices were evolved by the attackers to wear down the resistance of those within the fortifications. Catapults, battering-rams, moving towers on wheels show the resourcefulness of the attackers in developing new weapons of war. The Tseudo or Tortoise was brought into being and formed a useful means of giving shelter when pressing an attack to within close quarters of the armed citadel.

Pikes, lances, long-bow and cross-bow are weapons which have proved of great use in their day in bringing hostilities to a conclusion.

At the battle of Crécy victory went to the light archers over the more heavily-armoured horsemen, and at Falkirk the English bowmen broke up the finest spearmen of Scotland. It is common knowledge that the invention of gunpowder made obsolete for all time some of the weapons then in use for close-quarter fighting, and eventually swept away the feudal system.

Many visitors to Edinburgh Castle have seen the famous piece of ordnance named Mons Meg, which is constructed on the same principle as modern ordnance of large calibre. It is a relic of the fifteenth century and was constructed of iron coils or sections overlapping one another. It measures 13 ft. in length, 7 ft. in circumference, 20 in. calibre, and weighs some five tons. James II in 1455 granted to

Brawny Tim, the smith who made it, the lands of Mollance, and his wife's name being Meg—hence the corruption "Mons Meg." I mention this piece of ordnance as even in the fifteenth century rewards were given to the inventor of a new weapon.

Lord Palmerston was pressed to adopt a mechanically propelled vehicle invented by James Cowan in 1885, which was described in a provisional protection as a locomotive land battery fitted with scythes to mow down infantry in the same manner as Queen Boadicea's war chariot. Then Mr. H. G. Wells, in an article in the *Strand Magazine*,[1] visualized a "Land Ironclad" like a large blockhouse 80 to 100 ft. in length that could cross trenches by means of many Diplock Pedrails.

In the autumn of 1914 it appeared to many that the war Germany had forced upon this Country would last a very long time and not be over in a few months as some people at the time predicted. The waste of wealth in firing millions of shells was nothing when compared to our great losses in human life then becoming very heavy. The flower of our manhood was being sapped and we were up against the stiffest problem this Country has ever been called upon to face. The sacrifices made in the Nation's interest were superb. Many of us lost not only relatives but our best "pals" from boyhood days. Consequently several thinking men, such as the very able Secretary of the Committee of Imperial Defence, Captain Maurice Hankey, and others, began to consider whether any new device or new weapon of war could be introduced which would help to lessen our casualties and, if possible, assist in shortening the war.

From our Naval experience Hankey, and myself knew how much we rely on armour protection in our ships. Towards the end of 1914 I showed Hankey in my Admiralty Air Office the wooden mock-up of a mobile infantry shield that Mr. Buckham[2] of Messrs. Vickers had prepared for me. This demonstration showed that two men, widely separated from each other in war work, were discussing the necessity for the provision of some form of armour

---

[1] *Strand Magazine*, December, 1903.
[2] Afterwards the late Sir George Buckham, Chief Ordnance Designer and Director of Vickers Ltd.

protection for the infantry and thereby help to minimise our great losses in human life at the Front.

Although we are a mechanically-minded race and make the best machinery in the whole World, we never seem to excel at inventing new weapons of war, for did we not have to go to America for the famous Holland design of submarine boat and build five of this type at Messrs. Vickers' works at Barrow-in-Furness for the British Navy in 1901–2 when we commenced our Submarine Service?

Again, we went to America for the bolt-action rifle in the early 'eighties and adopted Lee's invention. Even our machine-gun designs, such as the Gatling, Maxim and Lewis, all had an American origin; also the Browning machine-gun is an American invention that is made under licence for the Air Ministry.[1]

Quite recently my very able colleague, Captain Douglas Hacking, when Financial Secretary to the War Office, announced to us in the House of Commons that the Army turning to Czechoslovakia was adopting the Bren gun as a light automatic because it has been found to be lighter than the Lewis gun, much easier to handle and is freer from the jambs which were always a serious complaint in the Lewis.

Therefore it is more than satisfactory to know that the weapon now commonly called the Tank was evolved from British ideas, by British brains, and built in British workshops. Undoubtedly the Tanks are a British invention, for did not His Majesty, the late King George V, allude to them as such in his Historic Message sent to Sir Douglas Haig in November, 1917, in these words:

> It is especially gratifying that the Tanks, a purely British invention, should have played so important a part in your victory.

But before the Tank idea became crystallized many proposals had to be looked into and sifted. Some wild ideas at first sight seemed attractive, but most of them, on close examination, were found to be of little value. A few merited action being taken to try them out, and even then

---

[1] As stated by Sir Maurice Hankey in his evidence before the Arms Commission, 8th June, 1936.

INTRODUCTION

a balanced judgment was necessary to determine whether they would be of sufficient use to justify the labour and cost of production.

Nothing is easier than to put ideas or schemes on paper. It becomes natural to many persons to do so. The only test of their worth is action.

Ideas alone are quite worthless in war. They must be followed up by some practical demonstrations or experiments to indicate quite clearly whether any one is of value to the fighting man and worth expenditure of labour, time and money.

In a close examination of the wars of the past I cannot find that any single weapon has ever achieved such a remarkable success in such a short time as the Tank, for has not the nephew of the late Field-Marshal von Hindenburg, President of the German Republic, in his biography of that great Soldier, written:

> But Foch stole a march on Ludendorff. With the greatest secrecy he had marshalled strong reserves at Villers-Cotterets and in the early hours of that fatal day which proved the turning-point of the war, 321 Tanks advanced under the joint cover of fog and gas clouds from the woods at Villers-Cotterets. The German positions were overrun at their very first onset. The soldiers were utterly helpless against the advance of these steel monsters. They fell back and their retreat quickly turned into helter-skelter flight. The Tanks followed so hot on the heels of the fugitives that they had not an opportunity of rallying. And still more and more Tanks, hidden by the dense banks of natural and artificial fog, rolled onward from the wood. The German artillery was helpless. To make matters worse the high corn combined with the fog to make it impossible to cope with the menace.
>
> After a few hours all the German artillery on this sector was in the hands of the French. Brass hats overtaken by the Tanks had to shin it for dear life from their billets. The ammunition columns and the stretcher-bearers, though they were far behind the German positions, were very soon overtaken by the onset of the

Tanks. There were no German reserves available and the few battalions that were rushed up in motor lorries were unable to stem the tide of disaster.[1]

The skill with which the large number of Tanks were handled at Villers-Cotterets won much applause from the Allies and the painful admiration of our great Enemy.

Several friends who have knowledge of my pioneer work in different directions have pressed me on many occasions to write the true story of the evolution of the Tank from the armoured car of the Royal Naval Air Service in much the same way as I wrote my book, the *Evolution of the Submarine Boat, Mine and Torpedo*. It was suggested to me that official letters should be included and names mentioned of all those persons who contributed most towards the natural evolution of this weapon. They say that after such a phenomenal success for the Tank, many people, not only of this Country but throughout the Empire, will be interested to know how these novel weapons of war were brought into being. My friends have also represented to me that unless I write this story from the notes and letters in my possession, it will be lost in much the same way as the early record of the difficulties that were experienced in the creation of the Canadian Pacific Railway has to some extent been lost through the death of those who played the chief part in the creation of that wonderful railway.[2]

Fortunately, in complying with the request of my friends to write this book, I have kept most carefully all the notes, minutes, letters from various people, photographs of the chief incidents in our armoured car and caterpillar experimental work, that paved the way to the construction of our successful caterpillar landship.

These have stood in the path of the scramblers for credit for the Tank invention, as these pages will disclose.

Also in this Country we are the proud possessors of a wonderful body of men in our Civil Service who, like

---

[1] *Hindenburg*, 1847-1934, p. 156 *et seq.*
[2] Excellent as the story of this railway is by John Murray Gibbons in his fascinating book *Steel of Empire*, those of us who remember Vancouver City before it was burnt down would like to have had the personal touch of the early pioneers in relating their own account of this great creation; the difficulties, misrepresentation, open hostility that they encountered, and how they surmounted their troubles when at their zenith. At times it must have been hard to retain their faith in a project that has proved such a triumph of good vision.

myself, have kept most assiduously at the Admiralty a true record of the evolution of the Tank and have with me resented and resisted the claims of those who had nothing whatsoever to do with its inception.

Some of their letters and the official papers are published in full for the first time to make my book of greater historic value to those who study the introduction of new weapons of war, and in doing so I place on record my admiration and sincere thanks to those Civil Servants who have helped so well in the defeat of the Scramblers for Credit for the Tank invention.

I feel confident that all Civil Servants, no matter in which Department they serve, after the contents of these pages are made public, will be all the keener and full out to assist the Pioneer of new ideas in the future. He will want all the help it is possible to give. Much guidance is required for those persons who have a creative sense. Unfortunately they often apply their minds to some difficult problem, then work out a partial solution and leave it there, as if Heaven would do the rest. Help in this direction should at all times be readily forthcoming.

It seems clear that in these modern days, with their great scientific developments, much thought and systematic large scale experiments will generally be necessary when evolving a new weapon of war.

For this class of experimental work there is no better training than that afforded by the Naval Torpedo School *Vernon*. Moreover, service in that establishment, with its great tradition, offers to any keen torpedoist an amazingly interesting time. Often new weapons of war have to be tried out in many experiments that cannot fail to add an interest in life. At least, I found they always did. It was through no merit on my part that I became connected with so much pioneer work. Being available when some original problem had to be tackled was just sheer good fortune. In all my interesting experiments in connection with the introduction of wireless telegraphy, gyroscope torpedoes, submarines, dynamo firing for guns, gun-fire control, aeroplanes, seaplanes, airships, kite-balloons, torpedo aircraft, aircraft carriers into the Navy and the creation of the Royal Naval Air Service, the first Anti-Aircraft Corps for defence of London and the Armoured Car Force, I was fortunate in having the very best Officers and Ratings to assist me that any Torpedo or Submarine Officer or Director of an Admiralty Department could ever have been blessed with. Many were *Vernon* men and all of them were most reliable. They all worked like Trojans, often far into the night on experimental work, and were good thinkers, fine doers and splendid fighters.

The only reward most of them ever received was to see our experiments turn out successfully. The thrills and narrow shaves we had were many. Not once did any one of my Officers or men lose his head or let me down in our often very difficult experimental work, or in emergency in the early submarines, or in our first aircraft. I can only record my grateful thanks to all those who are still living for their much valued assistance, and write that the devotion to duty of my gallant experimental crew, who were all lost in submarine "A 1" shortly after I handed over the command of her to Lieutenant Mansergh,[1] many of my first Air Pilots who gave their lives in our early experimental work in trying out new aeroplanes and seaplanes, also those intrepid Pilots who lost their lives in the War, and those associated with me in our armoured car and first caterpillar landship experiments is for ever fresh in my memory and I am mighty proud to have worked with such fine comrades who gave me unstintedly a wealth of loyal service.

This pioneer work in so many directions gave me an almost unique experience in handling the creative work and obtaining the confidence which is necessary when introducing a new weapon of war.

Also, being a mechanically trained Torpedoist, Submarine and Air expert, I was in an exceptionally good position to tackle the difficult problem set me by Mr. Churchill to get out a scheme for a new weapon for trench warfare that could cross No-Man's-Land, go over difficult terrain, and deal effectively with the wire entanglements and machine-gun nests of the enemy.

Great as the mechanical difficulties were in introducing

[1] This disaster occurred on 18th March, 1904, when she came into collison with the S.S. *Berwick Castle* off the Nab Lightship. Admiral Bacon calculated that only 15 seconds delay on her course by either "A 1" submarine or the *Berwick Castle* in her passage by the Nab Lightship would have prevented this most unfortunate disaster.

a new weapon of war, such as the caterpillar landship, I think the personal difficulties in having to win confidence by overcoming open hostility and prejudice to new ideas were even greater, as the following pages will indicate.

Some persons may think that information acquired by Officers in the course of their duties ought to be treated as confidential. For over twenty years the Noahs[1] have had their hostility to the development of caterpillar landships treated with great confidence. But much confidential information has in recent years been published by ex-Prime Ministers and ex-Ministers of State, Admirals, Generals and many other of our distinguished countrymen.

Further, the special conditions that attended the Great War should not let the Noahs have it all their own way. They should, in the interests of the Pioneer of the future, be exposed to the full ridicule of public opinion.

Moreover, responsible Officers must in times of National Emergency, such as the Great War, be prepared to risk their chances of personal advancement if the interests of the State demand that they should press certain developments or fight for the introduction of a new weapon of war. Otherwise they will be held in some contempt by most of their countrymen.

As defence problems are always with us, it is interesting to note that some four centuries of the Military History of London were drawn up in the Lord Mayor's Show of 1936.

To display the various weapons of war that had throughout this time been used in the Defence of the Realm was a happy thought.

This pageant was a great success and brought home to the many thousands of spectators the advance in armaments from the Pike to the Tank. There was general agreement that this was the best procession within living memory.

In Part I of this Book, I deal firstly with the foreshadowings, then the useful suggestions which were in the direct line of causation, as proved before the Royal Commission

---

[1] Francis Bacon gave a good description of Noahs when he wrote : "Men of age object too much, consult too long, adventure too little, repent too soon and seldom drive business to the full period."

on Awards to Inventors, that influenced or stimulated the construction of the successful Tank and point out the mechanical difficulties that arose in creating this novel weapon of war.

In Part II, I deal more with the personal difficulties, to show what a really uphill struggle it is for any Officer belonging to a Super-Conservative Service like the Navy to advocate the introduction of quite a novel weapon of war and get it taken up for use by another Conservative arm such as the Army.

My task in writing this volume is one of some difficulty owing to personal matters. After due consideration, and silence being no longer necessary, I think there is now little harm in letting our caterpillar work with the extraordinary difficulties we had to surmount see the light of day.

Also my singular experiences should help to guide many Pioneers of the future in their fight for progress and even strengthen their good effort to overcome much personal discouragement should it come their way from the Noahs.

May I draw particular attention to the gracious letter received from the Army Council, page 235. To learn officially from the War Office that we helped in the perfecting of a weapon which had so weighty an effect on the fortunes of the Great War will, I am certain, give considerable satisfaction to those Naval Air and Armoured Car Officers and Ratings associated with me in our armoured car and caterpillar landship experiments.

In making this further contribution to war literature I am fortified in no small way by my reading of Thucydides, for does he not remind us that " he wrote his history in order that whoever wished might have a clear view both of the events which had happened and of those which in all probability would happen again in the same way, or similar way. He hoped that the great men of the future would profit by example drawn from the exact record of the past."

In that spirit I beg to place before my Reader a true statement of facts and a chronicle of the experiments carried out with caterpillar machines that led to the building of the first Royal Naval Air Service Caterpillar Landship which was in the natural process of evolution followed by the construction of the successful Tank.

I mention the contribution of all those persons chiefly concerned in these experiments and who played such an important part in gaining the confidence of Authority in these new weapons. There were many difficulties both mechanical and personal to overcome by my little band of Naval Air and Armoured Car Officers when initiating such a novel weapon of war as the caterpillar landship for the use of the Army in the field, but none of them ever faltered in their faith in this weapon, commonly known as the Tank, which in the skilful hands of the Commanding Officers, their Captains and crews proved one of the determining factors in helping to win and end the Great War.

Part I

CHAPTER I

PRELIMINARY RESEARCHES AND IDEAS

(1) THE FIRST ROYAL NAVAL AIR SERVICE ARMOURED CARS AND SHIELDS.
(2) THE FIRST LANDSHIP PROPOSALS.
(3) FLIGHT COMMANDER HETHERINGTON'S GIANT LAND BATTLESHIP IDEA.
(4) MR. WINSTON CHURCHILL'S STEAM ROLLER SUGGESTIONS.

"In War, deeds not words."

(1) THE FIRST ROYAL NAVAL AIR SERVICE ARMOURED CARS AND SHIELDS

IN his interesting *Book of Reminiscences* Colonel Repington reminds us of a conversation he had with Winston Churchill in these words:

We had a great discussion about the famous Tanks which made their first appearance in the field in last Friday's battle. Winston said that though he had in his mind H. G. Wells's predictions about them, they really developed from the armoured motor car which trench warfare had rendered useless. They were taken up by the Admiralty. He found he had some money to spare and he applied it to this purpose.

To that extent the initiation and responsibility rested with him.

This conversation leads the way for a brief description of the Naval Airmen's armoured car which laid the seed for the construction of the first caterpillar landship that was successfully developed into the Tank.

On the 25th August, 1914, after obtaining the First Lord's approval I ordered Squadron-Commander Samson to report himself at the Admiralty, and gave him orders to take his air squadron to Ostend, as I thought at that time Ostend would be a good temporary advanced air base for keeping the Channel under close observation for enemy's submarines during the passage of the Expeditionary Force.

When Samson was at Ostend, I got into communication with Mr. Sarell, our very able British Vice-Consul at Dunkirk. He was the first person to telephone to me to suggest that we should form a permanent naval air station at Dunkirk, for working with the French, and also for certain diplomatic reasons which he did not disclose. He informed me that there was a small aerodrome that he had no doubt the Governor of Dunkirk would give us, if he was diplomatically approached. We were then considering Samson's recall, as the Marines, who had been operating near Ostend, had been recalled to Dunkirk.

I reported this conversation to Mr. Churchill. He had been approached by the Foreign Office with a similar request to keep our Naval Air Squadron at Dunkirk, and I asked permission to create a naval air station at Dunkirk. Mr. Churchill said he was not at all certain that we could hold Dunkirk, and suggested Calais as an alternative.

After some discussion, Mr. Churchill had the following minute drafted:

> The largest possible force of naval aeroplanes should be stationed in Calais or Dunkirk. Reports have been received, and it is also extremely probable, that the Germans will attempt to attack London and other places by Zeppelin airships, of which it is said a considerable number exist. The close proximity of the French coast to England renders such an attack thoroughly feasible. The proper defence is a thorough and continual search of the country for 70 to 100 miles inland with a view to marking down any temporary airship bases or airships replenishing before starting to attack. Should such airships be located, they should be immediately attacked. Commander Samson and Major Gerrard, as second-in-command, will be entrusted with this duty; and the D.A.D.[1] will take all steps to supply them with the necessary pilots, aeroplanes and equipment.

Mr. Churchill marked this minute, dated 1st September, 1914, in the following order to the Director of Air

---
[1] Short title for Director of Air Department.

PRELIMINARY RESEARCHES AND IDEAS 29

Department (myself), the Fourth Sea Lord and Chief of Staff. As soon as these instructions were made official, I dispatched some Air Officers to inspect the site of the Dunkirk aerodrome, and on receiving a favourable report, I went to Dunkirk to fix up matters with the French Authorities.

From my official reply to Mr. Churchill's minute of 1st September, 1914, and other instructions about speeding-up the delivery of aeroplanes, I extract the following :[1]

CARS FOR ATTENDING ON MACHINES

These should be armed with a light gun. They would assist in forming temporary bases for the machines so as to enable the aeroplanes to extend their flights to a greater distance. *Most important to proceed reporting scheme in detail.*

About 50 will be required; as the autumn wet weather will soon be coming on, it will be necessary to provide tents for the aeroplanes at Dunkirk. *100.*

It is anticipated that a system of special airship watchers from points connected to the telephone can easily be organized over the country which will greatly reduce the number of aeroplanes which need be left patrolling. An airship can be much more easily seen from the ground than from the air.

Attacks on airship sheds at Dusseldorf and Cologne. With four machines armed with 20 lb. bombs and petrol bombs a useful attack on these sheds might be brought off. The machines could operate near the frontier to eastward of Antwerp. *Make proposals.*

Motor cars would supply this temporary base with petrol bombs, etc.

The remarks in the margin are Mr. Churchill's instructions.

But the point I wish to draw particular attention to in my minute is the proposal to arm a large number of motor cars with a gun, and that Mr. Churchill altered my figure of 50 into 100. The First Lord's approval on this paper led to the building of the Naval Airman's Armoured Car Force that I created at Wormwood Scrubs, and we were fortunate in having such a good place as the *Daily*

[1] Dated 4th September, 1914.

Mail airship shed[1] which was soon adapted to our purpose.

My difficulty was to get guns for these cars.

But the Director of Naval Ordnance[2] kindly came to the rescue and raised some Maxims from different places.

As a first start Commander Samson was instructed to obtain ordinary mild steel plating from the firm of Chauteurs de France, Dunkirk, and bolt it on to the bodies and in front of the radiators of his cars. This was with the view to forming some slight protection for his crews when under the enemy's rifle-fire.

After some experience this plating, unless the thickness was very much increased so as to be excessive, was found to afford very little protection. It was reported to me that a German bullet had penetrated one of the 6 mm. plates on 26th September, 1914.

The War Office were then asked if they possessed any details of the necessary thickness of armour plate to resist rifle-fire at close range.

They possessed no information and had no data with regard to the penetrative qualities of various rifle bullets at less than one hundred yards.

Consequently I was forced to commence experiments at once in connection with the penetrative effect of the German rifle bullet on armour plates at close range.

The first experiments were carried out in September and October, 1914, consisting of firing the German bullet and a British service bullet at a special $\frac{3}{8}$-inch steel armour plate. The British service bullet failed to pierce the plate, whilst the German bullet made almost a clean hole through the plate, as shown (Plate I). The service bullet was tried on a $\frac{1}{2}$-inch nickel plate. Then an experimental bullet X and a Service bullet. The service bullet failed to penetrate, but the patent bullet X just got through a special 4 mm. plate with a 3 mm. wood backing (Plate II). These experiments were continued at Messrs. Beardmore's during the autumn of 1914 and spring of 1915.

Mr. Service of Messrs. Beardmore gave most valuable help to my Officers during the early experiments.

---

[1] Kindly placed at the disposal of the Royal Naval Air Service by Lord Northcliffe.
[2] Vice-Admiral Sir Morgan Singer.

PLATE I

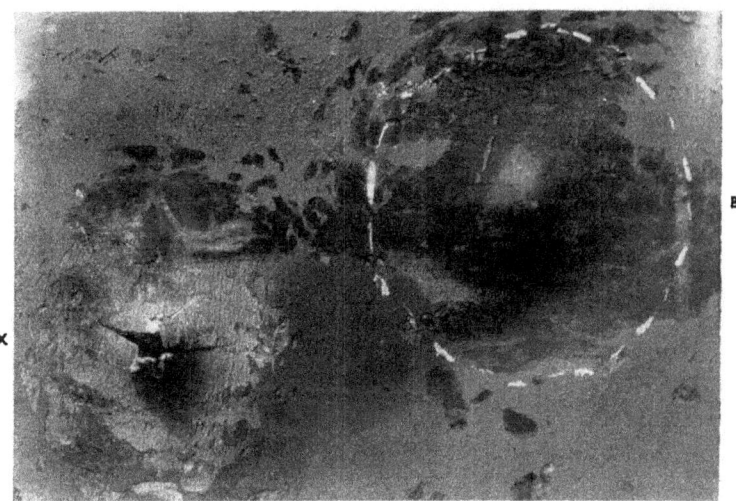

PLATE II

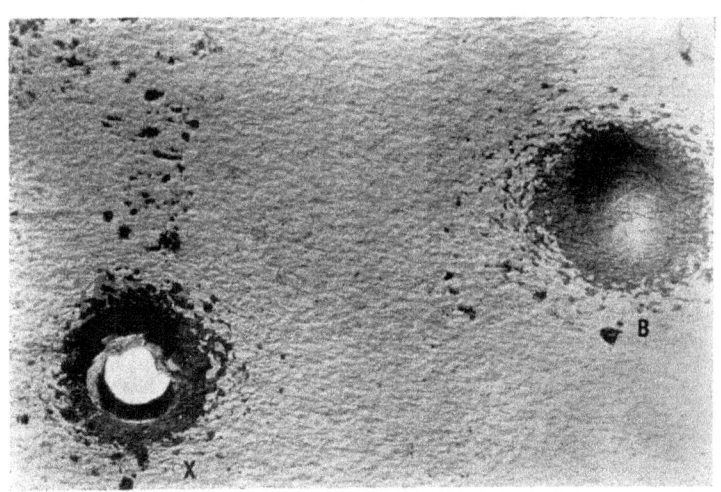

(*Above*) 4-MM. SPECIAL STEEL PLATE WITH 3-MM. WOOD BACKING
X. Patent bullet, 1914.   B. British Service bullet.

(*Below*) EXPERIMENTS WITH SPECIAL ⅜" STEEL PLATE, 1914, AT MESSRS. BEARDMORE
X. German bullet.   B. British Service bullet.

PLATE III

PLATE IV

(*Above*) EXPERIMENTS WITH SPECIAL ½" STEEL PLATE, 1914
X. Y. German bullets.   B. British bullet.
(*Below*) ¾" SPECIAL PLATE
X. German bullet "S" point first penetrated.
Y. German bullet "S" point first not penetrated.
Z. German bullet "S" point reversed penetrated.

PRELIMINARY RESEARCHES AND IDEAS

Later some further plate experiments were conducted at Wormwood Scrubs with a ¾-inch special plate. One rifle bullet, point first German, penetrated; second shot, point first German, did not penetrate; third shot, reversed German, penetrated (Plate III).

Another special plate test: one German rifle bullet point first did not penetrate; German bullet reversed penetrated (Plate IV).

Squadron-Commander Briggs and Flight-Commander Hetherington supervised this armour plate work from the Admiralty and I detailed Lieutenant Symes, one of my Armoured Car Officers, to supervise the necessary acceptance or rejection of all the plates required for our armoured cars.

In the Air Department we kept a complete record of the behaviour of armour plates under rifle-fire.

It was our custom to fire German ammunition at one plate in every heat. Lieutenant Symes became a great expert in armour-plate experiments and if he passed a plate I could be quite sure there would be no complaints from the Officers on active service that a German bullet had penetrated inside one of the armoured cars through the plating.

Lieutenant Symes carried on this armour-plate work from our first armoured cars down to and including the first Tanks. He performed really good service in supervising the rapid production and testing of armour plates for several years.

The firms we employed, especially Messrs. Beardmore, played up in a splendid manner to the necessity for producing these first armour plates with rapidity.

Quite soon I was able to send Samson a good quantity of ·3-inch armour plate that would keep out the Mauser bullet at point-blank range, to substitute for the mild steel plates he had obtained, as a temporary measure, from the Chauteurs firm at Dunkirk.

This could give the cars only flat armour plate protection because the art of bending these light steel plates had not then been acquired by any firm in this Country.

The first two Rolls-Royce armoured cars of the open type were delivered on 19th September, 1914, and by the

22nd October I had fifteen armoured cars ready for sending to Dunkirk (Plate V).

In this work of armouring the first cars, all creative work of a novel character, I was fortunate in having the assistance of Lord Wimborne and Mr. Macnamara.[1] Both of them and my Officers slaved to get something going to help our Airmen at Dunkirk.

On returning from Antwerp the evening before its fall, and having seen the work of the armoured cars in the villages between Antwerp and Dunkirk, I became convinced that both Lord Wimborne and myself were on the wrong lines with armoured cars. Our cars suffered from lack of overhead protection and the crew were open to rifle-fire from snipers at the upper windows of houses and in the arms of trees.

This impression then formed was shared by the late Admiral Horace Hood, the First Lord's very able Naval Secretary, who was with me at that time. Also we had attached to my Armoured Car Force at Dunkirk a Military Officer—Captain Arthur Nickerson, who had seen considerable service in the South African War. He was the first to impress upon me the necessity for providing overhead protection to the crews of the armoured cars, and pointed out quite rightly that it was not fair to the men cramped together in the cars unless they were protected from snipers who would soon find out the weak spots, and it was exposing the crews unnecessarily.

I informed Captain Nickerson that I had discussed this weakness in our armoured cars with Admiral Hood and as soon as possible after my return to London I would design some means of giving overhead protection to the crews, and instructed him to return to the Admiralty when he could be spared and lay his views before my little Committee then advising me on all armoured car matters.

This Captain Nickerson did and he placed before the Committee a rough sketch of the kind of overhead armoured protection he thought would meet the case. My Committee thanked him warmly for his good guidance.

At that time the former war experience of Captain Nickerson was most valuable as we had so few Officers or

---

[1] Son of the late Rt. Hon. J. Macnamara, P.C., M.P. for North Camberwell.

PLATE V

PLATE VI

(*Above*) THE FIRST ROYAL NAVAL AIR SERVICE ARMOURED CAR,
OPEN TYPE, DUNKIRK, 1914
(*Below*) ROLLS-ROYCE ARMOURED CAR, REVOLVING TURRET TYPE
First car constructed, December, 1914.

PLATE VII

PLATE VIII

(*Above*) ROYAL NAVAL AIR SERVICE HEAVY ARMOURED CAR. (SEABROOK 5 TON), ARMAMENT NAVAL 3-PR. GUN, 4 MAXIMS
First car delivered February 5th, 1915. Used at Ypres by Sir John French.

(*Below*) ARMOUR 8-MM. STEEL PLATE. SIDE ARMOUR PROTECTION DOWN, PORT BOW MAXIM IN POSITION

PRELIMINARY RESEARCHES AND IDEAS 33

men who had ever been under rifle-fire before, and he was the means of checking many a rash undertaking by inexperienced Officers in our first armoured cars. His knowledge of the tactics employed against mounted men proved helpful when Commander Samson was operating with his armoured cars against the bands of Uhlans that were overrunning the Cassel, Arras area, etc.

The Committee considered carefully Captain Nickerson's advice and after discussing several possible forms of cars with Lord Wimborne, Squadron-Commander W. Briggs, Flight-Commander T. Hetherington and Mr. Macnamara, a revolving turret, completely covered, was decided to be the only real solution, and accordingly a model car was made on these lines in three-ply wood.

The next difficulty to overcome was how to bend light armour plates without cracking them. After many experiments this was solved by Messrs. Beardmore's ingenious armour experts.

All the armour plate, armament, ammunition and crew weights were worked out carefully, and it was found possible to carry them on either a standard Rolls-Royce or Lanchester chassis. The work of making this car in armour plate then commenced, and after a certain amount of experimental work these cars were produced. The technical difficulties we had to overcome were many—the whole armour of the car, turrets, etc., had to be secured rigidly to the chassis without the bolts of the securing brackets shearing through jars or vibration when going over a roughish road; the fixing of the armour plate over the bonnet and roof of bonnet with necessary supporting stays caused at first a good deal of trouble.

At this time Mr. Scott of Messrs. Beardmore gave Flight-Commander Hetherington and Squadron-Commander Briggs much assistance in this detailed work.

With everybody working their utmost we had the first three revolving turret Rolls-Royce type of armoured car delivered on 3rd December, 1914 (Plate VI). At one period I had no less than fourteen Firms delivering armour plates and the necessary brackets, small internal fittings, etc., for the armoured cars.

At times it was difficult to keep Messrs. Beardmore

c

supplied with sufficient Mauser ammunition for testing the plates. The following firms supplied the Admiralty with special chassis for the first armoured cars:

>Rolls-Royce,
>Lanchester,
>Delauny-Belville,
>Wolseley,

and subsequently a large number of squadrons of armoured cars were fitted out which gave uniformly good service wherever employed under conditions at all suitable for their use (Plate VI). At the same time it was realised that such cars, carrying only machine-guns, required to be backed by some heavier weapon, and the question was approached of providing a motor lorry which could carry a three pounder or even a twelve-pounder, and the Vickers 1-inch Pom-Pom. Lorries were accordingly built protected by shields and armour plate to resist machine-gun fire.

The first Seabrooke Lorry to carry a three-pounder was delivered on 5th February, 1915, from the Portholme Aerodrome Co., Huntingdon (Plates VII and VIII). During our first tests we had great trouble with these heavier armoured cars, as the tyres, springs, back axles, etc., would not stand up to the heavy load so well as the turret armoured car type, and they gave us trouble enough. On flat roads all our armoured cars would just stand the weight. But on rough roads very many replacements became necessary. This was a constant source of anxiety to all of my Officers in command of these Squadrons. As can be imagined, it was very difficult to keep the weights down.

At this time the War Office suddenly became interested in our armoured-car work; it was shortly after I had turned over some sections of kite-balloons to the Army at Lord Kitchener's personal request as described in my Air Book. Colonel Fitzgerald rang up from the War Office and asked if I could send my "armour" expert to the War Office the next morning. Squadron-Commander Briggs was absent at Messrs. Beardmore's, so I instructed Flight-Commander Hetherington to call at Colonel Fitzgerald's office at 10 a.m. next day.

Flight-Commander Hetherington reported himself at the War Office and was informed Lord Kitchener wanted to see him. Then arose a humorous situation for my young Airman. Lord Kitchener sat at the head of a table with the Master of Ordnance one side, the Director of Artillery the opposite side, and one other Officer. Hetherington was dressed as a Cavalry Captain and looked extremely youthful. Lord Kitchener then put him through his armour plate and armour car knowledge. Fortunately my Airman was a most efficient young Officer with plenty of assurance and had been working extremely hard with Squadron-Commander Briggs and myself in developing armoured cars, and as Colonel Fitzgerald informed me afterwards, was quite capable of holding his own uncommonly well when answering the difficult questions put to him by Lord Kitchener. Hetherington was able to give much of the useful information we had gathered in our armour-plate experiments with the German bullet at point-blank range. He was given a note and instructed by Lord Kitchener to go to Woolwich and take it to the Superintendent of the Arsenal, then inspect and report upon an armoured General Omnibus chassis that had been constructed for experimental work to see if it would have any fighting value.

Hetherington reported the result of his visit to the War Office to me and in due course went to Woolwich and found an armoured car had been constructed with armour that would stop a German bullet at 100 yards but no nearer. Hetherington was naturally surprised that Woolwich was not better informed that armoured cars were required for close-range fighting, and their armoured car would be quite useless unless the armour afforded sufficient protection for close fighting. This was interesting, as it shows the value of all experimental work being approached from more than one angle, no matter from which side of Whitehall. This was a lesson always hammered into me by my old *Vernon* Chief, Admiral Sir John Durnford.

One of the early reports on the value of our armoured motor cars at the Front came to the First Lord from General H. Rawlinson dated October 14th, 1914, and he instructed me to circulate the following to all concerned:

During a short pause in this interesting situation and after having gained touch once more with Gen. Hqs. I must write you a line to express my very sincere thanks for your kindness in allowing me to keep the armoured trains,[1] armoured motors and aeroplanes under Samson. They have all done excellent work. The armoured motors pick up half a dozen prisoners a day and have instilled a holy terror into our opponents. We could do with double the number of them. Samson and his aeroplanes have obtained for us the most valuable information and though they have broken up several machines there have been no casualties amongst the Officers so far. Samson himself earns more of my respect and appreciation daily. To-day we had quite a sensational capture—as we were all standing in the market-place with the Household Cavalry Brigade, a Taube aeroplane flew over at about 2000. We opened on it with maxims and rifles and brought him down, capturing the two Officers who were unwounded.

Before the Germans dug themselves in, all our armoured cars did well. Major-General C. M. Kavanagh, commanding the Second Cavalry Division, reported as follows, on 27th May, 1915:

The section of armoured cars with Maxim guns that has been attached to this division have rendered excellent service during the late operations near Ypres.

They are most useful for reconnaissance and for conveying Staff Officers through dangerous zones and, although the opportunity has not arisen when they could fulfil the role of attack or pursuit, I consider them a valuable arm for this purpose in conjunction with cavalry.

The retention of the armoured cars with this division is, in my opinion, very desirable, and I would further recommend that each section should be supplemented by the addition of the following:

(*a*) Four cycle side-cars armed with Maxims.
(*b*) Two three-pounders on trailers drawn by armoured cars, which I believe exist.

---
[1] Page 243 footnote.

Also, General De Lisle's report is of interest, as he stated:

The section of armoured motor cars attached to the First Cavalry Division was employed in action on 24th May throughout the day and part of the night.

The situation that day was such that any movement from the support and reserve trenches to the forward trenches could only be made at considerable loss of life. All telephone communication was cut, and owing to the asphyxiating effects of gas, information by human means was not forthcoming from the front trenches. Under these circumstances the armoured cars proved of the greatest possible assistance.

Although the Ypres-Menin road was being heavily shelled the cars were taken up to the Birr cross roads and returned with valuable information. At another time the cars were called on for offensive action, and there is little doubt that their fire effect assisted in checking any further advance of the Germans. The crews and drivers behaved well under fire and could always be relied on thoroughly to carry out their orders.

The men in the fire trenches, who had been cut off from communication to Brigade Headquarters, state that the sight of the cars advancing up the Menin Road had a most inspiriting effect on their morale, as it was evident that the cars would prevent any attempt being made to turn their flank, once the gap in the line had been made.

It is considered that in trench warfare and in any future advance these armoured cars would prove a most valuable addition to a cavalry division.

This was the official account sent to:

Officer Commanding
    Armoured Car Squadron
        1st Cavalry Division.

Forwarded for your information. This is a copy of the report sent in by G.O.C., 1st Cavalry Division, on the operation of the 24th May.

        (Sgd.) A. F. Home, Lt.-Col.
            1st Cavalry Division.

Although Sir John French liked the R.N.A.S. three-pounder heavy armoured car, and asked Mr. Churchill for more, they were not really a success. The guns in our three-pounder cars were not powerful enough, and the cars could not cross even a small road trench except with the aid of planks, and only then under the most favourable conditions, as the crew had to expose themselves to snipers, shell-fire, etc., whilst laying the planks. The great difficulty we had to contend against was that our armoured cars, although fitted with these boards, as shown in Plate XII, for crossing ditches, were practically valueless for cross-country work when the Germans dug themselves in, and we had great difficulty in getting the tyres, springs, back axles and wheels to stand up to the load of armour-plating, gun, ammunition, crew and baggage.

The latter on active service is always an important item and must be taken into account quite seriously. The crew, in spite of all orders, will increase their baggage and hide oddments in all sorts of odd places.

I tried filling the tyres with Rubberine, but that was not very successful.

As Trench warfare developed on the Western Front, the armoured cars became of no further use, so we sent a squadron to Egypt under the command of the Duke of Westminster, and he carried out very valuable services. The gallant Duke was awarded a D.S.O. in recognition of his good work. I have an amusing recollection of seeing the Duke of Westminster looking extremely miserable when paying the men of his armoured car squadron in pouring rain at Wormwood Scrubs Naval Air Station, and getting a little mixed up with the small coins that are always such a bother on these occasions, in getting the amount payable to each man accurate.

Another armoured car squadron was taken to Russia by that intrepid man, Commander Oliver Locker-Lampson, C.M.G., D.S.O.[1]

Locker-Lampson is a born leader. He does not know such a thing as fear, or what a difficulty is. He likes overcoming them, and his work during the War in Belgium, Russia and Roumania would make most interesting reading,

[1] Now Member of Parliament for Handsworth.

could we persuade him to write a book giving the full story of his gallant deeds with his Royal Naval Air Service armoured cars, commencing from the time he went across the Channel, then to Russia and Roumania, and return to this Country.

I recollect being most interested in the Commander's dispatches from Russia, particularly in his interview with the late Czar, when he stated that His Majesty had the cause of the Allies very much at heart. This combated the view that had been basely circulated in this Country that he was faithless to the cause of the Allies.

The arrival of Locker-Lampson's armoured cars in Russia created no little stir, as the following interesting report that he sent me, dated 13th July, 1916, shows:

> At Archangel the Force met with the greatest kindness. By the special request of the Governor the Force marched with arms through the streets of Archangel and was presented with a valuable Ikon many years old representing St. Michael the Patron Saint of Archangel. This Ikon was specially taken from the Cathedral and was presented to the Force firstly as it was the first British Force to land in Russia, and secondly, out of gratitude for the return of the church bell taken by the British from Archangel during the Crimean War and sent back by them in 1911.

Commander Locker-Lampson's expedition with his armoured cars assumed a most important character, as the following telegrams disclose:

No. 1.
From . . . The Grand Duke Nicholas,
To . . . General Fleisher.

With my whole heart I welcome the arrival of the Armoured Car Detachment from England, the great Ally of our glorious Armies.

As the Hetman in command of the Cossack Armies of the Caucasus I greet them—ALAVERDEE—wishing health and prosperity to the brave British Army and Navy.

I warmly thank General Fleisher for his message of greeting and goodwill and I hope soon to see and welcome personally the British Armoured Car Division in Mschyet.

General Commander-in-Chief,

NICHOLAS.

No. 2.

From . . . General Trotsky, Director of the Vladicaucasian Cadet Corps and the Officers of the Corps,

To . . . His Excellency the British Ambassador, Petrograd.

Celebrating as we do the arrival of a British Force, with Commander Locker-Lampson at its head, to the home of the Vladicaucasian Cadet Corps and the Company of Polotsks Officers we, British and Russians, stand now united by a common feeling and purpose which I, for my part, may perhaps be allowed to translate into a message of goodwill from us to your Excellency as the Representative in Russia of our Great Ally Britain. We desire to send you and yours our heartfelt wishes for health and prosperity.

From . . . Sir George Buchanan, British Embassy Petrograd,

To . . . The Director of the Corps of Cadets General Staff's General Trotsky, Vladicaucas.

Deeply touched by your Excellency's telegram. I thank you sincerely for the goodwill and kind messages sent to me and my family and I am very grateful to you for the cordial reception given Commander Locker-Lampson and his detachment.

Locker-Lampson's Force was the only British unit to fight for Russia on Russian soil. Before this the Russians had very little evidence of British effort during the War. The presence of even a few Englishmen in khaki, with their photographs in the daily Press and on the cinema films, appearing in the villages and towns throughout Russia did a tremendous amount of good at that time amongst the ignorant peasants, and removed a false idea of England's contribution to the Allies' cause. Locker-Lampson worked right through Russia, taking his armoured cars where most needed, and then went to the help of Roumania, who was in the greater need of assistance.

Commander Locker-Lampson's dispatches from Roumania were equally interesting. In that Country his armoured cars performed services of great value, and he came into close contact with the late King of Roumania, who worked hard and did so much for his very interesting and picturesque Country.

I have heard that Admiral the Duke of Edinburgh's daughter, then the beautiful Queen of Roumania,[1] and her handsome daughter, the former Queen of Greece, were very interested in our Naval armoured cars and showed the crews much kindness.

Commander Locker-Lampson did not have it all his own way, as I extract the following from a German official communiqué on 1st December, 1916:

> In the Dobrodya the enemy attacked the Bulgarian left wing, the attacking masses breaking down under our fire. Even the English Armoured Cars were unable to mitigate that failure. Two of these are lying destroyed before our barricades.

A few more of our armoured cars were knocked out by the Bulgarians and their crews captured. Most of the prisoners were sent to Turkey, where they had a much better time than had they remained with the Bulgarians. The Turks employed several of our armoured car prisoners to teach their children English.

Many of us thought Commander Locker-Lampson's fine effort in taking his armoured cars, in spite of almost every official opposition that it is possible to imagine, to stiffen up the Russians, then the Roumanians, was really a great piece of independent work. This man is always out to help the bottom dog, and in making an endeavour to assist the Russians and Roumanians to keep up their spirits on the Allies' side, was true to type and performed a service of no little magnitude at that particular time to the cause of the Allies.

[1] Now the Queen-Mother of Roumania, who is not only admired for being a great Stateswoman, but is known throughout the world as the Author of many charming books.

I always impressed upon Commander Boothby, the Commanding Officer of my Armoured Car Force, that his crews should consider themselves an emergency unit and they ought to be like a Fire Brigade, available for any call day or night to rescue one of our Air Pilots who might have to make a forced landing in hostile territory.

This Armoured Car Force was composed of very fine mechanics largely recruited from London. They were all new to War operations and required some guidance. We encouraged them to be temperate with the result that we had a very small defaulters' sheet all the time this Force was kept under the good control of Commander Boothby.

On raising a new squadron for working under Commander Locker-Lampson I sent him the following letter:

THE AIR DEPARTMENT, ADMIRALTY,
27th July, 1915.

DEAR LOCKER-LAMPSON,

I hope you are now well established in your camp. As you are now on Active Service I cannot impress upon you too forcibly the need of conducting your camp properly in time of war. It is essential that no temptations should be offered either to men or to Officers in camp and that you should do everything to keep the health of those under you good for emergencies. Special regulations exist in the Navy limiting the wine bills of Officers on board ship and forbidding the provision of any drink for the men except the rum ration at night. It occurred to me that it would perhaps be best for you to treat your camp as a ship for this purpose and to limit, as far as possible, the temptation to men and Officers in the camp. The penalties at the Front for drunkenness are very severe and in a War like this, in order to win, everybody must exercise self-denial.

Let me know at any time if you require anything.

With best wishes for the success of your Squadron,

I remain,
Yours sincerely,
(Sgd.) MURRAY F. SUETER,
Director, Air Department.

PRELIMINARY RESEARCHES AND IDEAS 43

At a later date we were informed from a source in a good position to know that Commander Locker-Lampson's little Force of armoured cars went right through their service at Dunkirk, then Russia and Roumania, and were mostly teetotallers. I thought that one up to the gallant Commander for his good example. But some of his men nurse a grievance against him to this day and believe he left their ration of rum behind at the base on purpose !

Although the armoured cars we sent to the Dardanelles were not of great value, their crews and guns carried out fine service under the command of a very gallant Officer, Lieutenant-Commander Josiah Wedgwood,[1] a Cromwellian type of man with independent views on most things but a fine fighter. He received a D.S.O. for his good work with our R.N.A.S. armoured car crews at Gallipoli and most richly deserved it.

From our Royal Naval Air Station at Mak Tau, East Africa, Squadron-Commander Cull sent me an interesting report, dated 25th January, 1916, and enclosed some air photographs. In a postscript he states: "Since these photographs were taken and the report written, troops have occupied Mbuynui and Seringheti without much opposition, the armoured cars doing great execution."

Our military successes in East Africa during the Great War were due largely to the Germans' entire lack of appreciation of the value of armoured cars and mechanical transport for operations in that country.

Another authority mentions the good use of armoured cars, for Lowell Thomas[2] tells us: "The following day Lawrence dashed back to Azarak in an armoured car, then flew across the desert and northern Palestine to Allenby's headquarters at Ramleh. . . . The next day the infantry under General Jaffer Pasha, the jovial Commander-in-Chief of Colonel Joyce's regulars, went down to have a look at the first large bridge which Lawrence had dynamited in the vicinity of Deraa. They found it nearly repaired but after a sharp fight they drove off its guards who were persistent and game German machine-gunners; destroyed more of the line and then proceeded to burn the

---

[1] Now the Right Hon. Josiah Wedgwood, P.C., D.S.O., M.P.
[2] *With Lawrence in Arabia.*

great timber framework which had been erected by the Turks and Germans during the intervening seven days. In this rather sharp encounter the armoured cars, the French detachment under Captain Pisani and the Rulla Horse under Nuri Shablan, plunged into the heart of things."

From the above it will be seen that the Royal Naval Air Service armoured cars were of some use to our Army units in their Near Eastern operations.

Even as late as the autumn of 1920, the War Office in the following letter asked me for armoured car information:

War Office,
London, S.W.1,
2.9.20.

Dear Admiral Sueter,

We are trying to get the designs of the Rolls-Royce armoured cars which I understand were prepared by the R.N.A.S. in conjunction with the D.N.C. I would be very much obliged if you could assist us in getting on the track of them, as we are very anxious to get them. My telephone is Ger. 6920, Ext. 26.

Yours sincerely,
(Sgd.) J. T. Dreyer.

This request from the War Office was at once complied with, but I may mention that the Director of Naval Construction never had anything to do with the design of my revolving turret or three-pounder armoured cars.

Armoured cars to the old R.N.A.S. pattern are still in use in the British Army and form part of the military equipment in many parts of the Empire.[1] During the Army manœuvres of 1935 my turret armoured car was well to the fore. Plates VI and IX show our R.N.A.S. 1914 pattern and the armoured car in use in Palestine in July, 1936. There is little difference in design but certain mechanical details have been improved.

Infantry Armoured Shields

As I have pointed out previously Captain Maurice Hankey and myself were much concerned as to how we

---

[1] There are eight Armoured Car Companies now in India. See page 292.

ROYAL AIR FORCE MACHINE GIVING INFORMATION TO ARMOURED CAR SECTION NEAR TRANS-JORDAN FRONTIER, JULY, 1936

PLATE X

ROYAL NAVAL AIR SERVICE INFANTRY ARMOURED SHIELD
EXPERIMENT, WORMWOOD SCRUBS, 1915

PRELIMINARY RESEARCHES AND IDEAS 45

could help our comrades at the Front by the use of armour protection for reducing their enormous casualties. Both of us had considerable experience of armour protection for our guns and crews in casements, turrets, etc., in ships we had served in. Having been the Admiralty overseer for some time in the construction of our first submarines at Messrs. Vickers' Works at Barrow-in-Furness, I was naturally friendly with a good many of the Firm's experts in their Head Office in London, so I got in touch with Mr. Buckham, a great gunnery expert, and asked him to come and see me at the Admiralty towards the close of 1914.

He got out for me a drawing, No. 66133G[1] of my proposed infantry shield and made a mock up of the shield in wood. This was brought to my office at the Admiralty and I showed it to Captain Maurice Hankey. This was the first attempt made in a practical manner at the Admiralty to get armour considered for use of our troops at the Front.

In going into the detailed weight of this machine with Mr. Buckham we found the weight of armour was a heavy loading for the central wheel and we feared it could not be used with any success over soft ground. But it was all right on hard ground.

Having some knowledge of caterpillars from Scott's Antarctic sleigh with which I helped, I instructed Squadron-Commander Briggs to find out from whence we could get a caterpillar. He obtained some details of the Diplock Company caterpillar machine and I sent Major Hetherington, my armoured car Transport Officer, to Fulham to have a look at it. His report being favourable I got in touch with the Diplock Company and asked them to send their caterpillar truck to my armoured car headquarters. The caterpillar duly arrived at Wormwood Scrubs on 13th January, 1915, and I intended to mock up a caterpillar infantry shield for experimental purposes on the lines of the one Mr. Buckham of Messrs. Vickers had prepared for me.

Before I was able to give this experiment any attention, Mr. Churchill set me the task of finding a solution to his problem of getting out a suitable weapon for trench warfare, which is dealt with in Chapter II.

[1] This drawing is with Messrs. Vickers.

At our demonstration on 30th June, 1915, before Mr. Lloyd George, Mr. Churchill and many Military Officers, as described on page 75, we showed an improvement to my infantry shield prepared by Lieutenant Symes. He fitted wings to the shield and mounted it on my Diplock caterpillar (Plate X). This mock up was made of wood, but we loaded it with pig iron to make up the same weight as if built of armour plate.

From these experiments it appeared possible to manufacture an extremely useful and mobile infantry shield. Commander Boothby then wanted to give it a small power unit and utilize the engine from a motor bicycle. Without power we estimated the shield would cost about one hundred pounds.

The Third Sea Lord, Admiral Sir Frederick Tudor-Tudor, invented a different type of infantry shield from mine. His was a distinct improvement on my first effort with one central wheel. The Third Sea Lord had a model of his made, this showed the wheels carried at the extreme ends of the screen and not let in as my wheel was. He arranged for the wheels to be secured on the axles with linch pins and washers in the same way as the Naval field-gun wheels are fitted.

However, the Army did not take up our infantry shields so I ceased to experiment any further with them by fitting power, as suggested by Commander Boothby.

Reports have appeared in the Press that during the Italian Grand Military Manœuvres of the autumn of 1935 armour shields were provided for the use of their troops.

I still think the further study of light armour protection for our infantry should be made to ascertain if something could not be evolved to lesson the enormous casualties, if unhappily another war is thrust upon this country.

(2) The First Landship Proposals
No Action Taken

Serving with my Armoured Car Force at Wormwood Scrubs in the autumn of 1914 we had a skilled Engineer, Lieutenant Macfie, who became well known amongst his brother Officers as a caterpillar expert.

PRELIMINARY RESEARCHES AND IDEAS 47

On the 5th November, 1914, he sent me in a report that I have before me on how to use caterpillar machines for hauling heavy Naval guns, and enclosed a cutting from the *Daily Mail's* issue of 5th November, 1914, which showed a Holt Caterpillar Tractor at Antwerp. In concluding his memorandum, Lieutenant Macfie wrote:

It is the writer's conviction that with a group of six caterpillar tractors and with a competent crew manager, weights of 85 tons, i.e. the weight of a 12-inch naval gun, could be moved over the remains of roads (they will be destroyed) which will be encountered on the advance into Germany at a speed of 20 to 40 miles a day. It is also the writer's conviction that the construction of a "floating" foundation capable of dealing with the recoil of these guns, built up of short lengths (say 5 ft.) of 12-inch beams and angle brackets and bolts and nuts (not rivets), so as to be easily and rapidly assembled in a few hours by field labour, present no undue mechanical difficulties.

Flight-Commander Hetherington, in minuting this paper to Wing-Commander Boothby, stated:

I think much valuable information might be gained if this unit had one of these machines at advanced base. Also it would be very valuable in getting broken-down armoured cars back to base when the roads are bad.

As I was not taking on the hauling about of 12-inch naval guns I took no action on these proposals.

At the hearing of the Royal Commission on Awards to Inventors, it was disclosed that Mr. Churchill, in answer to a memorandum prepared by Captain Hankey dated 28th December, 1914, on the subject of special mechanical devices, such as heavy rollers propelled from behind by engines fitted with caterpillar driving-wheels, wrote to the Prime Minister a letter dated 5th January, 1915, from which I extract the following:

It would be quite easy in a short time to fit up a number of steam tractors with small armoured shelters, in which men and machine-guns could be placed, which would be bullet-proof.

Used at night, they would not be affected by artillery fire to any extent. The caterpillar system would enable trenches to be crossed quite easily, and the weight of the machine would destroy all wire entanglements.

This, of course, was a secret letter.

On being asked a question concerning this letter of 5th January, 1915, by the Attorney-General before the Royal Commission on Awards to Inventors, Mr. Churchill stated:[1]

"I have ascertained that Mr. Asquith, two or three days after receiving this letter, laid it personally before Lord Kitchener and urged him to prosecute research into all these matters with vigour. I think he also sent Colonel Hankey's Memorandum of a few days earlier. Lord Kitchener therefore remitted the matter to the Department of the Master General of Ordnance.

After the failure of the existing caterpillar tractor to fulfil the extremely severe conditions laid down by the War Office, further action was suspended. There are some official Minutes, but I do not think it is necessary to quote them, which sustain those facts as I have stated them."

Mr. Churchill was then asked: "Did that second attempt come to nothing?—It came to nothing: no action was taken. At what date was that—I lost touch with this particular sequence of events after writing my letter to the Prime Minister. It begins with Colonel Swinton; it goes on to Sir Maurice Hankey that was followed by my letter; then Mr. Asquith sent it to Lord Kitchener: and then Lord Kitchener remitted it to the Department of the Master General of Ordnance. Certain investigations were made, but the matter came to a dead end."

For some unknown reason neither the Committee of Imperial Defence nor the War Office took any definite action on these first proposals.

---

[1] Page 7, Minutes of Proceedings before the Royal Commission on Awards to Inventors, Tuesday, 7th October, 1919.

PRELIMINARY RESEARCHES AND IDEAS 49

But such suggestions showed that the Secretary of the Committee of Imperial Defence, Captain Maurice Hankey, was not satisfied with the trench warfare weapons that existed at that time, and was searching for a weapon with greater possibilities for dealing with the position that then arose at the Front.

Also at this time Mr. Churchill did not quite know what was required, otherwise he would have followed up his proposal by definite action. Being First Lord he had the whole Admiralty Office behind him, and could give orders, within limits, to build almost any mechanical machine he chose.

On the War Office side, Colonel Swinton in the early part of the War was, I understand, a Press representative at the Front, and like many who had inside knowledge of our terrible casualties, was anxious to do all in his power to lessen the loss of such valuable lives. When on visits to England in his official capacity he impressed upon Mr. Asquith and Captain Hankey that some mechanical weapon should be evolved for trench warfare, and as he had been made aware of the efficiency of Holt Caterpillar Tractors for haulage purposes previous to the War, he was not unmindful of their capabilities. He discussed the matter fully with Captain Hankey and also Major Tulloch, an ex-Artillery Officer, with the result that Major Tulloch on 19th January, 1915, forwarded a Memorandum to General Scott Moncrieff dealing with land cruisers and lighter land destroyers, the former type to mount ordnance and the latter machine-guns. Both types were to be mounted on a carriage supported by caterpillars of the Hornsby-Akroyd type that had been improved upon in the Holt Caterpillar.

Quite unknown to the Admiralty Air Department several Generals and other Military Officers had been considering these caterpillar proposals by Colonel Swinton and Major Tulloch. They were General Guthrie-Smith, General von Donop, Colonel Holden and Colonel Jackson. The *Attorney-General* before the Royal Commission on Awards to Inventors stated that General Sir Scott Moncrieff's Committee turned down caterpillar machines in these remarkable words, as recorded on page 3 of the

D

Minutes of the Royal Commission dated 7th October, 1929:

On the 13th January the Committee (General Sir Scott Moncrieff's) inspected two Holt Caterpillar tractors at Aldershot and it was thereupon arranged that a trial course of trenches, barbed wire and obstacles should be prepared at Shoeburyness. That plan was carried out and a Holt Tractor dragging a truck weight of 5000 lb. was tried over that track on 17th February, 1915.

The result of that preliminary trial was not such as to satisfy the War Office Committee that the scheme was practicable and the members of the Committee, being unable to suggest any Engineer competent to work out a fresh design, that project appears to have been abandoned on the 26th February, 1915.

(3) Flight-Commander Hetherington's Giant Land Battleship Idea

On the Admiralty side of Whitehall towards the end of 1914 Flight-Commander Hetherington, one of my Armoured Car Officers, brought me a proposal to construct a giant wheeled vehicle for cross-country travelling, which was to have wheels of such large diameter and to be provided with such great propelling power, that it could travel indiscriminately over all but the greatest natural and artificial obstacles. It was to be armoured against hostile gun-fire and to be armed with a naval 12-inch gun. The intention was to employ this land battleship, as it was called, to flatten barbed wire entanglements and to destroy trench systems, and more particularly to travel about behind the enemy's lines destroying his batteries with its gun-fire and breaking his railways by anchoring to the tracks and tearing them away bodily.

I sent for Squadron-Commander Briggs and Mr. Harris Booth, two of my assistants in the Admiralty Air Department, and instructed them to go into some weights with regard to armour, engines, armament ammunition, stores and crew, and suggested we should consider carrying Diesel engines of the submarine type, of which I had knowledge, to drive dynamos for supplying current to

PRELIMINARY RESEARCHES AND IDEAS 51

electric motors geared to the wheels. On going very carefully into all the weights based on our armoured car knowledge in the Air Department, we found Flight-Commander Hetherington's idea too ambitious, and he agreed that I should water down his original proposal.

This enabled me, early in January, 1915, to put forward the following Minute to the First Lord, Mr. Churchill:

Submitted:

With a view to providing forces operating on land with a method of breaking down the resistance of the enemy when he resorts to "siege warfare," a new weapon has been proposed by Flight-Commander Hetherington of the R.N.A.S.

It may be briefly described as a cross-country armoured car of high offensive power.

It consists essentially of a platform mounted on three wheels (of which the front two are drivers and the stern wheel for steering), armed with three turrets, each containing two 4-inch guns, propelled by a 800 h.p. Sunbeam Diesel set, electric drive to the wheels being employed. The engines as well as the guns and magazines would be armoured, but not the purely structural part, which would be fairly proof against damage by shell-fire if a good factor of safety is used and a superfluity of parts provided in the structure.

The problem of design has been cursorily examined by Air Department Officers and the following rough data obtained:

Armament, 3 twin 4-inch turrets, with 300 rounds per gun.
Horse-power, 800, with 24 hours' fuel or more, if desired.
Total weight, 300 ton.
Armour, 3 in.
Diameter of wheels, 40 ft.
Tread of main wheels, 13 ft. 4 in.
Tread of steering-wheel, 5 ft.
Overall length, 100 ft.
Overall width, 80 ft.
Overall height, 46 ft.
Clear height under body, 17 ft.
Top speed on good country road, 8 miles per hour.
Top speed on bad country road, 4 miles per hour.

The above particulars must be regarded as approximate and cannot be guaranteed, owing to the absence in the department of technical knowledge properly applicable to this problem. These particulars are, however, quoted in the belief that they can be readily worked to. The cross-country qualities of the machine would appear to be good. It would not be bogged on any ground passable by cavalry. It could pass over water obstacles having good banks up to 20 ft. or 30 ft. width of waterway if deep. It could ford waterways with good bottom if the water is not more than 15 ft. deep. It could negotiate isolated obstacles up to 20 ft. high. Small obstacles, such as banks, ditches, bridges, trenches, wire entanglements (electrified or not), it would roll over easily. It could progress on bottom gear through woodland of ordinary calibre.

The greatest disabilities of the machine appear to be as follows:

It cannot cross considerable rivers except at practicable fords, which practically means that it cannot operate as a detached unit in country held by the enemy where this involves the systematically opposed crossing of big rivers. It can be destroyed by sufficiently powerful artillery. It can be destroyed by land mines.

The machines might on occasion do good service by destroying railway lines in the enemy's rear, but its most important function would appear to be in destroying the enemy's resistance over any region where he does not possess other guns than field-guns or howitzers.

It would appear at first sight that the machine ought to be more heavily armed and gunned, but considerations of the disproportionate weight of the guns and of time of building have resulted in the proposal being reduced to the comparatively moderate one described above.

Mr. Churchill referred these proposals to Lord Fisher, then First Sea Lord, and he detailed Sir Percy Scott, one of our famous gunnery Admirals, to look into them.

Sir Percy Scott held a conference, at which I attended, accompanied by Squadron-Commander Briggs, Flight-Commander Hetherington, Mr. Harris Booth and other of my interested Air Officers. After some considerable discussion, Sir Percy Scott reported against the whole idea of land battleships of large dimensions on the ground that heavy artillery would wreck them before they could be brought into action.

(4) Mr. Winston Churchill's Steam-roller Suggestions for Crushing in Enemy's Trenches.

In the middle of January, 1915, talking the whole position over once more with Mr. Churchill in his room at the Admiralty, he desired me to carry out the following experiment. In making the suggestion he warmed up to his subject, and in fact got quite excited, being carried away by enthusiasm for his idea. Striding up and down his room, he outlined what was in his mind and drafted the following minute. Whilst doing this, at intervals, he would stop and say: "We must crush the trenches in, D.A.D.[1] We must crush them in. It is the only way. We must do it. We will crush them. I am certain it can be done."

He then proceeded:

> I wish the following experiment made at once. Two ordinary steam-rollers are to be fastened together side by side with very strong steel connections, so they are to all intents and purposes one roller covering a breadth of at least 12 to 14 ft. If convenient, one of the back inside wheels might be removed and the other axle joined up to it. Some trenches are to be dug on the latest principles somewhere handy near London in lengths of at least 100 yds., the earth taken out of the trenches being thrown on each side, as is done in France. The roller is to be driven along these trenches, one outer rolling wheel on each side and the inner rolling wheel just clear of the trench itself. The object is to ascertain what amount of weight is necessary in the roller to smash the trench in. For this purpose as much weight as they can possibly draw should be piled on to the steam-rollers and on the framework buckling them together.

[1] Short for my official title of Director of Air Department.

The ultimate object is to run along a line of trenches, crushing them all flat and burying the people in them. If the experiment is successful with the steam-rollers fastened together on this improved system, stronger and larger machines can be made with bigger driving wheels and proper protection for the complements, and the rollers of these machines will be furnished with wedge-shaped ribs, or studs, which can be advanced beyond the ordinary surface of the wheel when required, in order to break the soil on each side of the trench and accentuate the rolling process. The matter is extremely urgent, and should be pressed to the utmost. Really the only difficulty you have got to surmount is to prevent the steam-rollers from breaking apart.

The simplicity of the device, if it succeeds, is its virtue. All that is required is a roller of sufficient breadth and with wheels properly fitted and an unscaleable bullet-proof house for the crew. Three or four men would be quite enough, and as the machine is only worked by night it might not be required to stand against artillery. In a fortnight I wish to see these trials.

These steam-roller instructions were dated 18th January, 1915, and marked to Third Sea Lord, Admiral Sir Frederick Tudor-Tudor and Director of Air Department (myself).

As a first action I referred the First Lord's instructions to Lieutenant Barry, my motor car expert, and his report is as follows:

20th January, 1915.

D.A.D. *Submitted.*

With reference to the attached letter from the First Lord, I have to-day visited Aldershot and inspected trials made with an American Holt caterpillar. The machine is, I believe, the most efficient form of tractor in existence, and the manner in which it goes over rough ground, soft ground, ditches, inequalities, up hill and down hill, is nothing short of marvellous. I saw it hitched on to a traction engine weighing 16 tons in soft

PRELIMINARY RESEARCHES AND IDEAS

ground, and it walked away with this as if it were no weight at all; they then hitched it on to the front of the traction engine at an angle of 45 degrees with the direction in which the traction engine was pointing; with equal ease as before it hauled it away, the front wheels of the traction engine tearing up the ground.

From inquiries made with regard to the joining of two steam-rollers together, it appears that if this were possible to do, and this machine was driven along a trench and did not break in half, the middle wheels would be supported by the outside wheels and it would not have the desired effect of rolling down the trench. I might add here that steam-rollers would be absolutely useless for this, as they would immediately become bogged in any soft earth, being made only for hard road service. Agricultural tractors might be utilized, but they would also, if the ground was very soft, become easily bogged. Any steam-roller or tractor would be very hard to armour-plate sufficiently to give protection both to the driver and vital parts of the engine. This also applies to the caterpillar above referred to.

The only suggestion I have to make is that two caterpillars, one on each side of the trench, be harnessed to a very heavy roller, but as their pace would be so very slow, the occupants of the trenches would have plenty of time to get out and escape. It is also extremely doubtful if any form of roller sufficiently heavy could be made which would really and genuinely roll these trenches flat considering that they are 6 ft. deep and varying from 2 ft. to 6 ft. across the top.

I submit that a possible method of attacking trenches would be to choose a day when the ground was frozen and utilize our armoured cars and armoured three-pounder lorries. If the ground was hard enough and these were fitted with non-skid chains, it is quite practicable to get them close up to the trenches. The only method for really attacking Germans in their trenches seems to be to have an enormous machine with a plough attachment to it, with a roller behind it, which would walk along the side of the trench, smash in one side and then roll it down flat. All of this could be easily managed in connection with the Juggernaut, specification[1] of which is attached.

After a considerable amount of trouble, we succeeded in coupling up two steam-rollers together. But I was only able, with the assistance of Lieutenant Barry, to keep them coupled for a short time. This, however, was sufficient to enable me to make the following report to Mr. Churchill well within the time he had given me.

Submitted.

In accordance with your directions two steam-rollers were obtained for the purpose of testing the possibility of their use for rolling down trenches.

A section of a trench was dug at Wormwood Scrubs where the land consists of hard clay, at present in a damp condition, but by no means soft.

On starting up the engines, however, the steam-rollers broke apart. Three more trials were made with the same result, and it is not considered possible, on account of the design of the ordinary steam-roller, to securely fix two together without practically rebuilding the engines.

In order to test the possibilities of this scheme further, tests were then carried out with a single roller. This was first of all run at full speed against the face of the trench, which consisted of a bank about 2 ft. high composed of a portion of the clay thrown out in making the trench. It was only just possible for the roller to move over the ground, and on reaching this slight bank it stopped dead, the driving wheels merely revolving and digging themselves deeper and deeper into the earth despite the fact that they had been wound round and round with 3-inch hemp rope to give them a better grip.

This engine was extricated and got on to a prepared plank roadway again for further tests with the help of the second engine working from this roadway.

Several more tests were made, approaching the trench from different directions, with exactly similar results.

The steam-roller would not climb the slightest inclination.

[1] Given on page 51.

These experiments prove that the loading of a steam-roller is too high for it to be successfully used over agricultural land, and that a machine to perform this work must be specially designed of a greater total weight and with very much greater wheel surface, and particularly much greater diameter wheels.

A machine of this description would be very costly to produce and would probably be very difficult to bring into action. Also it could be easily mined.

As an alternative to Mr. Churchill's steam-rollers coupled together proposals, Squadron-Commander Briggs, in a Reference Sheet I have before me, stated:

> After carefully reading through the First Lord's Minute on the subject of the trench-crusher I can see no difference, as regards proving the practicability of the scheme, between using two engines coupled together or one engine singly so long as the width of the trench is not such as to allow the front roller to fall in.

I discussed this matter with Briggs and he proposed using one giant steam-roller and got out for me a drawing showing Mr. Churchill's proposal of two steam-rollers coupled together and his proposal of a single giant steam-roller. He wanted to multiply the ordinary steam-roller dimensions by twenty so, as he said, to make a real trench-crusher to meet the First Lord's wishes. But I could not agree that this was a solution of the problem of a weapon for trench warfare.

On carefully considering from every point of view the various proposals put before me by Lieutenant Macfie, Squadron-Commander Briggs, Lieutenant Barry and that Major Hetherington's giant wheel battleship idea had been turned down by Admiral Sir Percy Scott, I did not see my way to ask Mr. Churchill to incur expenditure on any one of them; consequently no further action was taken and landships were for a time dead.

That landships were not then being proceeded with is borne out by the evidence given before the Royal Commission.

After describing his steam-roller proposals the Attorney-General said to Mr. Churchill:[1]

So that up to this point there have been three quite separate efforts to bring about the manufacture and adoption of engines which were subsequently known as the Tank?

Mr. Churchill replied: "That is so."

And they all came to nothing and ended in a deadlock?

Mr. Churchill: "That is so."

[1] Paragraph 28 of the Royal Commission's Report.

CHAPTER II

THE FIRST CATERPILLAR EXPERIMENTS

(1) THE CREATION OF CONFIDENCE IN CATERPILLAR MACHINES FOR WAR PURPOSES.
(2) THE FIRST ROYAL NAVAL AIR SERVICE CATERPILLAR LANDSHIP.

> "Sitting still and wishing
> Don't make no country great.
> The good Lord sends the fishing
> But you must dig the bait."[1]

(1) THE CREATION OF CONFIDENCE IN CATERPILLAR MACHINES

WHEN first I could find time to give serious thought to Mr. Churchill's problem of evolving a weapon suitable to cross No-Man's-Land, I had collected an exceptional amount of useful data in the Admiralty Air Department to work upon.

We had got out the designs and produced the open armoured car, the revolving turret armoured car, then the three-pounder heavy armoured lorry and armoured shields. Exhaustive experiments had been conducted with different thicknesses of armour plates to resist the Mauser bullet at point-blank range, and our armour-plate experts in the trade had learned to roll light armour plates, a hitherto unknown art.

At short intervals I had to see Mr. Churchill upon Naval Air matters and when doing so he would nearly always swing round to the subject of producing a weapon for trench warfare. The necessity for producing such a weapon was very much on his mind at that time. He would not drop this matter and constantly told me it was up to me to do something to get out a Trench Warfare weapon which was so much required and would say: "Now, D.A.D.,[2] put your best brains into this problem."

---

[1] Quotation made by Poet Laureate, Mr. John Masefield, on 8th July, 1935.
[2] Director of Air Department.

Which I did. But I could never see, nor can I see now, what trench warfare had to do with my duties as Director of the Admiralty Air Department. I was a Naval and not an Army Officer. To produce or attempt to produce a weapon for Army use was surely outside my Naval duty. There was no mention of this sort of creative work in the duties assigned to me in printed Admiralty orders.

Naturally I was as keen as anybody to contribute my small share in helping to win the War and do my very utmost, if able, to reduce the heavy casualties our Army comrades were called upon to bear.

On studying Mr. Churchill's steam-roller proposals from every possible angle, I came to the definite conclusion that both he and Flight-Commander Hetherington, with his giant wheel land battleship proposals, were quite on wrong lines.

First it seemed to me we should work up to big landships by starting with small ones in exactly the same way as at Barrow-in-Furness we worked up to the larger dimension submarines of the "A," "B" and "C" class from the small Holland Submarines. Then I reasoned the Trench Warfare machine that was required to cross No-Man's-Land should be a low machine, to lessen the target from hostile gun-fire: of moderate dimensions in all directions: should carry a gun mounted as in our Turret Armoured Car, but the gun to be of heavier calibre than we had been able to provide in those cars.

To distribute our load over as great a surface as possible, the exact opposite to Mr. Churchill's steam-roller idea, seemed to me to be required. We had tried double wheels on our armoured cars to give a greater wheel surface. But this had not solved the problem, and we were still experiencing much trouble with the tyres, springs and back axles.

The heavy hammer-like blows of an armoured car fully loaded with gun, ammunition and crew on some of the roads in this country and Belgium that were not very resilient caused considerable vibration, and matters were not improved by the roads being broken up in many districts by the ravages of water and frost during the winter of 1914–15.

The water content was then high.

THE FIRST CATERPILLAR EXPERIMENTS 61

Our pneumatic tyres and the chassis, however well sprung, could not stand up to too many of these sort of hard blows.

Big bills for replacements were coming into the Air Department, as Admiralty documents will show. This expenditure was being criticized very severely by the then Fourth Sea Lord, who loathed the Armoured Car Force from its inception, and always considered that the armoured cars had nothing to do with the Navy and the Navy should leave all armoured car work to the Army.

My calculations showed definitely that our wheeled armoured vehicles would not stand any greater load.

By experience on Service we found that the loads apart from the petrol which varied on consumption, however strict the Officers were, always tended to increase rather than diminish by extra stores, spare parts, baggage, etc.; on rough roads the wheels and springs would not stand up to the heavy loading and had to be constantly replaced.

If armoured cars had to be developed for use over difficult terrain it seemed to me that some form of caterpillar track to replace the wheels was essential.

At this time caterpillar traction was not entirely unknown to me, as I advised Captain Robert Scott, of Antarctic fame, who was a brother torpedo-man and old station-mate of mine in the Pacific and Channel Squadron, how to get his caterpillar sleigh built, and what firm to go to. He knew I had had considerable experience in running the first Holland submarine boats that were fitted with American petrol engines. Also "A1" Submarine[1] was fitted with a petrol engine designed by Mr. Herbert Austin,[2] of the Wolseley Company, a very capable designing engineer. From what I remember, the Wolseley Company built two or three motor sleighs for Scott, and he carried out some trials with these machines in Norway (Plate XI).

Scott asked me my advice whether he should develop aeroplanes or caterpillar sleighs for his Antarctic work. I advocated caterpillar sleighs, as our aeroplane engines at that time were not very reliable for long flights over

---

[1] "A1" was provided with a 12-cylinder 600 h.p. horizontal engine for running on the surface.
[2] Now Lord Austin, the celebrated Chairman of Austin Motor Car Ltd.

difficult Antarctic conditions, where it would have been almost impossible to bring the Pilot in if he had to make a forced landing.

Also I gave Scott all my tips for starting petrol engines in our early submarines when we had to cut our way through the ice in the Barrow Docks on our way to the Irish Sea for diving trials. All through the severest weather in the winter we kept the submarine trials going, and it was in the coldest weather no easy task to get "A1" submarines' 600 h.p. petrol engine to "pip" in all 12 cylinders when it was freezing hard.

As recorded on page 47 Lieutenant Macfie, one of my Armoured Car Officers, had sent me in a scheme during November, 1914, for hauling 12-inch naval guns by means of caterpillar tractors. More than once I had mentioned our tyre difficulties to Mr. Churchill and had told him we would be forced to some form of caterpillar track to replace the wheels.

Lieutenant Barry in his report of 20th January, 1915,[1] had given me a good account of the Holt Caterpillar Tractor for going over rough and soft ground, irregularities, uphill, downhill, etc.

As previously mentioned Squadron-Commander Briggs was assisting me on the engineering side with all our difficult problems in connection with armour and fixing it to the cars. I cannot speak too highly of this Officer's services in the Air Department. He was most successful with aeroplane engines, airship engines, cars for the S.S., coastal airships and the armoured cars. His engineering advice all the time he served under me could not have been more helpful or more readily forthcoming. He was indeed a splendid Officer and skilful Engineer. I sent for Squadron-Commander Briggs to discuss my new caterpillar landship scheme with him. From my submarine experience I knew what confined space a crew could work in without much air for a prolonged period, for had we not, under Admiral Bacon, carried out breathing experiments in a completely sealed submarine in a practical manner when totally submerged in the Barrow Docks to the nth.

I took the 60-ft. Holland Submarine as a guide, and

[1] Pages 54 and 55.

cut it in two for my length dimension. This gave me 30 ft. and the diameter of the Holland was 9½ ft.; this gave me my approximate width and height. In a landship of this size constructed on submarine lines, with the necessary armour plating, turret, a crew of eight men could work, breathe and be fairly comfortable.

We found in the first submarines, with their petrol motors, our chief danger was the carbon monoxide that percolated through from the exhaust gases of the internal combustion engine. It is almost impossible to make a perfect joint. This dangerous gas is often as high as 3 per cent in the exhaust gases of an ordinary petrol-engine. That is why we submarine men in the early days pressed with success for the Diesel Engine which has so much smaller percentage of carbon monoxide in the exhaust gases when using heavier oil.

Even if the gun port-holes of my caterpillar landship had to be closed as much as possible when under rifle- or machine-gun fire, the air that would percolate through would keep the crew going without much ill effect for a considerable time, in spite of the carbon dioxide and carbon monoxide gases that are most difficult to eliminate entirely.

We armoured my proposed landship with the same armour as on our Turret Armoured Cars. This would keep out the latest German bullet at close range, provided a turret, and gave an armament of one twelve-pounder or two six-pounders with spares, ammunition, crew, etc. We had all the data of our turret and three-pounder armoured cars before us and the weights of the twelve-pounder or two six-pounders that we obtained from the D.N.O. Department. My main idea was to take a heavier calibre gun into action pointing the right way for engaging the pill-boxes and machine-gun nests of the enemy, thus differing from the many systems of hauling heavier calibre guns with the muzzle pointing the wrong way.

The information we had been able to obtain about caterpillar tracks enabled us to work out approximately the maximum and minimum load per square foot on both tracks, which was in the order of 800 to 1000 lbs. per square foot. This loading would allow for the weight of the tracks not being too excessive for practical work.

With all weights carefully worked out I found we could produce a 24-ton landship of reasonable dimensions and not be too large a target for hostile gun-fire. Admiral Sir Percy Scott impressed this upon me when he turned down Flight-Commander Hetherington's giant battleship scheme and said we were wasting time in considering big landships. Briggs procured a book on bridges that I still have in my possession, and we ascertained most bridges near towns are constructed to support a load of 25 tons.

My idea was to construct our landship with a turned-up bow and stern like the bow of a submarine and support the load on long track caterpillars driven by two Rolls-Royce engines. Each caterpillar track to be driven independently like the propellers in our first rigid airship—*Mayfly*. These could go ahead or astern or one ahead and one astern as required. This would give us a small turning circle. Also I had the particulars of all the productions of the Pedrail Transport Company, as on the 12th January, 1915, I had sent Squadron-Commander Hetherington to this Company's Works at Fulham to inspect their caterpillar machine with the view of using it for experimental purposes with the infantry shield, which Mr. Buckham of Messrs. Vickers was designing for me (page 45). Squadron-Commander Hetherington's report had been favourable and I asked the Pedrail Transport Company to send their caterpillar truck to Wormwood Scrubs where it arrived on 13th January, 1915.

Most of my Officers who had been assisting me to develop our armoured cars were well aware that the problem of distributing the weight of a highly loaded vehicle over a greater area than ordinary wheels provided had engaged the attention of Road Engineers for a great many years. We were faced with the same problems in developing landships.

It is quite true to say at this period of the War not only myself but most of my Staff were getting rather fed-up and exasperated at Mr. Churchill's policy of giving us all the hard nuts to crack, as anything new he wanted done was always given to the Air Department, a compliment we did not, with so much air work on hand, always appreciate. His action always recalled to my mind the title of one of

THE FIRST CATERPILLAR EXPERIMENTS

Mr. Cochran's earlier revues—"One Dam Thing After Another." Nevertheless, I was making every endeavour to get out a useful weapon for trench warfare to keep this forceful man quiet.

We searched much literature for caterpillar ideas and Squadron-Commander Briggs was fortunate enough in obtaining from one of the foreign booksellers off Leicester Square a copy of *Scientific American* of 18th February, 1911, which showed a good picture of a caterpillar agricultural machine mounted on a fairly long track for supporting a heavy load over bad agricultural land. Armed with this caterpillar information I had collected, on 16th February, 1915, I went to Mr. Churchill's room in the forenoon and reported to him I had solved his steam-roller problem in another way, and would he attend a demonstration on the Horse Guards' Parade that afternoon.

Mr. Churchill said: "I still believe there is something in my heavy steam-roller idea." But I told him my scheme was better, and he agreed to attend the demonstration. Mr. Churchill was most unreasonable at times in expecting me to do a great deal with air machines, armoured cars, anti-aircraft defence of London, etc., but he was quick-brained, and a good Chief to work for, and although we had a very limited amount of money and small staff, Mr. Churchill seemed to place extraordinary trust in the Air Department's ability to overcome obstacles.

I instructed Flight-Commander Hetherington to get in touch with the Fulham Firm and arrange for them to bring their Diplock Caterpillar truck to the Horse Guards' Parade on the 16th February, 1915. This caterpillar had no motive power of its own and had to be drawn by a horse. Although I had this machine at Wormwood Scrubs for experimental work in connection with my infantry shield, the Admiralty had not yet purchased it and the caterpillar was still the property of the Diplock Transport Company. We had no horse at Wormwood Scrubs so the Firm were asked to bring it for us (Plate XIII). Flight-Commander Hetherington arrived with the Diplock Caterpillar on the Horse Guards Parade on the 16th February, 1915, accompanied by Mr. Diplock and Mr. Brackenbury, Directors of the Diplock Transport Company, who I had invited to attend the demonstration. Then I gave Mr. Churchill my proposals for building a machine for crossing "no-man's-land" as follows:

With a long caterpillar fitted under one of our turreted armoured cars each side, you could do away with all the spring difficulties. The load would be better and more evenly distributed, and you could increase the armament, i.e. calibre of guns, amount of armament carried, etc. The planks we had fitted to our heavy armoured cars could be done away with. This would relieve the men from exposure to shell-fire when placing them across small shell-holes, ditches dug in roads, etc. (see photograph of planks, Plate XII). We had received complaints about exposing the crews when laying these planks.

Barbed wire could be easily rolled down or cut if a torpedo net cutter was used. The crew would be properly protected, and all the controls would be inside, as in our revolving-turret armoured cars, and not exposed, as in the three-pounder heavy armoured cars.

I pushed the caterpillar truck, loaded with large stones, about with my hands, to show Mr. Churchill how easily it could be manipulated, explained the caterpillar system as far as I knew it, and showed Mr. Churchill how our spring difficulties could be overcome (Plate XIII).

Mr. Churchill then pushed the caterpillar truck about the Horse Guards' Parade, and was amazed at the ease with which this truck with a full load of large stones could be moved. Although Mr. Churchill does not shine at his best in dealing with mechanical matters he has the sharpest brain for grasping a new idea that I have ever met and at once saw that my proposals were a better proposition than his steam-roller idea or Flight-Commander Hetherington's giant wheel scheme. After considerable discussion it ended in Mr. Churchill being quite satisfied that our turreted armoured cars could be constructed with caterpillars instead of wheels, and he gave me approval to build eighteen landships before any other department or firm came into the landship picture.

My scheme was quite practicable and only wanted working out by skilful designers and constructors, similar to those we had when building our first Naval Submarines at

PLATE XI

PLATE XII

PLATE XIII

(*Top*) CAPTAIN ROBERT SCOTT'S ANTARCTIC SLEIGH
(*Centre*) LANCHESTER ARMOURED CAR
Showing planks for crossing ditches, January, 1915.
(*Lower*) THE DIPLOCK CATERPILLAR TRUCK
Used by the Author on Horse Guards Parade, February 16th, 1915, to demonstrate to Mr. Winston Churchill how caterpillars could replace wheels of Armoured Cars.

DIAGRAM I

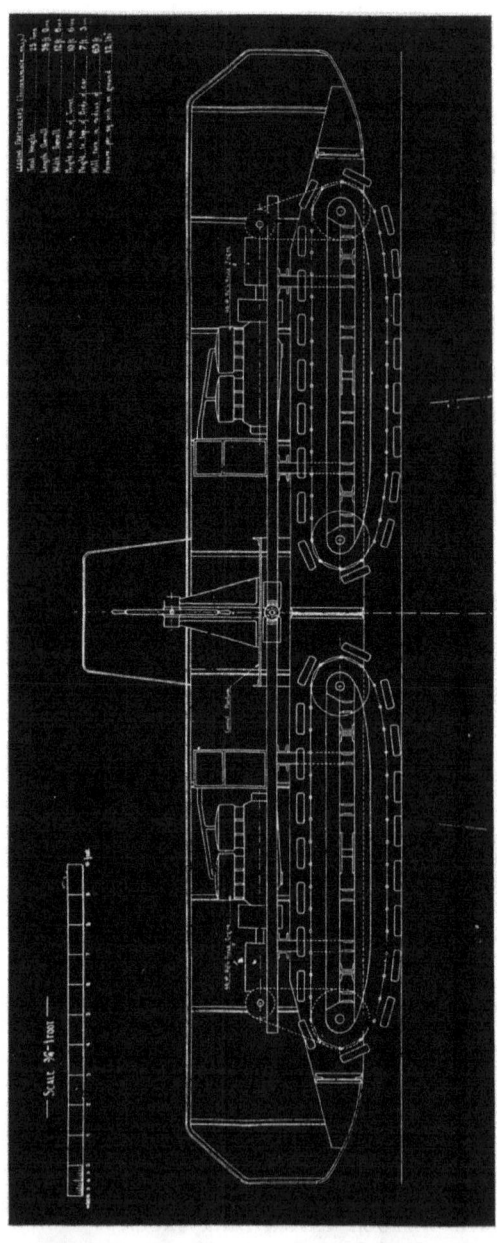

FIRST CONCEPTION OF ROYAL NAVAL AIR SERVICE CATERPILLAR LANDSHIP

This drawing was prepared from armoured car data furnished by Commodore Sueter (Director of Admiralty Air Department) to Mr. Diplock (Director of the Pedrail Transport Co.). It was laid before the Landship Committee on March 4th, 1915, for examination and discussion. Noticeable is the upturned Bow and Stern. Two short caterpillar tracks are shown because the Diplock Co. could not manufacture long caterpillar tracks. No guns are shown in Turret for secrecy purposes. Attention is drawn to the characteristics of the machine which are of interest. This is the first drawing of a Caterpillar Landship to be placed before responsible Authority during the War and is with its sectional drawing in Admiralty Office.

Published for the first time by permission of 1937 Board of Admiralty.

Messrs Vickers' works, Barrow-in-Furness. The problem was almost the same. The stresses thrown upon a vessel in a heavy sea are not unlike the problem of a landship on rough terrain when going in and out of a shell-hole.

I asked Mr. Tennyson D'Eyncourt to come down to the Horse Guards Parade and have a look at the Diplock Caterpillar machine and we manœuvred it about for him to see and made him acquainted with my proposal to build a caterpillar landship. I informed D'Eyncourt that Colonel Crompton, the big road traction expert, had been consulted and said my ideas were sound and that he was making more calculations with Mr. Le Gros, a friend of his, to verify his first opinion.

In talking to Mr. D'Eyncourt, I told him that the Fourth Sea Lord had ordered me not to devote too much attention to armoured cars and neglect the Air Service, therefore I could not take a very active part in the building designs.

Mr. D'Eyncourt, in spite of his enormous responsibilities and big work as Director of Naval Construction, saw the point and kindly agreed to run the show and I was to stay in the background and guide the experimental work with my Officers and men at our armoured car stations. On my advice, as proved before the Royal Commission on Awards to Inventors, Mr. Churchill approved of a Committee being set up consisting of

> The Director of Naval Construction, Mr. Tennyson D'Eyncourt, as Chairman,
> Colonel Crompton,
> Colonel Dumbell,
> Squadron-Commander Hetherington, representing the Director of the Air Department,
> Mr. Dale Bussell, representing the Director of Contracts

—to develop my caterpillar landship scheme, and all proposals were to be considered by that Committee no matter who they came from. My first action was to obtain Admiralty Board approval to appoint Colonel Crompton as technical adviser to this Landship Committee from first of March, 1915, for six months. I wanted this Committee to develop my caterpillar landship in exactly the same way as the Admiralty Committee of Experts developed the Whitehead Torpedo and made it famous as a great weapon of war.

After the demonstration to Mr. Churchill I asked Mr. Diplock to come to my office and then instructed one of my Officers, Flight-Commander Michell,[1] to go to the library and borrow my Submarine Book from Mr. Perrin, the Admiralty Librarian. I went through the illustrations with Mr. Diplock and showed him the plates of the Lake Submarine and Fontes Submarine. We decided that a landship should have an upturned bow and stern and that it should be mounted on caterpillar tracks. Mr. Diplock said his Firm could not construct long track caterpillars as I required, but they could build short ones. So I had to be content with that. I gave Mr. Diplock the data that Squadron-Commander Briggs had worked out with me and I limited our caterpillar landship to 25 tons. At first I wanted, if the weight per horse-power was not too great, two 70 h.p. Rolls-Royce engines. But Mr. Diplock said it would be wiser to keep to their standard type to avoid delays and keep weights down. This was their 46 h.p. engine, two of which would be required. Mr. Diplock was a man of considerable experience and had for many years carried out a large amount of difficult haulage work. He was a great road locomotive expert. We worked at the data I provided and went into the necessary details between 16th February and 27th February, 1915. The final dimensions for my caterpillar landship that Mr. Diplock agreed upon with me before he imparted them to his draughtsman, Mr. Lowe, for my armoured caterpillar landship drawings were:

Total length	38 ft.
Width	12 ft. 6 ins.
Height to top of turret	10 ft. 6 ins.
Height to top of body	7 ft. 3 ins.
2 Rolls-Royce engines, 46 h.p. each	92·6 h.p.
Armament	1 12–pounder.
Crew	8 men.
Pressure per square inch on ground	12 lb.
Turning radius	65 ft.

[1] Minutes of Proceedings, The Royal Commission on Awards to Inventors, page 48, para. 720, 8th Oct., 1919.

Turret provided.
Upturned bow and stern.
Total weight of armour armament,
    ammunition, crew, baggage, etc. 25 tons.

With this data before him and the particulars I had given Mr. Diplock, a drawing of a caterpillar landship was made for me on 28th February, 1915, by Mr. Lowe (Diagram I).

A photo-print of this drawing was prepared on 4th March, 1915, and I instructed Mr. Diplock to have it taken to Colonel Crompton's private house and ask the Colonel to lay it before the Landship Committee as a first idea for examination and discussion. Mr. Lowe took this drawing to Colonel Crompton and he was pleased with it. A meeting of the Committee was summoned that afternoon at the Admiralty and Mr. Lowe presented my landship drawing. I claim that this was the first turret armoured caterpillar landship drawing got out in the War, and placed before a responsible authority, i.e. the Admiralty Landship Committee.

At this meeting was shown a blue print of an armoured tractor machine mounted on wheels which was Mr. Tritton's of Messrs. Fosters' idea of a landship.

Mr. Brackenbury in his letter to me dated 30th May, 1919, states:

> "Sir William Tritton's claim as the originator of the idea can readily be disposed of by the production of the drawing which he submitted to the Admiralty Landship Committee on the 4th March, 1915, at the same time we submitted the design which you have.
>
> This design of Tritton's shows a tractor engine on wheels with a kind of armoured shield in front of the driver.
>
> This design was rejected in favour of our own and it was only months later that Tritton came forward with any other suggestion."

At first Mr. Tritton did not seem to be favourably impressed with caterpillars for landship work and my armoured-car Officers were always of the opinion that he had more than once stated that barbed wire would jamb the tracks and throw the whole machine out of action when required to flatten down the formidable criss-cross barbed-wire entanglements that the Germans had erected when they commenced to "dig in" at the Front. The progress reports in my possession bear out this opinion, page 86.

At a later date through contact with my armoured-car Officers, such as Squadron-Commander Hetherington, Lieutenant Stern and Lieutenant Wilson, Mr. Tritton came round to the caterpillar idea for landships. He realized fully when a mock-up of a large machine on wheels was built that it was an impossible solution of the problem as the wheeled landship offered too great a target to hostile gun-fire. This was the same opinion as expressed at an earlier date by Admiral Sir Percy Scott when he examined Squadron-Commander Hetherington's giant wheel battleship proposals.

A short time elapsed and I made certain administrative arrangements with the Landship Committee, in which the Director of Naval Construction and Director of Contracts concurred, before I issued the following orders:

REFERENCE SHEET

From—
    DIRECTOR OF AIR
        DEPARTMENT AT ADMIRALTY.
To—
    O.C. ARMOURED CARS (COMMANDER BOOTHBY),
    FLIGHT-COMMANDER HETHERINGTON,
    COLONEL CROMPTON, R.E.,
        THRIPLANDS,
            KENSINGTON COURT.

Dated: 30th March, 1915.
5672.

INFORMATION REQUIRED, OR NOTIFIED.

The following routine is to be observed in organizing and ordering material for the three new Squadrons of Armoured Cars.[1]

---

[1] We called the caterpillar machines under various names, as armoured cars, pedrail machines, juggernauts, landships, and eventually Tanks, for secrecy purposes during the experiments and their construction.

All questions of designs will be considered in Committee with D.N.C. and D. of C., O.C. Armoured Cars, Flight-Commander Hetherington, and Colonel Crompton.

Colonel Crompton to supervise the design and generally to assist, but should place no orders himself.

Flight-Commander Hetherington is to supervise the construction of the Cars. He is to forward copies of all drawings, when complete, to me, through O.C. Armoured Cars. He is to forward all proposals for purchase of material, etc., to O.C. Armoured Cars, who will bring them to me for approval and signature before forwarding them to the Director of Contracts.

The O.C. Armoured Cars is responsible for organizing the personnel of the new Squadrons and that I am kept informed of the progress of the work in a weekly report.

The new Squadrons are to be organized on exactly the same lines as the present Armoured Car Squadrons.

(Sgd.) MURRAY F. SUETER,
Director of Air Department.

30th March, 1915.

The arrangement I made with the Chairman of the Landship Committee at that time was that my Armoured Car Officers and Ratings would under my general direction conduct all the experimental work and I would place at the disposal of the Landship Committee our armoured-car organization. The Committee was purely advisory and had no executive authority. All executive orders had to come through myself.

To hasten the construction of a Caterpillar Landship I instructed Commander Boothby and Flight-Commander Hetherington to ascertain if we could not get quick delivery of caterpillar tracks from America. For some time I had been ordering a large number of aeroplanes and seaplanes from the well-known firm of Curtis and Company in America. These machines I used for training purposes and also to have a second string should many of the employees of our Aircraft Firms have to join the Colours. Also the policy of employing American Firms to construct our school machines allowed our aircraft manufactuers in this country to devote all their attention to the production of war machines.

The American aircraft were quite good for the purposes required and I thought the Firms that manufactured caterpillar agricultural machines in the United States would be equally good for constructing experimental caterpillar tracks for our landships. Colonel Crompton, under instructions from the Landship Committee, had been collecting all the information he could in connection with the development of caterpillar tracks in America from various United States representatives then in this country. He ascertained that a "creeping grip" Bullock Caterpillar Tractor had arrived at Greenhithe. I arranged that Flight-Commander Hetherington and Lieutenant Wilson should inspect this machine. They went with Colonel Crompton on 28th April, 1915, to Greenhithe, and after this inspection we ordered through the Director of Contracts two creeping grip Caterpillar Tractors and two specially lengthened standard Bullock tracks from America for landship experiments. On Colonel Crompton's advice, I was fortunate in being able to obtain the services of Mr. Field who had been a technical assistant to the Colonel in former days. The Board of Admiralty gave me approval to grant him a commission as a Lieutenant R.N.V.R. for service with the Armoured Cars, and I sent him in May, 1915, to America to supervise the building of the lengthened standard Bullock tracks that we had ordered for the Landship Committee through the Director of Contracts. The instructions I gave to Lieutenant Field were that a caterpillar landship would have to cross a 5-ft. trench and go over a 2-ft. 6-in. parapet, and he was to study and collect caterpillar information in America and send reports home as speedily as possible.

After doing a considerable amount of caterpillar investigation in America Lieutenant Field sent in some valuable reports on Killen Strait and Bullock Caterpillars, which I sent immediately to the Landship Committee.

In one report received on 6th July, 1915, he enclosed a drawing showing special angularized caterpillar tracks got out for him by the Killen Strait Company in America.

THE FIRST CATERPILLAR EXPERIMENTS 73

The drawing was of considerable interest and importance because it showed that Lieutenant Field in his work in America came to the conclusion that angularized tracks were necessary for caterpillar landships. This drawing was almost identical with the angularized track invented by Lieutenant Macfie and Mr. Nesfield, and shown on the Macfie-Nesfield Model that I had given orders[1] on the 29th June, 1915, to be placed before the Landship Committee.

Unfortunately for Lieutenant Field, Macfie and Nesfield had anticipated him by a very short time and the Royal Commission, after hearing all the evidence, decided to give Mr. Nesfield and Lieutenant Macfie a small award for drawing the attention of the Landship Committee to this important invention in caterpillar track development.

In May, 1915, Colonel Crompton desired the following information for the Landship Committee and asked if I could help him to obtain it :

"To enable us to fix the minimum turning circle and maximum width of these vehicles and the minimum loaded weight of the mile run we require to know the width, curves and weight carrying capacity of the existing roads and bridges and the general nature of the ground surface between our own and the enemy's trenches.

We wish to have specimen sections of the most recent form of German trenches giving width, depth, nature of revetments and parapets to compare with our own. Particulars of the most recent and most difficult type of wire entanglements were also required."

I tried to obtain some of this information through Squadron-Commander Gregory, my Armoured Car Officer at Dunkirk, but he was unable to get anything accurate from G.H.Q., and the War Office had no information of any value to impart to us.

So in consultation with D'Eyncourt I decided to send Flight-Commander Hetherington and Squadron-Commander Gregory to accompany Colonel Crompton to G.H.Q., France, to obtain at first hand the information required. Everything at this time seemed to be working

[1] Page 109.

against all of us who were so interested and bent on developing landships.

When Colonel Crompton and his party arrived at St. Omer they were met by a Staff Officer who promptly sent them back. This was done in a very curt manner because they had no official pass from the War Office.

Colonel Crompton was very bitter at his treatment and wrote me a strong letter of complaint. It took me some time to pour oil on his troubled feelings.

There is no doubt that certain Noahs at the War Office, all Services seem to breed Noahs for the sole purpose of thwarting progressive men, were determined to block the use of mechanical weapons by the Army in exactly the same way as the Admiralty Noahs were retarding Naval Air development.

Acting upon Colonel Crompton's and Flight-Commander Hetherington's advice, I purchased a Killen Strait Caterpillar Machine through the Admiralty Contracts Department for the Landship Committee to commence practical experiments and handed it over to Commander Boothby to place it upon the Armoured Car establishment at Wormwood Scrubs.

In the Torpedo School *Vernon* when about to introduce a new type of mine or gyroscope torpedo or some novel electrical fire-control instruments, it was usual to obtain confidence in the new weapon or piece of electrical apparatus by inviting Admiralty Officials and interested Officers from the other Torpedo Schools to attend a practical demonstration. I had to arouse the confidence of Authority and attract technical thought to my landship scheme. Once this was accomplished there would be a definite and forceful effort by all concerned to try caterpillars out to see if they would be of use on active service. On Commander Boothby's return from inspecting the armoured cars we had sent overseas, I instructed him[1] to prepare a big demonstration at Wormwood Scrubs to try and establish confidence in my Caterpillar Landship proposals before Authority. After some consultation with his Officers, Flight-Commander Hetherington, Lieutenant Stern and

[1] Minutes of Proceedings before Royal Commission on Awards to Inventors, paragraph 302.

PLATE XIV

PLATE XV

PLATE XVI

(*Top*) EXPERIMENTS WITH KILLEN STRAIT MACHINE
Hetherington, Stern, McGrath, June, 1915—Royal Naval Air Service Officers.
(*Centre*) KILLEN STRAIT OVER RAILWAY METALS
(*Below*) KILLEN STRAIT OVER RAILWAY SLEEPERS

PLATE XVII

PLATE XVIII

(*Above*) DEMONSTRATION BEFORE MR. LLOYD GEORGE, MR. WINSTON CHURCHILL AND MILITARY OFFICERS
Flight-Commander Hetherington driving Killen Strait Caterpillar Machine through barbed wire obstructions at Wormwood Scrubs, June 30th, 1915.

(*Below*) KILLEN STRAIT CUTTING THROUGH BARBED WIRE

others, the Commander and myself agreed that we should erect at Wormwood Scrubs the following obstacles:

    Railway metals in piles;
    Railway sleepers heaped up;
    Various depths of wire entanglement;
    Improvised shell-holes and trenches.

Commander Boothby also agreed that we should fit the Killen Strait Caterpillar Machine with Pioneer naval net-cutters like we use for the Whitehead Torpedo. I obtained two of these Pioneer Net-Cutters from Admiral Dumas, then Director of Torpedoes. These were fitted to the Killen Strait Machine. The Officers and men of the Armoured Car Force worked hard in building up our obstructions, etc. (Plates XIV, XV and XVI).

The demonstration was arranged for 30th June, 1915. Mr. Lloyd George, then Minister of Munitions, Mr. Winston Churchill, Chancellor of the Duchy of Lancaster, General Sir Scott Moncrieff, General Phillips, Colonel Crompton, Colonel Jackson, and several of my Armoured Car Officers, Admiralty officials, etc., attended at Wormwood Scrubs.

Flight-Commander Hetherington was selected to drive the Killen Strait Caterpillar because he was formerly a Cavalry Officer, a fine steeplechase rider and one who had considerable nerve in tackling most fences on a horse. Being a great lover of horses, I always doubted whether it occurred to Hetherington at that time that our Caterpillar experiments would lead, if successful, to the construction of Caterpillar Landships which might mean the partial elimination of the horse from our Army.

Hetherington drove the Killen Strait Machine with great skill, negotiating various and difficult objects, and impressed all those who witnessed these tests that there was something in Caterpillar Landships (Plates XVII and XVIII).

The torpedo net-cutters clipped the wire entanglements as if they were made of twine. Some defects occurred towards the end of this demonstration, one of the rods connecting the two net-cutters together sheered and allowed some of the barbed wire to get round the steering member. This did not occur until the caterpillar machine had been once completely through the barbed-wire entanglements and two-thirds through another large wire entanglement of the same dimensions. The Military Authorities expressed themselves very enthusiastically about the cutters.

Mr. Lloyd George seemed impressed with the whole demonstration and thought we should continue the caterpillar experiments for landships. He was very much taken with the naval net-cutters that had cut through the barbed-wire entanglements (Plate XVIII) and the way the caterpillar had negotiated the difficult obstructions we had prepared.

The whole demonstration was an undoubted success, and I congratulated Commander Boothby most warmly for the good work he and his Staff had done. In these experiments we found the Killen Strait Track had no destructive nut-cracker action as Colonel Crompton rather expected.

It consisted of an endless chain of heavy steel links, joined together in such a way as to form an absolutely smooth track. Hardwood tread blocks sheathed with heavy steel channels were bolted to these links to form the treads. The wood blocks formed the "ties" of the track and absorbed a large proportion of shocks and jars. The links were joined together with case-hardened steel pins 1 in. in diameter and 13 in. long. These pins had bearing surface over their entire length. The machine was carried on large iron idler wheels. These wheels served to carry the weight and keep the track in line, but were not used to transmit any power. The power was positively applied to the track by driving sprockets with detachable case-hardened rims. Three links of the chain engaged the sprocket at one time, thus minimizing the wear. Ample provision was made for tightening the chain when necessary, by moving the front set of idler wheels. If the chain became stretched out of pitch by long service it could be adjusted by bolting on new sprocket rims with increased pitch.

Had it not been for Hetherington's skilful driving of the Killen Strait over these various obstacles shown in Plates XV, XVI and XVII, which won Mr. Lloyd George to our side, and the support of the Third Sea Lord, Admiral Sir Frederick Tudor-Tudor, in generally encouraging our armoured car efforts, I fear the whole landship idea would not have matured.

THE FIRST CATERPILLAR EXPERIMENTS 77

Hetherington's services all the time were splendid. He made me think whilst we were developing our armoured cars in terms of landships and had much to do with the success of the armoured cars. All through the difficult times after Mr. Churchill left the Admiralty this young Airman kept up his belief in landships and never wavered for one minute. This had much to do in keeping confidence from wavering or entirely fizzling out. His services were of very great value and it always seemed to me he was rewarded very inadequately with a C.B.E. for his big share in much landship experimental work.

A short time after our demonstration to Mr. Lloyd George I was sent for by a Member of the Board of Admiralty and instructed to send in my reasons in writing for daring to use the Pioneer Torpedo Net-Cutter at Wormwood Scrubs on our caterpillar machine. I explained that the Assistant Director of Torpedoes, Admiral Dumas, had raised no objections when I asked him to allow two Pioneer Net-Cutters to be used for our landship experiments and said no real objection could be taken as I had removed the secret part! Poor landships, how we had to struggle to get them going. I had the greatest difficulty in persuading Authority that no harm had been done to the Naval Service in showing Mr. Lloyd George how a Naval Net-Cutter could clip wire entanglements like grass.

The papers in connection with this objection to the use of these Pioneer Net-Cutters at the demonstration for Mr. Lloyd George are really amazing; one would have thought he was a German spy instead of our great Minister of Munitions who did so much by organizing the production of supplies at that critical time to help us win the War in 1918.

Crush all initiative was then a favourite pastime for the Noahs. These airmen with their awkward ideas must be put in their proper place. This attitude of mind was scarcely helpful in the greatest War the World has ever seen.

In his design for a caterpillar landship Colonel Crompton departed from my 38-ft. caterpillar landship drawing and made his 60 ft. in length. Then he ascertained from Army sources that 60 ft. was too long, so he proposed to cut his original design in halves and arranged for the two parts to be coupled together in an articulated type of landship.

To fully test out Colonel Crompton's articulated landship idea a whole series of experiments were carried out by my Armoured Car Officers under his general guidance with the two creeping grip Caterpillar Tractors (Plate XIX) when coupled together at Burton. An idea of the stresses thrown on the coupling that would have to join two 30-ft. machines together can readily be imagined by a close examination of Plates XIX, XX and XXI.

As these machines were crossing trenches the experiments clearly showed that an articulated machine had little or no prospect of success. Over and over again I discussed the whole question of articulated landships with Commander Boothby. We were both Torpedoists and preferred a single unit to any double type of landship. Being able to fire down one street in a Flanders village whilst at the same time being able to engage an enemy down another did not seem to either of us a very practical proposition.

I gave Commander Boothby instructions to oppose this waste of time on articulated landships that were not likely to possess any value for fighting purposes, as they were too complicated, and get Colonel Crompton to design a single unit landship on the Bullock trucks we were obtaining from America, and the Commander opposed articulated landships as opportunity offered.

(2) THE FIRST ROYAL NAVAL AIR SERVICE CATERPILLAR LANDSHIP.

After Mr. Churchill left the Admiralty in May, 1916, Mr. Arthur Balfour became First Lord, and as soon as he commenced his important duties more than one Sea Lord urged him to disband the Royal Naval Air Service Armoured Car Force and discontinue all caterpillar landship experiments.

Then my struggle to retain No. 20 Squadron that I had created specially for caterpillar experiments commenced in earnest.[1]

Naturally I kept Commander Boothby informed of my new difficulties and how the Fourth Sea Lord was working

[1] Page 246.

PLATE XIX

PLATE XX

(*Above*) EXPERIMENTS WITH BULLOCK CREEPING GRIP TRACTORS COUPLED TOGETHER AT BURTON-ON-TRENT, JULY, 1915

(*Below*) FLIGHT-COMMANDER HETHERINGTON AND LIEUTENANT WILSON—R.N.A.S. ARMOURED CAR OFFICERS—
conducting these experiments with Bullock Creeping Grip Tractors.

PLATE XXI

PLATE XXII

PLATE XXIII

(*Top*) EXPERIMENT WITH BULLOCK TRACTORS. FRONT WHEELS OFF GROUND
(*Centre*) SHOWING SAG OF CATERPILLAR TRACK BULLOCK TRACTOR
(*Below*) TWO BULLOCK CREEPING GRIP TRACTORS COUPLED TOGETHER IN CONNECTION WITH ARTICULATED LANDSHIP EXPERIMENTS, JULY, 1915
Colonel Crompton, Flight-Commander Hetherington and Lieutenant Wilson.

at his very best to wreck our caterpillar experiments that we were both so keen about. I told him that I had persuaded Mr. Balfour to allow this experimental work to continue and the First Lord approved that our caterpillar experiments should be pressed forward so that one caterpillar landship could be constructed as soon as possible. If the Officers and Ratings had a landship to handle it would counter the large amount of criticism then being made that they were idle. I instructed Commander Boothby, as opportunity offered, to get a move on the Landship Committee and get something done. They were appointed towards the end of February and here it was the end of June and no machine had yet been built. Commander Boothby was a great Officer. He had commanded the Armoured Car Force, working directly under my orders, since its inception. No Officer could have worked harder or been more loyal. If Plate XXIV shows a smiling face it must not be assumed he was always in that mood. As Carlyle would have said he was a man with "fire in his belly."

On 1st July,[1] as stated by D'Eyncourt in his evidence[2] before the Royal Commission on Awards to Inventors, that difficulties had arisen, I myself[3] gave evidence that D'Eyncourt told me he would remain the President of the Committee only if I removed Commander Boothby. D'Eyncourt also said he did not think that there was much of a future for landships. I made a careful note of this statement at the time as it struck me as being exactly the same sort of view as that expressed by the late Admiral Sir W. H. Henderson after I had dived him in a Holland Submarine at Barrow-in-Furness, when on landing he turned to me and said: "Lieutenant Sueter, I am very much interested in your submarine and as I have inspected the Holland boat in America I want to inform you that in my opinion they are perfectly useless."

It is a habit of mine to take note of important conversations, and I had to deal with Commander Boothby[4] after-

---
[1] 1915.
[2] Page 108, par. 1692, Minutes of Proceedings of Royal Commission on Awards to Inventors, 10th October, 1919.   [3] Page 40, par. 477.
[4] Page 40, par. 475, Minutes of Proceedings of Royal Commission on Awards to Inventors, 8th October, 1919.

wards when I had to dismiss him from the Landship Committee. So many strange happenings, such as burning important papers, occurred at the Admiralty in those days that careful notes, copies of minutes and sometimes photographs of a particular decision on a docket became necessary.

D'Eyncourt was exceedingly nice. I had to explain to him my difficulties and all the criticisms that were being hurled at my head to the effect that No. 20 Squadron were an idle lot and not pulling their weight in the War. At least that was the opinion the Fourth Sea Lord was freely circulating round the Admiralty Office, and it was all my fault for trying to develop these stupid caterpillar landships that nobody wanted.

During this conversation I asked D'Eyncourt if he could not without delay build an experimental landship roughly of the dimensions of my first Diplock Caterpillar drawing and use the lengthened Bullock Caterpillar tracks that had been ordered in America. If this was done this landship could be handled by No. 20 Squadron and used to see what sort of trenches and parapet she could get over. I explained that in No. 1 Holland Submarine we blanked up the torpedo tube for nearly a year and used her in an unfinished condition for under-water experiments in the Irish Sea just to get our crew trained, and we wanted to do much the same with a landship for the Officers and Ratings of No. 20 Squadron to handle when crossing trenches.

I gave D'Eyncourt the opinion Commander Boothby and myself had formed that time was being wasted over Colonel Crompton's articulated design, as it was complicated and we would prefer a single unit type of landship on the lines of my first Diplock Caterpillar drawing, and not a caterpillar landship that was to be worked in two halves, this was to our mind unnecessarily complicated. Even one of the halves of Colonel Crompton's landship would be better, for our men to handle, than nothing. D'Eyncourt agreed to do this and turn down, after a few more experiments, the less promising designs. But he said he must be given a free hand. I told him he would have no interference from me. He could run No. 20 Squadron as he liked provided they got a caterpillar landship going for No. 20 Squadron to handle as soon as possible. I reminded

D'Eyncourt that in the early days of the Landship Committee they had considered building a machine on the Bullock tracks. Then I reluctantly agreed to remove Commander Boothby from the Committee. No Officer had worked harder or been more successful in building up our Armoured Car Force than Commander Boothby. Both he and myself had learnt in the Torpedo School *Vernon* that there always must be some finality in experimental work.

Boothby always held the opinion that D'Eyncourt did not like him encouraging Lieutenant Macfie with his caterpillar machine at Mr. Nesfield's works. The value of this independent experiment that gave us the angularized track is given on page 109.

In a reference sheet now before me, Commander Boothby urged Lieutenant Stern, then Secretary of the Landship Committee, to stop the work on the articulated landship experiments as I had instructed him to do and urged that the Bullock tractors should be plated over and used as single units for experimental purposes. But I had already discussed this matter of the articulated landship designed by Colonel Crompton with D'Eyncourt and had convinced him that a single unit caterpillar landship was a better proposition than any articulated type.

I then issued instructions that Commander Boothby was to discontinue attending the Landship Committee meetings, and informed him that the Chairman of the Landship Committee had agreed to build an experimental landship on the Bullock tracks that we had ordered from America for No. 20 Squadron to handle and carry out experiments over trenches to see what it could do. Once the experimental work was started we would soon overcome the criticisms that these Officers and men were remaining idle for so long in the War.

When I explained these orders personally to Commander Boothby, he took my action in good part, like the sterling fellow he was, and said:

It is all very fine for D'Eyncourt to object to me trying to get a hustle on his Committee as you ordered me to. But he doesn't get all the hostility and criticism that you and I have to put up with about No. 20 Squadron doing nothing. Only last week the Fourth Sea Lord sent for me and wanted to know what my "damned idlers" in No. 20 Squadron were doing and when did I propose that they would take some part in the War.

Words fail me in expressing how much I regretted having to take this action with regard to Commander Boothby's services on the Landship Committee. I should like to have seen him serving with landships for the rest of the War, but Boothby had to go. However, our great consolation was that we had got a move on the Landship Committee.

Commander Boothby's contribution to the evolution of the Tank is given in the finding of the Royal Commission on Awards to Inventors, page 198, and is a pretty shabby acknowledgment of the good work he carried out in helping to build the Armoured Car Force, supervise the first caterpillar experiments for me, and generally helping to create confidence in Authority that there was something in the Naval Airman's caterpillar landship idea.

At this time I instructed Commander Boothby to draw up orders for the care of experimental landships in connection with who would be responsible in case of fire, for placing sentries on the machines, etc. I did this from my experience with submarine boats, as one cannot be too careful in all experimental work, particularly when it is of a novel nature.

Also I saw D'Eyncourt in connection with the charge of the caterpillar machinery at Burton-on-Trent, and early in July, 1915, gave instructions through Commander Boothby, the Commanding Officer of the armoured cars, as follows:

> Lieutenant Wilson is to take charge of the caterpillar machines as soon as they have passed their tests satisfactorily. He will be the Landship Committee's representative on the ships and will be responsible to the Commanding Officer of the Armoured Car Division for their efficiency and cleanliness of the machines under his charge in the same way as any other Squadron Leader.
>
> Lieutenant Commander McGrath, Officer commanding No. 20 Squadron, is to place the necessary men at the disposal of Lieutenant Wilson for the maintenance and upkeep of these machines.

PLATE XXV

PLATE XXVI

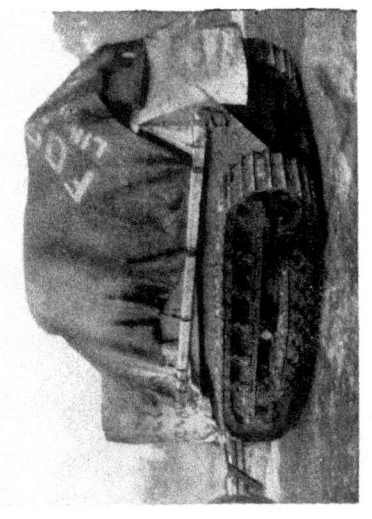

(*Above*) THE FIRST ROYAL NAVAL AIR SERVICE CATERPILLAR LANDSHIP, SEPTEMBER, 1915

(*Below*) THE NAVAL AIRMEN'S FIRST CATERPILLAR LANDSHIP ON THE (MODIFIED) BULLOCK TRACKS
Obtained from America on advice of Colonel Crompton, R.E., after they had been lengthened and given more camber, September, 1915.

PLATE XXIV

CAPTAIN F. M. BOOTHBY, C.B.E., R.N., COMMANDING OFFICER OF ROYAL NAVAL AIR SERVICE ARMOURED CAR FORCE, 1914–1915

PLATE XXVII

EXPERIMENTS WITH THE FIRST ROYAL NAVAL AIR SERVICE
CATERPILLAR LANDSHIP

Flight-Commander Hetherington supervising. Canvas covers were kept over
our first landship for secrecy purposes.

The Chairman of the Landship Committee kept his promise to me and on 29th July, 1915, Messrs. Fosters of Lincoln received a definite order from the Director of Contracts to build the first Royal Naval Air Service landship to be mounted on the Bullock tracks that I had sent Lieutenant Field to obtain in America. This was a purely experimental machine for No. 20 Squadron to try over small trenches, etc., and we used the 105 h.p. Daimler engine with its transmission gear, the same as that used for the heavy howitzers' tractors. The turret was made of correct weight, but was a dummy and could not revolve. The body was constructed of boiler plates to get the correct weight. The armament was one 2-pounder automatic and several Lewis guns for firing through the portholes, with their necessary ammunition to make up the full weight. The height of this first caterpillar landship from the ground was 10 ft. 2 in. and the total weight was 18 tons (Plates XXV and XXVI). This machine was first tried on a ground just outside Lincoln early in September, 1915. Flight-Commander Hetherington came to my office and informed me that the experimental trials with this first landship were quite successful, but the special Bullock tracks we had obtained from America were not of sufficient length to allow big trenches to be crossed, and we must construct longer tracks. Also the material with which they were built was of poor quality.

Lieutenant Stern in his book states: "This trial gave great satisfaction." Also my satisfaction can be imagined, as this was the first trial of a caterpillar landship in the history of the World, and it was undertaken before responsible authority, Mr. D'Eyncourt, the Chairman of the Landship Committee.

My Armoured Car Officers, and representatives from Messrs. Fosters attended this trial. In these caterpillar experiments we did what had never been done before. They compare to the great achievements of the late Mr. Louis Bleriot in July, 1907, when he flew across the channel in his crude self-constructed 25 h.p. Monoplane and the success that we had when first diving No. 1 Holland Submarine at the time we introduced under-water vessels into the British Navy. Although this first caterpillar landship was slow and could only cross a 4 ft. trench (Plate XXVII), it was an experimental success and showed that caterpillar landships, if constructed with efficient tracks made with suitable material and given a good armament, had great possibilities. The experiments with this landship were valuable, as we were able to ascertain the supporting power of the Bullock tracks over soft ground, the tractive effort and other data that is necessary before any draughtsmen could commence to design a Tank in a practical manner for construction in an engineering workshop.

Whilst our first landship was being built a second design was got out by Mr. Tritton of Messrs. Fosters and Lieutenant Wilson. Some delay occurred in completing this landship owing to difficulties that arose in trying out the new Tritton-Wilson caterpillar tracks that these two engineering experts had designed (Plate XXVIII).

One of our armoured car Officers, Lieutenant Stern, was following every move in this caterpillar work from the time of our first experiments at Wormwood Scrubs. Nobody could question the accuracy of his evidence. In his interesting article in the *Strand Magazine* of 19th September, 1919, Lieutenant Stern gives an illustration which is shown in Plate XXIX, with his exact wording.

As Lieutenant Stern was the Secretary of the Landship Committee at that time, and it is largely through his energy and direction on the supply side that Tanks were so successful in the War, we can take it on his authority that these early caterpillar landship designs and experiments led directly to the Rhomboidal Tank, which is dealt with in the next chapter, being constructed.

CHAPTER III

THE TANK TAKES FORM

(1) MR. TRITTON'S AND LIEUTENANT WILSON'S FINE SUCCESS.
(2) COLONEL CROMPTON'S AND MR. LE GROS' CONTRIBUTION.
(3) LIEUTENANT MACFIE'S AND MR. NESFIELD'S ANGULARIZED CATERPILLAR TRACK INVENTION.
(4) COLONEL SWINTON'S SPECIFICATION.

"After me cometh a Builder—
Tell Him I, too, have known."
KIPLING.

(1) MR. TRITTON'S AND LIEUTENANT WILSON'S FINE SUCCESS

WHEN we commenced caterpillar landship investigations my representative on the Admiralty's Landship Committee reported to me that Mr. Tritton, then Managing Director of Messrs. Fosters, preferred wheeled landships to the caterpillar type. Independent evidence is provided by Mr. Brackenbury, one of the Directors of the Pedrail Transport Company, in his letter to me dated 30th May, 1919, in which he stated: "Tritton's claim can readily be disproved by the production of the drawing which he submitted to the Admiralty Landship Committee on the 4th March,[1] at the same time we submitted the design[2] which you have. This design of Tritton's shows a traction engine on wheels with a kind of armoured shield in front of the driver."

To show that Messrs. Fosters first submitted a Big Wheel Tractor design when my caterpillar landship proposals

---
[1] 1915.
[2] This was the first drawing of a caterpillar landship that Mr. Diplock prepared for me.

were being further developed. The following report is, by permission of the Admiralty, now published:

D.N.C.'s COMMITTEE
Report of progress—19th March, 1915.

(1) LANDSHIP.—Pedrail[1] design.

The design has been further developed, and a scale model has been made which can demonstrate the capabilities of the machine.

The model can be shown at the Admiralty if desired.

(2) BIG WHEEL TRACTOR.—Designed by Messrs. Fosters of Lincoln.

In addition to the Pedrail, we have received from Messrs. Fosters of Lincoln a Big Wheel Tractor (proposed) which is a development of some very successful Tractor designs now in use at the Front, to carry about seventy men and machine-guns, all protected from rifle- or machine-gun-fire. This will be able to negotiate ordinary trenches, etc., without any bridging device. The model is at the Admiralty, and can be seen.

At a rough estimate an experimental machine of this type would cost between £2000 and £3000.

Messrs. Fosters already have the engine ready and could put the rest of the work in hand at once. They estimate the time necessary for completion at about three months. The length of time stated is due to the difficulty of securing the steel sections for the wheels, and this might possibly be reduced.

(Sgd.) E. H. T. D'EYNCOURT,
20.3.15.

Also in a memorandum before me, Colonel Crompton writes, when referring to the caterpillar experiments which he assisted to arrange for Mr. Lloyd George to see on 30th June, 1915: "the correspondence shows at that date Tritton was corresponding with me on the advantage of using for this purpose (landships) large-wheeled machines driven by electricity," and I have a report stating Mr. Tritton was not in favour of caterpillar landships for fear that barbed wire would jamb the tracks. To satisfy Mr.

[1] Caterpillar.

THE TANK TAKES FORM

Tritton's views the original order for 18 caterpillar landships, that I had obtained approval from Mr. Churchill to construct, was altered to 12 caterpillar landships and 6 wheel landships. This was done against my wishes by Mr. Churchill.

Before the latest War Office requirements came to hand that a 5 ft. trench would have to be crossed and a parapet 4 ft. 6 in. high had to be surmounted by a landship, a mock-up of a 15 ft. diameter wheel machine was made, but on the first sight of it my Armoured Car Officers and others came to the conclusion that a vehicle with wheels of that dimension would offer too great a target for enemy's artillery fire.

This was a similar opinion to that given early in 1915 by Admiral Sir Percy Scott, without him seeing any full-sized model of a wheel supported landship.

At that time most of my Armoured Car Officers who were with me were disposed more favourably towards my caterpillar landship scheme than any giant or large wheels proposals.

From a memorandum in my possession that I sent to Flight-Commander Hetherington, the following is extracted: "My orders to you were to press for long track caterpillars and only to agree to big wheels for experimental purposes." When we first commenced caterpillar work I had secured the services of a skilled engineer, Mr. Wilson, whom the Admiralty gave me approval to enter for duty with the Armoured Car Force as a Lieutenant R.N.V.R.

This Officer had served formerly in the Navy as a Midshipman, and was when war broke out a consulting and designing engineer of marked ability. He had devoted much time, with considerable success, to developing road traction.

I gave instructions to the Commanding Officer of the Armoured Car Force that Lieutenant Wilson was to be specially detailed for landship work, and he was to attend with Colonel Crompton and Flight-Commander Hetherington the first experiments with the Bullock creeping grip tractor at Greenhithe, and the experiments with this type of tractor for Colonel Crompton's articulated landship design.

Also he had been following the design of the first Royal Naval Air Service landship to be built on the Bullock tracks we had obtained from America, and all designs and suggestions for improving upon the first caterpillar landship were freely discussed by my Armoured Car Officers, Commander Boothby and myself. I have little doubt that Lieutenant Wilson, after I had sent him to supervise landship work at Messrs. Fosters in many discussions with Mr. Tritton, won him to our view and persuaded this able Engineer to discard all ideas of a wheel type landship and go full out for a caterpillar landship that would meet the requirements of the War Office. These had been at first rather nebulous, but were now beginning to take a more definite form.

In practical experiments, as previously mentioned, our first caterpillar landship on the Bullock tracks would only cross a small trench and the material of the tracks was none too good. With the new War Office requirements before them that a 5 ft. trench—this was the average dimension of an enemy trench—would have to be crossed, and that a 4 ft. 6 in. parapet would have to be surmounted, Mr. Tritton and Lieutenant Wilson got out a new design.

It was, if I may say so, in the natural process of evolution once the principle of caterpillar landships was established and accepted by Authority, and followed on the designs of the first two experimental landships in exactly the same way as the designs of "A", "B" and "C" Class Submarines followed on from the first Holland Submarines when we were developing under-water vessels for the Navy at Barrow-in-Furness in 1902. To give a second very reliable opinion, may I quote more fully what my former Armoured Car Officer, Lieutenant Stern,[1] who had, as previously mentioned, followed caterpillar landship development from the demonstration we gave to Mr. Lloyd George on 30th June, 1915, at Wormwood Scrubs, says with regard to the evolution of the rhomboidal type from the first Royal Naval Air Service caterpillar landship, which I take from the *Strand Magazine* of September, 1919:

> A number of experiments were made, and in August Mr. Tritton, of Messrs. Foster and Company, of Lincoln,

[1] Now Sir Albert Stern, K.B.E.

PLATE XXVIII

PLATE XXIX

(*Above*) EXPERIMENTS WITH THE SECOND DESIGN OF CATERPILLAR LANDSHIP ON WILSON-TRITTON TRACK, BURTON PARK, LINCOLN, NOVEMBER, 1915

(*Below*) THE MACHINE KNOWN AS "BIG WILLIE," WHICH EVENTUALLY DEVELOPED INTO THE TANK CALLED "MOTHER"
(The first Royal Naval Air Service Caterpillar landship.)

PLATE XXX

PLATE XXXI

(*Above*) THE FIRST RHOMBOIDAL TANK, BURTON PARK, LINCOLN
Designed by Mr. Tritton and Lieutenant Wilson.

(*Below*) TANK EXPERIMENTS, HATFIELD PARK

THE TANK TAKES FORM

and Lieutenant Wilson had started to draw out a machine on the same lines but of stronger material and better design. On 26th August Mr. Tritton, Lieutenant Wilson and I viewed the full-sized wooden model of this machine. It was known as the "Tritton" Machine, and later as "Little Willie." On the same day, at a meeting at the White Hart Hotel, Lincoln, we discussed fresh requirements which he had just received from the War Office. They asked that the machine should be able to cross a trench 5 ft. wide with a parapet 4 ft. 6 in. high. Lieutenant Wilson and Mr. Tritton thereupon started work on a type designed to do this. It would, they told me, require a sixty-foot wheel.

The contour of this sized wheel became more or less the shape of the underside of the new machine.

In the wording underneath the photograph given in Plate XXIX Lieutenant Stern states definitely how Mother Tank—the rhomboidal caterpillar landship of Mr. Tritton and Lieutenant Wilson—was evolved from the first Royal Naval Air Service Caterpillar landship.

The Tritton-Wilson Tank was a completely armoured vehicle with two specially constructed tracks, encircling the body, which was of rhomboidal form with turned-up bow, as in my first Diplock drawing of a caterpillar landship.

The tracks were angularized after the manner of Lieutenant Macfie's and Mr. Nesfield's invention.[1]

The dimensions were:

> 31 ft. 8 in. 28 tons 8 cwt.
> Speed, ¾ mile to 4 m.p.h.
> Foster Daimler Engines, 105 h.p.
> Armament, 2 6-pounders. Crew, 8 men.

For making small turns she had an elastic tail of two wheels, which also absorbed the shock in passing over banks or rough ground. Quick turns were effected by throwing one or other track out of gear. She could climb a perpendicular parapet 4 ft. 6 in. and cross a 9 ft. trench (Plate XXX).

The most notable departure from my idea of a caterpillar

---
[1] Page 109.

landship Mr. Tritton made was to make the caterpillar run round the periphery of the machine instead of as shown in the photograph of the first R.N.A.S. Tank. The French Tank was more like the R.N.A.S. design than the Tritton-Wilson Tank. The sponsors of this landship were specially designed by Mr. Tennyson D'Eyncourt for mounting the two 6-pounder guns for getting a right ahead and right astern fire. But they were not as satisfactory as my revolving turret system adopted in our improved armoured cars. The Rhomboidal Tank was taken to Hatfield Park and the first trial was made before many distinguished Military Officers and others (Plate XXXI). At Mr. Tennyson D'Eyncourt's special request I attended this trial on 26th January, 1916. Amongst those who also witnessed the demonstration were:

>Vice-Admiral Sir Frederick Tudor-Tudor, Third Sea Lord.
>Vice-Admiral Sir Morgan Singer, Director of Naval Ordnance.
>Mr. Tennyson D'Eyncourt, Director of Naval Construction.
>Brigadier-General Jackson.
>Brigadier-General Nanton.
>Brigadier-General Hill.
>Colonel Crompton.
>Colonel Maurice Hankey.
>Colonel Swinton.
>Mr. Dale Bussell.
>Lieutenant Wilson.
>Lieutenant-Commander McGrath.
>Lieutenant Symes.
>Lieutenant Field.
>Lieutenant Stern.
>Lieutenant Barry.

Several other distinguished people attended, but they were unknown to me and I regret being unable to name them.

    Commander McGrath tells a good story against me when I went round telling every person of importance at these first Hatfield experiments we would want 3000 Tanks. One Military Officer seemed to get rather annoyed at my

THE TANK TAKES FORM

action and said very waspishly: "Who is this damned Naval man saying we will want 3000 Tanks? He talks like Napoleon!" But I was right, we did need them, and before the War concluded we had over a 1000 Tanks delivered and some 5000 on order in this Country alone, also France had thousands delivered and on order.

A little later in answer to a private letter of mine urging the necessity for providing hundreds of Tanks, Captain Maurice Hankey,[1] in his reply of 7th February, 1916, wrote: "I shall get as many Tanks as they will let me have. Hundreds, I agree, are necessary."

After attending the Tank experiments at Hatfield, I asked Commodore de Bartolomé to persuade Mr. Balfour to have a trip in a Tank, and he went to Hatfield on 2nd February, 1916, when Lord Kitchener desired to see the Tank cross a 9-ft. trench. Mr. Balfour inspected the Tank, and, much to the amusement of my Armoured Car Officers, had to be removed feet first with Commodore de Bartolomé's assistance, as he was too tall to get through the sponson door in an elegant manner. On regaining his feet Mr. Balfour said to Commodore de Bartolomé that he was perfectly sure there must be some more artistic method of leaving a Tank.

During this trial the Royal Naval Air Service Officers of No. 20 Armoured Car Squadron were rather perturbed, as Lord Kitchener seemed so strongly adverse to the employment of mechanical weapons of war. He declaimed in a loud voice that the war would not be won by such machines, as they could so easily be destroyed by enemy's gun-fire.

Lord Kitchener had at that time many matters of moment on his mind, and in referring to the Tank as "a pretty mechanical toy" did himself much injustice. I am quite certain this great General would have appreciated the possibilities of the Tank if it had been first explained to him by an Officer who was in sympathy with mechanical weapons of war. Instead, a military Noah probably gave a bias to Lord Kitchener's line of thought, and made him antagonistic to all mechanical weapons. When I turned over my kite-balloon sections to Lord Kitchener he grasped their utility in a second, and was extremely nice to me in the interviews I had with him. At the time of the first Tank

[1] Secretary of Committee of Imperial Defence.

trials there were many Noahs at the War Office opposed to mechanical weapons, and the Tank having been developed by the Admiralty did not exactly help matters, as Lord Kitchener did not like Mr. Churchill.

This, I think, explains Lord Kitchener's attitude in being so sceptical about the Tank and all mechanical weapons of war.

These Hatfield demonstrations before Military Authorities were highly successful, and Mr. Tritton, thanks to my Armoured Car Officers, who pressed upon him the desirability of caterpillars for landships instead of wheels, became one of the great successes of the War and was Knighted for his valuable services.

The financial award made to Mr. Tritton and Lieutenant Wilson for evolving the successful Tank from our first R.N.A.S. caterpillar landship and other caterpillar experiments by the Royal Commission was laughable. In my considered judgment they should have received ten times that amount.[1] Commander Burney received twenty times more from Messrs. Vickers for the Paravane than the award made to Mr. Tritton and Lieutenant Wilson, which would hardly seem to be fair!

But the man who received the greatest insult from the Royal Commission on Awards to Inventors was Sir Tennyson D'Eyncourt.[2] For our skilled Director of Naval Construction to receive £1000 for his hard work and good guidance as Chairman of the Landship Committee in developing these caterpillar machines was deplorable. In my opinion, and in the opinion of most of the Airmen associated with me in Tank work, the Admiralty should have seen that he was better rewarded. The amount was disgusting and despicable!

On 8th February, 1916, No. 20 Squadron, who were detailed for the Hatfield Park experiments, were warned that His late Majesty, King George V, would make a visit of inspection of the Tank, and a special demonstration was arranged. His Majesty took a ride in the Tank, and expressed the view "that such a weapon would be a great asset to the Army possessing a large number."

There is no doubt that King George's long experience in

[1] Page 200.   [2] Page 199.

the Navy taught him to appreciate the possibilities of this new mechanical weapon of war.

On the conclusion of the Hatfield experiments, which had shown the chief Military Officers that there was something in these novel machines, an order was given to Messrs. Fosters for 125 caterpillar landships, and in order to preserve the utmost secrecy the name Tank was adopted, because the second caterpillar landship bore a close resemblance to an oil-tank cart which could at any time be seen in the London streets (Plate XXVIII).

Another order was placed for Tanks with the Metropolitan Carriage Works, Birmingham. This Firm did great work in Tank construction, and earned the gratitude of the whole Nation for their enterprise in entering so wholeheartedly into the production of a new weapon of war.

Eventually the Tanks arrived at the Front, and on 15th September, 1916, they were used in action for the first time in history, in the great Battle of the Somme, officially known as the Battle of Flers-Courcelette, in which High Wood and Flers were taken. The Tank crews handled their new weapons with great gallantry.

The work of the Tanks in action, described more fully in Chapter IV, shows how successful they soon became; then a large number of Tanks were placed on order to meet our ever-growing war requirements. I understand that the Metropolitan Carriage Works of Birmingham produced nearly seventy per cent of the Tanks used by the British Army.

Other firms that built Tanks were Kitson, Clarke Company of Leeds, Messrs. Armstrong Whitworth and Company, Marshall's of Gainsborough and the North British Locomotive Company of Glasgow. As these mechanical weapons were developed they were known, like our Whitehead torpedoes in the Navy, by naming them Mark I, II, III, IV.

But the chief effort was concentrated on making the heaviest Tank a success. This was the Mark V, that was much easier to control, and had a smaller turning circle than the earlier types. It weighed 27 tons and was 26 ft. in length, 8 ft. in width, had a maximum speed of 5 miles an hour, and an armament of two special short six-pounder guns and four Hotchkiss machine-guns. The Female Mark V carried six machine-guns and no six-pounders. The power unit in the Mark V was a 150 h.p. Ricardo engine.

Meanwhile the Medium Mark A Tank, commonly known as the "Whippet," had been designed. It weighed 17 tons, carried two 45 h.p. Tylor engines, had a maximum speed of 8 miles an hour, and was armed with four Hotchkiss machine-guns. The crew comprised one Officer and three men. In this design the sponsons were abandoned and the turret as fitted to my Royal Naval Air Service armoured cars was reverted to.

After having had such a strenuous struggle to keep our caterpillar landship work from being stopped, and in saving No. 20 Squadron when the Armoured Car Force was disbanded in August, 1915, I was very pleased to learn from an Admiralty docket that the Director of Naval Construction had received the thanks of the Army Council in the following letter from the War Office, dated 10th February, 1916:

> SIR,
>   I am commanded by the Army Council to request that the Lord Commissioners of the Admiralty will convey the very warm thanks of the Army Council to Mr. E. H. Tennyson D'Eyncourt, Director of Naval Construction, and his Committee for their work in evolving a machine for the use of the Army, and to Mr. W. H. Tritton and Lieutenant W. G. Wilson, R.N.A.S., for their work in design and construction:
>
>   I am to state that their efforts in this connection have been highly appreciated by the Army Council. I am to add that the work of the Officers and men of No. 20 Squadron, R.N.A.S., in assisting by construction of trenches, etc., in the experimental work necessary to the production of the machine, have been of valuable service.
>
>   I am, Sir,
>   Your obedient Servant,
>   (Signed) B. B. CUBITT.

Mr. Arthur Balfour, then First Lord, minuted this docket, enclosing the above letter,

"The thanks of the War Office are thoroughly well deserved."

THE TANK TAKES FORM

No body of men worked harder than my R.N.A.S. Officers and Ratings of No. 20 Squadron in making caterpillar landships a success when conducting experimental work, testing every type of Tank and making all arrangements for their transport, etc.

Also some thanks were then due to Mr. Arthur Balfour and his Naval Secretary, Commodore de Bartolomé, for keeping the caterpillar landship experiments going in spite of the advice of some of the Sea Lords to scrap them.

The only Sea Lord who gave us encouragement during the early War period in armoured car and caterpillar landship work was Admiral Sir Frederick Tudor-Tudor. We felt that our efforts to initiate a new weapon for trench warfare always had his support and this helped us in our difficult struggles to prevent all landship work going on the scrapheap after Mr. Churchill left the Admiralty. Sir Frederick's encouragement at that difficult time was of great value, and I am certain he helped to restrain some of the hostility of the other Sea Lords to their Airmen's creative caterpillar work.

Two of my Officers of the Royal Naval Air Service Armoured Car Force, whom I have mentioned previously, did wonderfully well.

From the earliest experiments with the Killen Strait Caterpillar, Lieutenant Stern had the greatest faith in these machines, and pressed for them all he was able. He can be seen looking very agreeable (Plate XIV). This support from a sound business man, with no axe to grind, was worth its weight in gold for caterpillar landship development. Lieutenant Stern has written articles in the Press and is the Author of an interesting book.[1] But some of his remarks are not quite accurate. He knew nothing about my demonstration of a caterpillar machine for Mr. Churchill on the Horse Guards Parade on the 16th February, 1915, as he was not there. Neither did he know anything about my interviews between 16th February and 27th February with Mr. Diplock that led to the first caterpillar landship drawing being got out and taken before the Admiralty Landship Committee on 4th March, 1915, as he was not in my confidence, whereas Squadron-Commander Briggs

[1] *Tanks, 1914–1918. The Log Book of a Pioneer.*

and Flight-Commander Michell were. They knew all about how I had this drawing prepared by Mr. Diplock. Neither was it within his knowledge what Commander Boothby and myself arranged to do at any time, as we did not consult him.

Lieutenant Stern was the Secretary of the Landship Committee. This Committee was presided over by Mr. Tennyson D'Eyncourt. Neither he nor anybody on the Committee could give a single executive order or move a single Officer or man without my authority or the authority of Commander Boothby, who in most cases I delegated this authority to. Lieutenant Stern had no executive authority except over the few people who may have been directed to assist him in any particular job he was given to undertake, all the time he served under me when I was Director of the Admiralty Air Department, and he was a Lieutenant in the Royal Naval Air Service Armoured Car Force. Then I was in charge of the Royal Naval Air Service and the Armoured Car Service, and issued orders direct from the Board of Admiralty.

Lieutenant Stern should not say he arranged the caterpillar experiments for Mr. Lloyd George to see at Wormwood Scrubs, as he had not the power or rank to do so. He had then to carry out any instructions that were given to him by a Senior Officer.

After all landship work was turned over by the Admiralty to the Ministry of Munitions to develop, Lieutenant Stern became a Colonel, and from being Secretary of the first Landship Committee became Chairman, then Director of Tanks Supply. In these important posts he did great work in keeping up Tank supplies. Afterwards he held the post of Director-General of Tank Supplies. Stern had great tenacity and good vision to foresee the ultimate success of the caterpillar landship, and was not to be put off by the hostile criticisms of the Military Noahs who were working against mechanical weapons. In all his important work he had a sorry time in fighting the reactionary Noahs at the War Office who were against mechanical warfare. I had been forced to think in thousands when ordering aero engines, whereas my Army Air Colleagues thought in hundreds, and were always coming to me for engines. That is why I asked for 3000 Tanks at the Hatfield experiment. What I most liked about Stern was he thought in thousands of Tanks, not hundreds, and proved right as I was. It was very difficult in those days to get anybody to "Think Big." Stern thought "Big." Men with big ideas were then scarce.

In his interesting book on Tanks Colonel Stern informs us that in 1918 a powerful Tank Board was formed to deal with production. This creation, he says,

"Received new ideas with enthusiasm, old-fashioned obstructions found no sympathy, and the programme for the year of 5000 Tanks had every chance of being completed."

It was a real grief to me when I learnt from one of my Armoured Car Officers that Colonel Stern had been suddenly hurled from the high post that he had obtained and, as a sop, was given a K.B.E.[1]

Very often I have wondered whose path Colonel Stern was standing in!

Few men in the War discharged the duties they were called upon to perform with greater devotion to duty and courage than Colonel Stern.

The intrigue that led to Colonel Stern being added to those who were done down for their Tank work was, to me, of some interest.

The other Officer I should mention, who backed the caterpillar landship from start to finish, was Commander McGrath. His work was not spectacular: but it was none the less important for that. Never once did he waver in his faith. No. 20 Squadron owe him a great debt of gratitude. I have met many of his men. They tell me when things were most difficult in Tank development Commander McGrath was always cheerful, ready to do any job that came along, and he set a fine example to his men. The exceptional work carried out in experiments, testing and transport by No. 20 Squadron under his command was of great value for Tank development.

One day he took my Wife and myself for a trip in a Tank at their testing-ground. I never minded how long I stayed

[1] See *Tanks, 1914–18. The Log Book of a Pioneer.*

under water in a submarine or up in the air in an airship or aeroplane; but my experience in a Tank left far more of a lasting impression than most of my submarine or air trips. There was not much room inside. We started. The Tank glided. When I least expected it, we entered a shell-hole, and I was literally hurled from one side to another. Then no sooner had I recovered my vertical position than McGrath made her stand on her tail. It was a hateful experience for me. My Wife loved every minute of it. But she was given a special position with Mrs. Briggs. In one lurch Squadron-Commander Briggs was hurled against me with such force that he was winded, and his hand came in contact with the exhaust-pipe which was hot! After that we clung on to the nearest fitting and declined to move whilst we went up and down a steep bank.

I was glad to get out of that Tank. Both Briggs and myself were much bruised, and I told McGrath submarines were palaces compared to Tanks, and airships were super palaces.

Never again do I go over big shell-holes in a Tank.

But those who read of the great deeds of the Tanks in the War should always remember the fine crew inside breathing the sickening fumes from the exhaust-pipe that cannot always be eliminated. They, like our submarine crews, deserve some admiration.

Colonel Crompton's and Mr. Le Gros' Contribution

Torpedoists in the Royal Navy do not design their Whitehead torpedoes, mines or submarines. They make known their requirements to the technical designers, who endeavour to meet and, if possible, improve upon the original requirements laid down by the technical torpedo Officers.

In searching for a road Engineer of repute to develop my caterpillar landship, the name of Colonel Crompton was brought forward by Hetherington. I knew Colonel Crompton to be a very skilled Electrical Engineer, because he was the head of the Firm who supplied the Navy with much electrical equipment, as searchlights, arc-lights, etc., that I had to deal with whilst serving for some years as

Electrical Commander on the Staff of the Director of Naval Ordnance at the Admiralty.

I asked Colonel Crompton to come and see me. In discussing the whole question of mounting our turret armoured cars on caterpillar tracks, he assured me that the building of a landship on these lines was quite possible, and should offer no very great difficulties. The only problem was to get a Firm capable of producing suitable caterpillar tracks in this Country.

After this interview I obtained Board approval to appoint Colonel Crompton as Consulting Engineer to the Landship Committee that Mr. Churchill, on my suggestion, had approved should be set up to develop caterpillar landships. Colonel Crompton was then appointed for six months, commencing his duties on 1st March, 1915.

On taking up this work the Colonel was fortunate in securing the services of Mr. Le Gros to assist him in design work, making calculations, etc. Mr. Le Gros was a very skilled consulting Engineer, who had a great deal of experience in motor car building, and was at one time President of the Institute of Automobile Engineers.

This able Engineer confirmed Colonel Crompton's opinion that caterpillar landships could be built, and that there were no technical difficulties in designing tracks that would stand up to the heavy load necessary with armoured vehicles that had to carry a gun armament, ammunition and crew. At the meeting of the Landship Committee on 4th March, 1915, the first caterpillar landship drawing got out for me by Mr. Diplock was produced by Mr. Lowe. On this drawing the approximate dimensions were given in regard to weight, length, diameter, armament, turning circle, etc.[1] Previous to this meeting this drawing had by my instructions been shown to Colonel Crompton, and he was pleased with it.

In due course Colonel Crompton produced a larger design to what he thought the military requirements were. This was a 60 ft. landship mounted on two central caterpillars.

Any information Colonel Crompton could at that time obtain was contradicted usually a short time afterwards by

[1] Page 68.

somebody with greater authority. At the War Office there seemed to be a good many Officers of high rank who were distinctly against developing mechanical weapons of war, and we could get mighty little encouragement from that quarter in our first efforts to develop caterpillar landships.

Colonel Crompton advised Flight-Commander Hetherington and myself to purchase a Killen Strait Caterpillar Machine that had just arrived in England from America. This we did. The demonstration with this machine before Mr. Lloyd George is described on page 75.

Working for the Landship Committee and following up all caterpillar work he could with various agents in this country, Colonel Crompton ascertained that Bullock Creeping Grip Caterpillar Tractor had arrived from America and was at Greenhithe. I sent Flight-Commander Hetherington and Lieutenant Wilson to accompany Colonel Crompton on his inspection of this tractor.

They carried out certain experiments with this machine to ascertain its capabilities. These were satisfactory, and American firms having been most useful to us with the construction of aeroplanes, it was decided to order two Bullock Creeping Grip Caterpillar Tractors from America, also two of their standard caterpillar tracts lengthened to 9 ft. I sent Lieutenant Field to America to supervise this work, as explained on page 72.

Certain difficulties occurred with Colonel Crompton's 60 ft. caterpillar landship. The military requirements altered and Colonel Crompton conceived the idea of constructing his landship in two halves and coupling the two portions together. This was known as his articulated landship.

On the arrival of the two Bullock Creeping Grip Caterpillar Tractors various experiments to demonstrate the possibilities of an articulated landship were carried out at Burton-on-Trent (Plates XIX, XX and XXI). Early in May, 1915, Colonel Crompton ascertained from the Bullock Company in Chicago that steering by driving caterpillar side-tracks independently was a complete success. This method of steering I advocated in my first demonstration to Mr. Churchill. At this time Colonel Crompton and

Mr. Le Gros spent much time and thought in carrying out many calculations, as to the best means of varying the contour of the under surface of the articulated machine he was designing:

(1) By use of the universal joint between the two halves of his landship;
(2) By tilting and controlling the tracks themselves;
(3) By providing a sloped-up climbing-nose to prevent it digging into the front of a parapet.

It may be remembered that in my Diplock caterpillar design I provided an upturned bow and stern like a submarine of the Fontes type. As I was uneasy about the time being taken over the articulated landship experiments I sent Commander Boothby to inspect the two Bullock Creeping Grip Tractors at Burton-on-Trent and report progress.

Both Commander Boothby and myself were strongly in favour of a single unit, and wanted Colonel Crompton to construct one. Before Boothby's visit D'Eyncourt had promised me to turn down the less promising designs and build an experimental landship on the Bullock tracks I had sent Lieutenant Field to obtain in America. Any Officer who had to use a caterpillar landship on active service in the field would, I feel certain, have felt as strongly as Boothby and myself did, that a single unit was preferable to any form of articulated landship.

After the Bullock Tractor experiments in connection with his articulated landship design did not prove the success Colonel Crompton anticipated, the landship work was taken out of his hands by the Committee, and when his six months' engagement expired it was not renewed.

In July, 1915, the Metropolitan Carriage Wagon and Finance Company asked to be relieved of their contract to build Colonel Crompton's landship, and it was cancelled. Both Colonel Crompton and Mr. Le Gros had worked like niggers at this landship, but it was turning out too heavy to be of practical value for use on active service. At a later date Colonel Crompton wrote to me about his services not having been properly recognized, and I sent him the following reply:

AIR DEPARTMENT,
ADMIRALTY,
28.10.16.

MY DEAR COLONEL CROMPTON,

I have been doing a round of Air Stations or would have replied to your letter sooner. First I want you to read my official report, copy herewith. You will see in it I mention your name and Colonel Dumbell.

As I thought you were still on the Committee it was not for me, but Mr. D'Eyncourt, to record your services in connection with the Tanks, and I can only say, Colonel, how deeply I regret that this was not done.

When I asked you through Major Hetherington to come in to advise us on pedrails[1] for land battleships, and place your great knowledge of road traction at our disposal, I had little idea that you would be so shabbily treated.

It is many years, some fourteen I think, since I first came in contact with you and your firm over coaling arc-lamps, etc., when I was in the Naval Ordnance Department.

After such a long acquaintance I feel very heavily that an injustice has been done to you.

When you are next in town will you look me up, as I should like to see you about the matter.

Yours sincerely,
(Sgd.) MURRAY F. SUETER.

In the following month Colonel Crompton again wrote and asked me to assist him with some of his new designs for high-speed Tanks. But I had on this date ceased to have anything to do with Tank designs. The Ministry of Munitions had taken over from the Admiralty all work in connection with the production of Tanks in numbers. Consequently I sent Colonel Crompton the following letter:

AIR DEPARTMENT,
ADMIRALTY,
4.11.16.

MY DEAR COLONEL CROMPTON,

Many thanks for your letter of 1st November. I am afraid I can do nothing in the way of helping any

[1] Caterpillars.

new designs, as I have nothing more to do with land battleships.

If I had there would be some radical changes in design. When you are this way please look in.

In haste, Yours sincerely,

(Sgd.) MURRAY F. SUETER.

In this letter I refer to radical changes in design, as I always held the opinion that Mr. Tennyson D'Eyncourt made a profound mistake in discarding my revolving turret and fitting sponsons for mounting the guns, as was done in the rhomboidal Tank. My opinion proved right, as sponsons were soon discarded and turrets have been substituted in modern Tanks, as can be seen in Plates XXXV, XXXVI, LIV and LV.

In discussing a paper read by Mr. L. A. Legros, M.I.M.E., before the Institute of Mechanical Engineers, Colonel Crompton remarked:

All those who had worked on the caterpillar problem in order to get a very extended flat foot in contact with the ground, knew that the principal wear took place at two points, at the pin-joints where there was the greatest angular motion, that is, at the point where the chain came down from the leading wheel on to the ground surface. There was little motion on the pin during the time it was passing over the flat surface of the ground, but when it was lifted up at the back of the track, there was another large angular motion on the pin, and all experience had been to go back as nearly as possible to the original wheel, that was, to make both the front wheel and back wheels of the tracks of very large diameter.

He was not able to say very much on this subject, because it was closely connected with developments in the Field. The limitation of angular pin movement was one of the things to which attention had to be directed. It was necessary to get the happy mean between a short track with a short flat foot, which was almost the same as a very large wheel, and the other extreme, the very long track with a very large angular movement at each end.

Colonel Crompton also alluded to the second great difficulty with caterpillars, that of taking up the slack due to the chain area at the pin joints and remarked:

> To-day it was possible to do a great deal better in the utilization of chains owing to the wonderful development of roller chains by various makers. The magnificent workmanship rendered possible by automatic tools allowed roller chains to be turned out of the very highest class of material, case hardened all over and with very little play to allow mud and dirt to get in. This was very hopeful. Now that the caterpillar makers had had the advantage of the knowledge of these things, it was hoped that by sheer good workmanship a great deal of the troubles experienced in the use of those kind of chains in those early days would be avoided.

The aforesaid notes indicate roughly the knowledge of caterpillars Colonel Crompton and Mr. Le Gros brought in when I asked them to advise the Air Department on whether my idea of caterpillar armoured cars was a practical possibility.

Although Colonel Crompton's articulated design of landship did not mature, he guided the Landship Committee on the line of caterpillar thought against the wheel landships first proposed by Mr. Tritton. We Airmen owe Colonel Crompton and Mr. Le Gros a great debt of gratitude for their valuable assistance. Colonel Crompton's sound advice led to the purchase of the Killen Strait Caterpillar Machine, the two Bullock Creeping Grip Caterpillar Tractors and the specially lengthened Bullock Caterpillar tracks I sent Lieutenant Field to obtain in America. This was good service. But a greater contribution to the evolution of the Tank was made by Colonel Crompton and Mr. Le Gros in the backing they gave to the Naval Airmen in pressing for caterpillar landships.

I could never have faced up to the antagonism of some of the Sea Lords had I not been aware that these two great road traction Experts had assured me that caterpillar landships were a practical proposition. Neither could I have persuaded Mr. Arthur Balfour, when First Lord of the Admiralty, to save No. 20 Squadron and continue caterpillar experimental work when the Fourth Sea Lord was doing his level best to have all our armoured car and caterpillar work stopped and all our men disbanded, had I not had the backing of Colonel Crompton and Mr. Le Gros.

These two Experts at a very difficult time guided us well as these pages disclose. They deserved some reward for their Tank work. The Royal Commission stated that Colonel Crompton and Mr. Le Gros worked loyally and very hard, and no doubt supplied the Committee with useful data and sound advice.

The Royal Commission seemed to me to miss the real value of the services of Colonel Crompton and Mr. Le Gros. We could never have kept the caterpillar work going without establishing confidence. In this these two road Engineers assisted so much, and their great contribution towards the evolution of the Tank was in helping to get the principle of caterpillar landships firmly established and accepted by Authority.

Recently I was informed that this fine old pioneer of electrical engineering and road traction, Colonel Crompton, had entered his ninty-first year. Some eighteen years have elapsed since I wrote to a high Authority submitting Colonel Crompton's name for a reward for his Tank work, as I was responsible for his appointment to the Admiralty Landship Committee. The Statesman I wrote to was then in a high position, but alas! my letter remained unanswered.

Surely our great Engineering profession, even at this distant date, might endeavour to obtain for Colonel Crompton some suitable reward for his good work in backing the Naval Airmen's first caterpillar landship proposals that were brought to fruition in the successful Tanks.

Lieutenant Macfie's and Mr. Nesfield's Angularized Caterpillar Track Invention

As previously mentioned one of my Armoured Car Officers, Lieutenant Macfie, was recognized amongst all of us as a caterpillar expert. He wrote a paper on the Evolution of the Tank idea and circulated it to all members of the House of Commons.

From this paper I extract the following:

On 19th October, 1914, I (Lieutenant Macfie) was appointed to the Armoured Car Brigade and a few days afterwards took up the caterpillar question with Lieutenant-Commander Boothby. This Officer took me up in his car to the Air Department to see Captain Murray Sueter, who owing to pressure of work could not see me but requested that I would write out a report.

In due course Lieutenant Macfie sent me a report on how to use caterpillar machines for hauling guns, dated 5th November, 1914. In concluding his memorandum, Lieutenant Macfie wrote:

"It is the writer's conviction that with a group of six caterpillar tractors and with a competent crew manager weights of 85 tons, i.e. the weight of a 12-inch gun, could be moved over the remains of roads (they will be destroyed) which will be encountered on the advance into Germany at a speed of 20 to 40 miles a day. It is also the writer's conviction that the construction of 'floating' foundations capable of dealing with the recoil of these guns built up of short lengths (say 5 ft.) of 12-inch beams and angle brackets and bolts and nuts (not rivets) so as to be easily and rapidly assembled in a few hours by field labour, presents no undue mechanical difficulties."

I repeat this extract[1] to show there is no mention of a caterpillar landship here or in any part of the Memorandum.

In a recent issue of the *Aeroplane*, under the heading of "A Neglected Pioneer," a statement is made in reference to Lieutenant Macfie's pioneer Tank work which cannot surely be quite accurate.

Mr. G. C. Grey's paper states:

"He (Lieutenant Macfie) brought to this office in September or October, 1914, general arrangement of a machine exactly like the Tanks which went into action in France in July, 1916, and at intervals for weeks he discussed with us his various efforts to get support for the idea."

[1] Given on page 47.

In Lieutenant Macfie's report dated October, 1914, that is now before me there is no mention of a rhomboidal type of landship fitted with sponsons for mounting the guns. It deals with the hauling of 12-inch Naval guns, and his other report, dated 27th October, 1915, was well after we had embarked upon caterpillar landship experiments. It is as follows:

POSSIBILITIES OF ARMOURED CATERPILLARS

"There exists a type of vehicle known as a caterpillar which runs on an endless chain instead of wheels, is capable of travelling over the roughest ground and up or down or across the steepest slopes. Some few of an inferior type have been used experimentally for transport work only by the Army, but their possibilities have not been realized by those in Authority.

It is within the scope of immediate practical mechanics to construct armoured caterpillars driven by improved mechanism, capable of pushing through barbed-wire entanglements and of travelling over trenches. They may easily be armoured against field-gun-fire. Front shield armour may be fitted up to 8 or 9 inches."

Before the date of this Memorandum I had my first Diplock caterpillar landship drawing laid before the Landship Committee (4th March, 1915) and Mr. Tennyson D'Eyncourt had agreed to build the first Royal Naval Air Service landship on the Bullock tracks I had sent Lieutenant Field to obtain in America. That is some three months before Lieutenant Macfie's proposals to build caterpillar vehicles with armoured shields. Lieutenant Macfie does not in his second Memorandum mention a rhomboidal type of landship with sponsons.

If Lieutenant Macfie had these drawings Mr. C. G. Grey writes about, it seems so strange that he did not produce them to the Landship Committee that I sent him before,[1] soon after they commenced their deliberations, or bring them to me.

Both Lieutenant Macfie and Mr. C. G. Grey were probably aware I was full out to get a caterpillar landship

[1] During the Landship Committee meeting of 22nd February, 1915.

built. But they never brought me any drawings to guide me in my efforts. The Admiralty Registry keeps a very careful record of all papers that are submitted to that office, and there is no record of any drawings of a caterpillar landship submitted by Lieutenant Macfie.

Whether he showed caterpillar landship drawings to any private person is not within my knowledge.

It is possible Lieutenant Macfie preferred to keep them for a more favourable opportunity. This I gave him in the following way. I wanted as many strings to my bow as possible in an endeavour to get a successful caterpillar landship built.

We had Colonel Crompton designing a caterpillar landship for the Landship Committee. We had sent to America for two creeping grip Bullock Tractors and two specially lengthened Bullock tracks.

Knowing Lieutenant Macfie to be a capable Engineer and interested in caterpillars, I found I could spare a little money and limited him to at first an expenditure of £700. Then I gave him a free hand to select whatever firm he liked for building an experimental caterpillar landship and issued the necessary instructions to Commander Boothby, the Officer commanding the Armoured Car Force.

This is a copy of Lieutenant Macfie's first report to his Commanding Officer, and is dated 25th April, 1915:

> "Immediately on receiving your instructions I proceeded to Lieutenant Barry[1] to discuss arrangements. Lieutenant Barry requested that, if possible, I should arrange for the work to be carried out in London so as to be within easy reach of the Admiralty. Wednesday, Thursday and Friday morning I spent in looking for a suitable firm, with the result that arrangements were made with Lieutenant Barry on Friday afternoon for the work to be carried out at Messrs. Nesfield and Mackenzie, 274 Uxbridge Road, Ealing; on Saturday, one Alldays 5-ton truck was towed from Lieutenant Hetherington's depot at the Talbot Works to Messrs. Nesfield and Mackenzie and working drawings commenced."

[1] My very efficient Transport Officer of the Royal Naval Air Service.

To place Lieutenant Macfie's work on a proper footing I placed a contract with Mr. Nesfield for converting an Allday chassis into an experimental caterpillar landship and appointed Lieutenant Macfie as the Admiralty Overseer in charge of this experiment.

Lieutenant Macfie had now the chance of a lifetime with a perfectly free hand to develop his ideas. Let us examine how this capable Engineer availed himself of this unique opportunity to produce a caterpillar landship for me to carry out further experiments at Wormwood Scrubs. Two months later Lieutenant Macfie had brought to my office a model (Plate XXXII) showing an angularized caterpillar track turned the opposite way to the Killen Strait caterpillar track. This was quite new to me and at once I saw the value of this angularized track invention for climbing over parapets, obstacles, etc. It was just what we required for our climbing machine. I gave orders to have the model taken immediately before the Landship Committee. A memorandum was the same day sent to the Commanding Officer, Armoured Car Force, from the Air Department and was signed by Lieutenant P. Barry, my Transport Officer, dated 29th June, 1915. It read:

Commodore Sueter instructs me to inform you that he has a small working model in his room of a Trench attacker worked on the caterpillar system which he thinks should be brought before the Committee dealing with Land Battleships, etc. Lieutenant Arthur is fully conversant with the manner in which this model works. Will you kindly make what necessary arrangements you think fit to carry out the Director's wishes.

Unfortunately serious differences soon arose between Lieutenant Macfie and Mr. Nesfield. A regular dog-fight ensued over this model.

I declined to enter into this fight and ordered Commander Boothby to do what he could to pour oil upon the troubled waters. But he failed in his endeavour. The discord continued and reluctantly I was forced to issue instructions to Commander Boothby to stop all the caterpillar work on the Allday chassis at Mr. Nesfield's Works, and he sent the following orders to Lieutenant Macfie:

The lorry under your charge and all parts of the caterpillar are to be removed to Headquarters forthwith.

Lieutenant Macfie in his report to the Commanding Officer of the Armoured Car Force, dated 19th July, 1915, stated:

> Your orders in connection with the removal of the "Allday" Chassis together with the semi-completed caterpillar mechanism from Messrs. Nesfield's Works to here[1] have been noted, and I am now getting it done.

Thus ended one of my efforts to produce a caterpillar landship. I expected great things from Lieutenant Macfie and was sorry that this experiment which at one time seemed so hopeful, did not mature. Quarrels in Peacetime are not helpful, in War-time they may mean disaster. Later I asked the Minister of Munitions to take over Lieutenant Macfie and his caterpillar designs and work. But for some reason unknown to me they declined to do so.

The Royal Commission went into the claims of Lieutenant Macfie and Mr. Nesfield and awarded them £500 each. It is not for me to say who first thought of the angularized track. The Royal Commission could not decide, but I think Mr. Nesfield had his attention first drawn to caterpillar work when I gave him, through the Director of Contracts, his first order for converting the Allday Chassis into an experimental caterpillar landship, his Firm had done no caterpillar work before the placing of my order.

The angularized track as shown on the Nesfield-Macfie model, as demonstrated before the Royal Commission, was undoubtedly the first proposal of this nature brought before myself and many Armoured Car Officers. Mr. C. G. Grey, the Editor of *Aeroplane*, thinks Lieutenant Macfie was very badly treated. I agree, his award of £500 was, in my opinion, an insult to both Lieutenant Macfie and Mr. Nesfield, when one considers that Commander Burney and Captain Usborne received £304,800 from Messrs. Vickers for the Paravane invention. No one regretted it more than I did that Lieutenant Macfie failed me in producing an experimental landship, but the angularized track invention,

---
[1] Talbot Works.

I am certain made the Tank the great success it became on active service.

What an opportunity Lieutenant Macfie and Mr. Nesfield had. It was no fault of mine that they did not become as successful as my other Armoured Car Officer Lieutenant Wilson and Mr. Tritton of Messrs. Foster and Company were with their Tank work.

Colonel Swinton's Specification

The whole question of who was responsible for inventing the Tanks was gone into by the Royal Commission on Awards to Inventors, and they elucidated that Colonel Swinton, R.E., and Major Tulloch had placed before the Army Authorities a scheme for building land cruisers and destroyers mounted on caterpillars. But after severe tests by General Sir Scott-Moncrieff's Committee, caterpillar tractors were turned down on 17th February, 1915.[1]

Further, it transpired that on 1st June, 1915, Colonel Swinton submitted to the Chief of Staff certain definite proposals for building armoured machine-gun destroyers on petrol tractors on the caterpillar system. This paper was sent to Sir John French on 22nd June, 1915.

At that time there was considerable opposition at the War Office to Colonel Swinton's proposals. But Sir John French was definitely in favour of creating a caterpillar machine with a turret to be used as a surprise weapon against the enemy. As can be seen on page 65 I had already demonstrated to Mr. Churchill on the Horse Guards Parade on 16th February, 1915, what advantage to our turret armoured cars would accrue if we replaced the wheels by caterpillars, not only on these cars but the 3-pounder heavy armoured lorries.

Further, my Diplock caterpillar landship drawing had been placed before the Admiralty Landship Committee on 4th March, 1915, which was some three months before Colonel Swinton's paper was sent to Sir John French.

Although Mr. Evans in this letter[2] of 26th September, 1916, was of the opinion that Colonel Swinton was claiming

---

[1] Minutes of Proceedings, Royal Commission on Awards to Inventors, 7th October, 1919.
[2] Page 186.

the Tank invention and the writer of the Memorandum given in Part II, Chapter I, held similar views, I did not share that opinion because Colonel Swinton knew he had nothing to do with the Admiralty Airmen who had carried out the Diplock, Killen-Strait and Bullock caterpillar experiments. Neither did he have any connection with my first Diplock Caterpillar landship drawing, giving approximate dimensions that was placed before the Admiralty Landship Committee on 4th March, 1915, or the first Royal Naval Air Service caterpillar landship built upon the Bullock tracks. It may be assumed that he knew his caterpillar proposals were turned down by Sir Scott-Moncrieff's Committee.

Colonel Swinton relieved Colonel Maurice Hankey and acted for a short time as his deputy. When Acting-Secretary of the Committee of Imperial Defence, he had the right and it was part of his duty to enquire into what was being done to develop new weapons of war, and see if he desired all the reports of the Admiralty Landship Committee and the caterpillar experiments my armoured car Officers were engaged upon. When he did make enquiries he found the Admiralty Naval Airmen had stolen a march on the War Office Generals and had carried out many caterpillar experiments.

In his evidence[1] before the Royal Commission Colonel Swinton stated in August, 1915: "Lieutenant Stern, Major Wilson and Major Hetherington, all Armoured Car Officers, called on me at the War Office and informed me that the Admiralty Landships Committee was bringing out the design of a machine based on a definite specification which had at last been received from the Army. I did not then pay much attention to the drawings; it was not my work...."

"After enquiring it seemed to me at that time that there was some confusion between the War Office, the Ministry of Munitions and the Admiralty in regard to the question of caterpillars—I will not call them Tanks. They were not called Tanks then. They were caterpillar motor cars for crossing the country.

I obtained sanction to call a conference between the

[1] Page 18, Report of Royal Commission on Awards to Inventors.

three departments in order to find out which department had done what, and which department should carry on the matter. That conference sat on 28th August, 1915. It was called the first Caterpillar Machine-Gun Destroyer Conference. The net result was that we agreed to press on with all information and facility for the Admiralty Landship Committee to carry on that work."

From the information in my possession that date, 28th August, 1915, is the first official connection Colonel Swinton had with the Landship Committee. It was after the Diplock and Killen Strait Caterpillar experiments and the decision to build the first R.N.A.S. caterpillar experimental landship on the Bullock tracks had been taken at my request by D'Eyncourt, the Chairman of the Landship Committee. Later, in connection with the trials of the first caterpillar machine, Colonel Swinton stated:

"On September 19th I was engaged to go down to see the trial of the machine known as 'Little Willie.' I went down there not as representing the War Office, but on behalf of the War Office Committee. I saw Little Willie tried and I was asked my opinion, and I said that Willie would not do. Little Willie did not comply with all the details of the specification I had sent home in the previous month from France. One thing Little Willie could not do was to climb a 5 ft. vertical height. The reason being that Little Willie was a steel box."

But surely the machine then undergoing trials was the first Royal Naval Air Service landship built on the Bullock tracks for purely experimental purposes. This machine was like, if I may give an analogy, the first Holland Submarine whose maximum speed was 6 knots, whereas "A1" Submarines', the next design in the evolution, speed was 10 knots when we put her on the measured mile.

This R:N.A.S. caterpillar landship was a beginning and the first machine to be handled by my Armoured Car Officers. They showed by practical demonstration what an armoured vehicle mounted on caterpillars could do.

The photographs, shown in Plates XXV, XXVI and XXVII, speak for themselves.

Colonel Swinton was then shown the mock-up of the successful Tank on 19th September, 1915, which he thought would comply with the specification he had got out, which was:

Armoured Machine-Gun Destroyers

"These machines would be petrol tractors on the caterpillar principle of a type which can travel up to 4 miles an hour on the flat, can cross a ditch up to 4 ft. in width without climbing, can climb in or out of a broader cavity and can scramble over a breastwork. It is possible to build such tractors. They should be armoured with hardened steel plates proof against the German steel-cored armour-piercing and reversed bullets and armed with, say, 2 Maxims and a Maxim 2-pounder gun."

If the characteristics on my Diplock drawing, page 68, are compared with Colonel Swinton's specification it will be seen how a Naval man and a Military man were working quite separately and unknown to each other to get out a suitable weapon for trench warfare.

Such a coincidence is not unknown and has many precedents when Scientists and others have been attacking the same problem. But I claim priority as my caterpillar landship drawing was got out on 28th February, 1915, and presented to the Admiralty Landship Committee on 4th March, 1915, whereas Colonel Swinton's specification is dated 1st June, 1915.

Colonel Swinton's contribution towards the evolution of the Tank was acknowledged by the Commission on Awards to Inventors in their finding, which is given on page 197.

It is not within my knowledge whether Colonel Swinton ever carried out any caterpillar experiments for the Army at Aldershot or Shoeburyness before the construction of the first R.N.A.S. caterpillar landship. If he did so, no doubt there are photographs of these experiments at the War Office which can be made public, but they were quite unknown at the Admiralty.

Colonel Swinton is undoubtedly the Army Tank pioneer,

and should receive every possible credit for that. It was mighty hard luck on him to see his ideas carried to success by others. But Colonel Swinton, to his everlasting credit, instead of being jealous, as he reasonably might have been, swung round and supported Tank development with all his might. I admired him immensely for this action. It was in accordance with the very best traditions of an Officer of that distinguished corps—the Royal Engineers. The initial successes with Tanks on active service were due in a large measure to Colonel Swinton's great ability,[1] initiative, and determination to make this new weapon a success.

But his friends should not claim that Colonel Swinton had anything to do with initiating the Admiralty Air Department's caterpillar experiments that were proved before the Royal Commission in the direct chain of causation that led to the successful Tank.

May I pay tribute to the splendid way in which the young military Officers took to the Tanks? Their action was very much the same as the young Naval Officers under Captain Bacon, some twelve years before, took to the submarines when we first developed them for the Navy.

The Senior Officers placed in charge of the Tanks had to evolve a new system of training. Colonel Swinton rendered a great service to the Nation in this direction at the Tank Training Ground at Thetford, in Norfolk, where he was entrusted to raise and train in secret the first military corps to man the Tanks. Both Officers and men had to be trained not only in fighting with the Tank but in looking after the engines, tracks and all mechanical details, and it has been noted that men trained in these mechanical weapons become very much sharper and quicker than those who have not the benefit of this training.

We all know that tradition plays a very large part in our conservative Army, and precedent perhaps a still larger part. There was no precedent for mechanical weapons of war. So there is cause for very much satisfaction at the way the Military took up so quickly the Naval Airmen's novel idea of a caterpillar landship. Generally a new weapon of war takes years and years to introduce. But in this case only months elapsed from the first caterpillar

[1] Now Major-General Sir Ernest Swinton, K.B.E., R.E.

machine being shown on the Horse Guards Parade to a completed machine being used at the Front.

But far the most important of all was to build up a feeling of confidence, enthusiasm, etc., for caterpillar landships and establish an *esprit de corps*. It was a great opportunity for all. Thanks to Generals Elles and Fuller, the Tank Corps rose to the occasion to their everlasting fame.

Colonel Swinton's work in this connection was of a high order and he obtained extraordinary results in a short time. New tactical ways for using the Tanks had to be devised by the Senior Tank Officers, whole establishments had to be created for training organization and engineering details.

The British public have appreciated the work of the Tanks on active service, but all this training, organization, etc., behind the scenes at home and in France was carried out with extraordinary efficiency by those who were detailed for this important duty. The Tank is mainly an offensive weapon and many problems had to be studied before it was first used in action. Lieutenant-General Elles and his Staff won the sincere admiration of the Naval Airmen who initiated caterpillar landships and who pressed so hard with success for Tank development. Both he and Major-General Fuller had wonderful initiative, courage, energy and good brains in tackling the new tactical problems that arose and in teaching the Tank crews not only how to handle these mechanical weapons, but also to be the masters of the emergency on active service.

Tanks in their early days had almost exactly the same mechanical troubles as we experienced in working the first Holland Submarines. All new weapons of war, such as submarines or Tanks, have to be understood by Senior Officers of very high rank, and they have to acquire a due appreciation of their limitations and potentialities. Before the War Senior Naval Officers neglected not only to study submarine warfare, but take the advice of their under-water experts. During hostilities over six and three-quarters million tons of British shipping and many Naval vessels were sunk by German submarine action. Clearly this lack of vision was disastrous. After some experience our great Generals learned to appreciate the value of the Tank as an offensive weapon of great power. Major-General Fuller, in his recent very interesting book,[1] states: "It is strictly and historically correct to say that the Tank made Lord Haig." Whether this view is quite accurate is not within my knowledge. But there is no doubt from all the reports, despatches and books on the War that I have read, the Tank did play a big part in Lord Haig's victories towards the close of the War, and he seemed to be highly appreciative of their great services, as shown by the extracts given in the next chapter.

[1] *Memoirs of an Unconventional Soldier.*

CHAPTER IV

TANKS IN ACTION

(1) British Opinion on Value of Tanks.
(2) French Opinion on Value of Tanks.
(3) German Opinion on Value of Tanks.

"The great value of Tanks in the offensive has been conclusively proved."
General Haig.

THE Tank idea arose solely from the desire of a few thinking men to save the lives of our very gallant infantrymen that were being so severely punished at the Front in France. Although Mr. Winston Churchill's ideas about using steam-rollers coupled together as trench-crushers proved unworkable in practical experiments, his efforts to obtain some sort of weapon for trench warfare inspired his Naval Airmen to press forward and endeavour to meet his wishes by developing a new weapon of war. I pay tribute to his great foresight in visualizing that something new was required in the way of a weapon to enable our comrades in the Army to become masters of a situation that was causing intense and ever-increasing anxiety in many homes in this Country whenever major operations of an offensive nature were being launched, by our Army Chiefs, on the Western Front. On 30th September, 1916, whilst sitting in my Admiralty Air Office, I received an agreeable surprise by a call from Mr. Tennyson D'Eyncourt and Colonel Stern. They had just returned from G.H.Q., France, and came to tell me all about the Tanks that had gone into action on the Somme for the first time on 15th September, 1916. They said 49 Tanks took part. Out of that number 16 or 17 broke down through sinking too deeply in soft ground or shell holes, or had mechanical troubles with their tracks. Thirty-two successfully reached the starting-point. Mr. Tennyson

D'Eyncourt was beaming at the thought of the success of the Tanks at the Front and was delighted. He said they had surpassed all his expectations. Reports had come into G.H.Q. that at Deville Wood, Flers, Gueudecourt and several other places whose names I could not remember, that the new mechanical weapon had done well and proved more than a match for the Germans, as one Tank had captured, single handed, three hundred Germans.

D'Eyncourt's information was most pleasing news to me at that time, because Air matters at the Admiralty had come almost to a standstill.

Colonel Stern informed me that General Haig said:

"The advance would have been impossible without Tanks and we have had the greatest victory since the Marne. Wherever the Tanks advanced we took our objectives and where they did not advance we failed to take our objectives."

That was indeed high praise for the new weapon from our great General.

Stern went on to say the crews had fought their Tanks with much gallantry, and the Officers were splendid. Many prisoners were taken with fewer casualties on our side due to the Tanks, also the Tanks had proved a good ally to the infantrymen, and although the mud of the Somme battle-field had proved too much for some of the caterpillar tracks, and caused several breakdowns, which prevented them doing much in the attacking line, undoubtedly they kept up the spirits of the men, which at that time were a little on the low side. Our conversation finished by Colonel Stern saying General Haig wanted more and more Tanks, and I was quite right at the Hatfield trials in telling the Military Officers that we would require 3000 Tanks.

I congratulated D'Eyncourt and Stern on their big success, which was earned so mightily well in getting the Tanks built in numbers and defeating those who sought to block mechanical weapons. I told them both I felt sure Tanks would make history, and they would become famous.

Shortly after this interesting conversation a wounded New Zealander arrived in a London hospital. He was behind and followed the Tank that did make history by manœuvring up Flers High Street. In giving his interesting experiences, this gallant soldier said:

The Tank refused to wait for our barrage fire to lift, and lolloped along through it all as if such a little shower of shells were beneath contempt. We were amazed.

We saw not a single member of her crew—not even a head or hand once.

Just on the outskirts of the village the "Tank" approached a German stronghold—a barn crowded with machine-guns, which were playing havoc among our men.

"What's this?" the travelling fortress seemed to ask. Then she pounded away with her guns for five minutes and then heaved forward.

First the wall crashed down, and then the barn was crushed out of existence. She just walked over it in her own peculiar, impertinent way.

She smashed everything that came in her way, and we of the infantry, scarcely believing our own eyes, just followed and did the rest.

She walloped straight along to the Flers High Street, over shell-craters, bringing down ruins and trees, and turning no corners, but taking the shortest cuts.

We are told that the Hindenburg Line was completed in the winter of 1916–17, when the Germans were not having it all their own way, and they feared a collapse on the Somme.

Whilst this colossal undertaking was being completed the Tank was used in small numbers on frequent occasions, but the softness and flatness of the terrain selected was not always advantageous to these mechanical weapons. They do better in hill country, where the rain rapidly drains off and the surface quickly dries (Plates XXXIII and XXXIV).

Both on the Somme and near Arras in 1917 the German gunners had much success in knocking out our Tanks.

If more Tanks and faster types had been available at that time the Germans would not have been so successful.

In all the small attacks wherever Tanks were used several hundred casualties would ordinarily have been expected, but they were reduced to unit digit figures.

My Staff in the Admiralty Air Department and at

PLATE XXXII

MR. NESFIELD DEMONSTRATING THE ANGULARIZED
CATERPILLAR TRACK MODEL BEFORE THE ROYAL
COMMISSION, LINCOLN'S INN

(By permission of the *Sphere*.)

PLATE XXXIII

PLATE XXXIV

(*Above*) TANK IN ACTION "BOW ON"
(*Below*) TANK IN ACTION—ROUGH TERRAIN

Taranto were exceedingly thoughtful and brought me much Tank information that I kept in a special book. They knew all the communiqués were of deep interest to those of us who had initiated the Tank weapon at the Admiralty, and a few seem worth recalling to our memories.

When in Southern Italy with No. 6 Wing of the Royal Naval Air Service, I noticed on 27th April, 1917, it was reported from Paris that:

> The German losses are estimated here at twenty per cent in the past three days' fighting on the Scarpe of the troops engaged. A Pomeranian division of at least 10,000 men was almost annihilated, and a regiment of a Prussian division, say 2000 bayonets, was mown down almost to the last man. When the Bavarian divisions were exhausted they were replaced by the Prussian Guard.
>
> One of the most gratifying features of the furious conflict is that most of the British wounds were comparatively slight.

The *Matin* then said:

> The Tanks did wonders. Three were engaged without a stop for eight hours. Besides their customary good work they exercised a salutary impression on the enemy. The new German anti-Tank guns do not seem to have sensibly interfered with their operations.
>
> Near Fontaine-lez-Croisilles the British carried at the end of the day a portion of the Hindenburg Line. Here the first belt of barbed wire was 20 yards deep, and the wire was two-fingers thick. Behind this was a series of ditches wired at the bottom. Then came reinforced concrete trenches perforated at regular intervals and provided with loopholes. The machine-gun emplacements communicated every 20 or 30 yards with connecting and supporting trenches. Lastly, tunnel shelters linked up the first and second lines of defence.
>
> Great things were expected from this formidable system of obstacles, but the British were equal to them.

Several of our Tanks were attacked by German flamethrowers, but on the whole these did little damage.

Mr. W. Beach Thomas,[1] the War Correspondent of the *Daily Mail*,[2] gave us a most interesting account of the endurance of a Tank, which is as follows:

The capture of Wancourt and Heninel (south-east of Arras) will always be famous if only for the journey of a Tank. It had a 40-hour duel with Hindenburg which outdoes all the stories of St. George and the Dragon. Nothing like it had been done before by any engine of war with a human crew. Only those who have heard what the hold of a Tank is like can understand the feat of endurance by its cabined and padded crew.

Our infantry were held up by heavy machine-gun fire from pits and trenches dotted over a slope on their left. They were attacking from the farthest point south where we had crossed the Hindenburg Line in the Arras sector. In their plight a Tank was called to their help and elected to go forth unaccompanied on a lone mission. It started by a direct advance along the line of Hindenburg's wire and flattened out one belt at its leisure while bullets rattled on its hide like hail on a tin roof. They flattened, fell, or glanced off, while the crew laughed, jested, and asked them to come in whenever a particularly loud one hit the door.

When one belt was flattened St. George the Tank turned in a graceful curve and proceeded with stately pomp to come back on a parallel course down the second net of wire. After this preliminary work St. George set out northwards to search the lairs of machine-gunners on the slope. For a while the gunners had ceased firing, but now again ordinary bullets and armour-piercing bullets rattled on his visor. He had already, with his own machine-guns, shot a number of infantry along the trenches behind the wire. He now picked off a quantity of machine gunners, though some burrowed into dug-outs and stayed there till subsequently taken prisoner.

From the warren of machine-gunners he went on to the village fortress of Wancourt, snaked a serpentine course in and around it, spitting fire—for he has the dragon's gifts as well as St. George's gifts—whenever a good target offered.

---

[1] Now Sir William Beach Thomas.   [2] *Daily Mail*, 14th April, 1917.

For a day and a night and a day he continued his quest, nosing out German machine-gunners and groups of infantry in two villages, in the valley, and along the slopes. At last, bumped and battered and worn as a shipwrecked crew, almost every pigeon-hole of ammunition used, the valiant crew turned their bows homewards.

Their ship covered much country and spent 40 hours on the adventure. It had flattened many hundred of yards of wire, cowed or knocked out a number of the enemy against whom our infantry had been powerless, and filled the mouth of a dug-out. I should doubt if any single feat in the war equals this record, and I have given no more than the skeleton.

Victory followed in its wake; the way was smoothed for the infantry, though some machine-guns were left both on the hill and in the village.

In May, 1917, a considerable section of the Hindenburg Line fell into our hands and on examination by our military experts was found to be in addition to the first, second and third line of trenches, composed of tremendous belts of criss-cross wire entanglements. In some places the wire was found to be thicker than a man's finger and possessing great tensile strength with barbs an inch long. The line was reinforced by concrete pill-boxes, machine-gun emplacements, etc. It must have been a tremendous task for our gallant Army comrades to have to dislodge the Germans from such a formidable line of protection.

Before the Cambrai Battle on 20th November, 1917, the Germans had been reinforced by a large number of Regiments from Russia. In this attack, surprise was to be attempted without previous bombardment by artillery. The Tanks were to be used instead of artillery to break through the wire entanglements and open up large passages for the infantry to pass.

Secrecy was the great feature of the attack. Tanks had to be brought up at night and were hidden in specially selected spots in advanced positions.

The main Hindenburg trenches had been made wider than usual and in some places had been increased to 16 ft. in breadth to prevent the Tanks passing over them. The ground chosen for the attack was sloped with a gradient of not more than 1 in 50.

The day of 20th November, 1917, broke and the Germans were unaware of any attack being launched, as no preliminary bombardment by artillery had been made. The attack commenced at 6.20 a.m.

The arrival of the Tanks in the German advanced line was the first the Germans knew that the British were attacking. The Tanks crashed over the barbed wire entanglements, cleared out a large number of German machine-gun batteries in the advanced line and then attacked the Hindenburg main line.

Over 400 Tanks took part in this attack. They had never been used in such large numbers before.

It will be remembered at the Hatfield Tank trials I asked for 3000 Tanks. Numbers of Tanks for attacking were always advanced by the Naval Landship Pioneers,[1] but a lack of vision had prevented them being used in numbers before this great attack took place.

The Tanks were most gallantly led by Brigadier-General H. J. Elles in his own Tank, and on taking his landships in numbers into action for the first time in the history of the World, with true Nelsonian touch, signalled "Every Tank is to do its damnedest."

The crews responded to a man and did their utmost in playing a big part in gaining a victory that has become historic.

The Tanks did fine work in the capture of Havrincourt.

The net result was that the Hindenburg main line and reserve line were broken through to a distance of 4½ miles on a 10-mile sector; 8000 prisoners were taken and 100 guns.

A high Military Authority informed me that before the arrival of Tanks a small indent made in the line cost us 5000 casualties. The losses in making a 4½-mile indent without Tanks would have been tremendous.

In this attack, thanks to the Tanks, the losses amongst the infantry were unprecedentedly light.

This was splendid news to receive, and I felt well justified for the fight I made to develop caterpillar landships when

---

[1] Page 91.

serving as the Director of the Admiralty Air Department.
The Tanks going into action in numbers must have been fine sight. One writer likened them to Hannibal's battle elephants that used to go into action ahead of the infantry with cavalry on either flank, about 218 B.C.

A Norfolk Officer writing an account of the Cambrai battle stated:

> In a few minutes after the attack commenced there was a rumbling behind us, and the Tanks crawled at an astonishing pace across No-Man's-Land. There were Tanks everywhere. One could count a score going across at once in our sector, and there were hundreds more besides. We let them get a little bit in front of us and then advanced at a walk, with rifles slung and everyone smoking merrily.
>
> The Boches had got belts of wire 25 ft. thick, but the Tanks strolled over them as if they were crops, and we wandered behind in their tracks. I had arrived with my platoon on the parapet of the Hindenburg Line without a casualty when an unlucky shell dropped almost between my legs and put sufficient shrapnel into one of them to bowl me over.
>
> When I got out of the dug-out again the guns were still thundering away, and a few Tanks were hauling supplies over the grass on rafts.

A distinguished General on returning from the Front informed me that our high Military Command was taken completely by surprise at the success of the Tanks.

As one who was following every stage of the War, may I recall that after several days' heavy fighting towards the end of March, 1918, our Third Army had been badly mauled and was retreating, and the Fifth Army had been severely punished. But to the everlasting fame of our great Armies, though badly smashed up, they were not beaten. The Defence offered by General Gough and his gallant men was magnificent and taught the Germans what a tough proposition the British Soldier is when he has his back to the wall. Most Sailors who followed closely the fortunes of our Armies at that time were full of admiration for the stubborn resistance the Fifth Army put up against vastly superior numbers and the way they took the very "guts" out of the German attack. After this severe setback a short rest became necessary, and the spirits of the men in the course of the next few months began to rise. The critics who said we were battering our heads against an impenetrable line forgot Britain's might in her factories and, thanks to Mr. Lloyd George's good vision, munitions were beginning to come in well to assist the infantrymen.

The "Whippet" Tank made its début during the great German push in March, 1918, and filled the German Brass Hats with dismay at—

> ... machines "which could outpace cavalry and were too quick for field-guns to put them out of action." Although the enemy, as usual, had an exaggerated notion of the mobility of the Whippet, it certainly accomplished notable feats. Near Villiers-Bretonneux, after the German bid for Amiens had failed, a few Whippets routed a German brigade, causing 400 enemy casualties, at a cost of five British casualties and one Whippet *hors de combat*.

From the time the Tank made its first appearance, the possibility of using Tanks in squadrons, like we do warships, in the Navy, to attack enemy Tanks, appeared feasible.

For example, *The Times* correspondent, writing from the British Front on 25th April, said of the fighting in the Villiers-Bretonneux area:

> Four of five enemy Tanks fell in with two of ours, and the first engagement between land ironclads took place. One of our machines was crippled, when a third British Tank hove in sight and joined in the attack. The newcomer knocked out one of the enemy, and the rest appear to have made their escape. On another part of the battle-field British light Tanks were engaged, and did fine work, some of them coming back with sides splashed with blood, for, besides using their guns, these Tanks were able to get home into bunches of Germans. They were evidently handled with great skill and gallantry, and have proved themselves a very useful weapon.

Here we have the first example of squadron actions between Tanks.

The closest co-operation between the Airman and the Officer in command of Tanks is necessary, because Tanks, though fairly immune from machine-gun and rifle-fire, are vulnerable to artillery.

It was, therefore, of great importance that our Airmen should endeavour to knock out all aircraft whether kite-balloon or aeroplane that were helping to control the enemy's gun-fire or could attack the Tank with bombs.

It is not, I think, generally known when His late Majesty King George V paid a twelve days' visit to his Armies in France, a special demonstration behind the front line was arranged for him and the Prince of Wales to see the latest weapons of offence. On the King arriving at a special screened spot, not a Tank was to be seen. Then Tanks suddenly made their way through brushwood, trees toppled over and the machines forced their way through wire entanglements and crossed trenches. His Majesty and the Prince of Wales got inside a Tank and manœuvred in her for some ten minutes. The crews were inspected operating the controls, engines, guns, and look-out arrangements were tested. During the inspection one Tank was ordered to go down an extra steep slope and His Majesty thought, when the machine arrived at the bottom, the force of the impact which was great had hurt some of the crew. But the smiling face of the young Captain of the Tank soon reassured him that all was well. The encouragement of this new method of warfare and interest his late Majesty took in the Tank Corps not only raised their prestige, but was appreciated most highly by all Ranks in that new Service.

After both sides had dug well in on the Western Front a long period of stalemate occurred and we are informed the Tanks played a big part in bringing back open warfare. Wherever the Germans anticipated the employment of Tanks they felled many roadside trees and laid these across any likely path of advance besides destroying most of the crossings over the many intersecting canals.

At that time the silver lining in the cloud began to show, for in his War Memoirs[1] Mr. Lloyd George states:

[1] *Daily Telegraph*, 2nd July, 1936.

Once more the Allies benefited by the new method of attack first attempted, but bungled at Cambrai—a short bombardment followed by the advance of a large force of Tanks.

The utmost secrecy was observed in the preparations for the Amiens offensive and when on August 8 it was launched, it took the Germans completely unawares.

Six to eight miles of ground were won by the evening of the first day. The French extended the attack to the south, and two days later they recaptured Montdidier. In a week's fighting 30,000 prisoners were taken—the British Fourth Army took 21,000 prisoners at a cost of only 20,000 casualties. German reinforcements were hurried up...

Four hundred and fifteen fighting Tanks went over the top at zero hour that morning and in all the engagements of the succeeding days Tanks played their part in smashing a way for the infantry, crashing through entanglements, sweeping across trenches, everywhere scattering and stampeding the enemy forces, circumnavigating machine-gun nests and receiving as little hurt from their sting as from antheaps in the path of a rhinoceros.

The reasons given by the apologists of the German Army Command for their failure to develop Tanks are in themselves a condemnation of the Staff policy in Britain and German of combing out all your able-bodied men from industry and thrusting them into the trenches. A few battalions more or less would not in fact have turned the scale between defeat and victory, whereas if they had been employed in manufacturing Tanks the effectiveness of the remaining battalions would have been multiplied manifold, and might have proved decisive.

This British attack before Amiens inflicted upon Ludendorff the severest defeat, up to that date, of the whole War.

On the 14th August, 1918, it was reported that during the heavy fighting our gallant Canadians did fine work.

The Tank "Dominion" led the Tanks into action in their sector with a piper of a Manitoba unit sitting astride the top skirling his pibroch. He came through unscathed, but another piper who piped his battalion into battle was killed.

Outside Bapaume in August, 1918, many Saxon prisoners were taken. One party came upon twelve Tanks in line and promptly surrendered. But one Officer naïvely remarked it was mighty difficult to surrender to an invisible enemy, whilst another Prussian Officer grew enraged because a Tank refused to take him on board.

The Officers in charge of Tanks soon learned good teamwork with the infantry and their general utility became a great feature of the War. One Tank covered between 8th August and 26th August, 1918, a distance of over 400 miles.

As the width of the trenches in many parts of the Main Hindenburg Line had been considerably increased in width, special cribs were constructed for laying down to assist the Tanks when necessary whilst advancing.

In the great attack made by American troops in September, 1918, when they wiped out the famous St. Michel Salient and General Pershing took over 13,000 prisoners, the Tanks working with the Americans made an excellent impression. The whole operation was carried out in a scientific manner. The success was due, in some measure, to the use of Tanks and a great extension of Air power.

The Tanks preceded the infantry at several points, smashing through the wire entanglements and rendering excellent services in dealing with those in the German trenches whom they soon had on the run.

One of our Staff Officers informed me that the Tank crews working with the Americans were most courageous, but it was unfortunate the Americans could not have fought with their own Tanks which, for reasons unknown to him, were not provided.

An American soldier who took part in the victory of French and American troops in the St. Michel Salient described[1] the following incident of Tank tactics when Tank met Tank:

> At first everything went without a hitch until we got bogged in some soft ground and enfiladed by machine-guns. It was a helpless feeling waiting for orders or for

[1] *Morning Post*, 19th September, 1918.

something to happen, but they held us in until a couple of Tanks flattened out the opposition. We could see they were making a stand well ahead, and our fleet of iron-'buses spread out just like a lot of battleships. They "got off" the scratch a bit jerkily, but were going good. We went after a few hundred yards away, and I saw something that tickled me to death. What appeared to be a strong point beyond Fritz's line began to move, and then I tumbled that it was a German Tank. One of ours nearest to it turned his nose around and made for it as fast as he could lick. He lurched into and out of holes like a ship in heavy seas. Afterwards when I went over the ground I could see the trap into which the Hun was trying to lead our "bird." This was a wide trench, knocked about so that it looked quite like the rest of the ground. But it would have bogged our man hopelessly. When he reversed and came back we had the same feeling you have when your friend does something you are ashamed of. It really seemed as if he was too proud to fight. But he made a détour, and the Hun had overstepped himself. Before he could get away our man had got abreast of him and fired all his guns. Then he seemed to go all out for him, and when the collision came he reared up nearly over the Fritz, which was a lower machine. But he slipped back flat, while poor Jerry completely capsized. He must have got near the edge of a crater in trying to dodge, and the impact pushed him right in. I saw what remained of the crew. They were nearly drowned, and I'll bet they never want to "loop the loop" in a Tank again. We marked that Tank "Huneater."

In the *Gazette* of Wednesday, 28th November, 1918, a most interesting record of valour is given of a Military Officer's leadership in which a Tank played some part. This account shows that these weapons in moments of emergency can be of great value.

Captain and Brevet Major (Acting Lieutenant-Colonel) John Standish Surtees Prendergast Vereker, Viscount Gort, D.S.O., M.V.O., M.C., 1st Battalion Grenadier Guards.

For most conspicuous bravery,[1] skilful leading and devotion to duty during the attack of the Guards Division on 27th September, 1918, across the Canal du Nord, near Flesquières, when in command of the 1st Battalion Grenadier Guards, the leading battalion of the 3rd Guards Brigade.

Under heavy artillery and machine-gun fire, he led his battalion with great skill and determination to the "forming-up" ground, where very severe fire from artillery and machine-guns was again encountered.

Although wounded, he quickly grasped the situation, directed a platoon to proceed down a sunken road to make a flanking attack, and, under terrific fire, went across open ground to obtain the assistance of a Tank, which he personally led and directed to the best possible advantage. While thus fearlessly exposing himself he was again severely wounded by a shell. Notwithstanding considerable loss of blood, after lying on a stretcher for a while, he insisted on getting up and personally directing the further attack. By his magnificent example of devotion to duty, and utter disregard of personal safety all ranks were inspired to exert themselves to the utmost, and the attack resulted in the capture of over 200 prisoners, two batteries of field-guns, and numerous machine-guns. Lieutenant-Colonel Viscount Gort then proceeded to organize the defence of the captured position until he collapsed: even then he refused to leave the field until he had seen the "success signal" go up on the final objective.

Some eleven years after the War terminated a tribute by a French General, General Debeney, was paid to a British unit for its assistance to a French Division. It was circulated by the War Office and reads:

Citation on behalf of 9th Battalion Tank Corps during the Great War. It is notified in an Army order that the Army Council have approved of the publication of the following citation, which appeared in general Army order number 83, by the General Officer commanding the First French Army on August 15, 1918, on behalf of the 9th Battalion Tank Corps which:

[1] Awarded the V.C.

In the actions of July 23, 1918, under the experienced and able command of its commander, Lieutenant-Colonel Woods, rendered most effective assistance to a French division and by its bravery, boldness and fighting spirit combined with its high standard of training, set an example which roused the enthusiastic admiration of its French comrades.

G.H.Q., August 15, 1918.

Le general de division Debeney commanding First Army.

(Signed) DEBENEY.

PALESTINE

Towards the end of 1916 eight Tanks were sent to the Near East for work in Palestine.

These Tanks were highly successful in France, but scarcely suitable for warfare in that rocky country.

Nevertheless, they played an effective part in the second Battle of Gaza.

In his very interesting book, *Airman Friday*, Mr. William Courtenay tells us from his own experience that the Turks put one Tank

out of action between our lines and theirs which meant that for weeks afterwards until the autumn campaign opened we had nightly patrol-work to do in searching this Tank in case the Turks got there first and made a machine-gun post of it.

Some additional Tanks were sent out from England and they did useful work in the third and victorious Battle of Gaza.

In these operations the Tanks did not do all that was expected of them, but they materially helped our infantrymen and their moral effect was great on the Turks, who had heard about, but never seen, these novel Weapons of War.

(1) BRITISH OPINION ON VALUE OF TANKS

"Tanks in the last three months of the War played a greater part than any other particular weapon."—D. LLOYD GEORGE.

It would be absurd for me to give any opinion as to whether Tanks were of any value in the Great War. I must leave that in abler hands and merely quote a few opinions.

That great Master of Tank Tactics, Major-General J. F. C. Fuller, D.S.O., after giving us details of the Cambrai fighting in November, 1917, and the important part played by the Tanks, writes:

"Thus ended the first great Tank Battle in the whole history of warfare, and, whatever may be the future historians' doctrine, as to its value, it must ever rank as one of the most remarkable battles ever fought. On November 20th, from a base of some 13,000 yards in width, a penetration of no less than 10,000 yards was effected in twelve hours ; at the third Battle of Ypres a similar penetration took three months. Eight thousand prisoners and 100 guns were captured, and these prisoners alone were nearly double the casualties suffered by the IIIrd and IVth Corps during the first day of the battle.

It is an interesting point to remember that in this battle the attacking infantry were assisted by 690 Officers and 3,500 other ranks of the Tank Corps, a little over 4000 men, or the strength of a strong Infantry Brigade, and that these men replaced artillery, wire-cutting and rendered unnecessary the old preliminary bombardment. More than this, by keeping close to the infantry they effected a much higher co-operation than had ever before been attainable with artillery.

When on November 21st the bells of London pealed forth in celebration of the victory of Cambrai, consciously or unconsciously to their listeners they tolled out an old tactic and ran in a new—Cambrai had become the Valmy of a new epoch in War, the epoch of the Mechanical Engineer."[1]

Major-General Sir Hugh Elles, the intrepid Commander of the Tanks in action, informs us:

The Germans lacked the means to move and supply their guns rapidly. They lacked Tanks to produce surprise or to carry forward the battle as an alternative to guns. They lacked lorries, they lacked cross-country vehicles.

[1] From *Tanks in the Great War*, by General J. F. C. Fuller, D.S.O.

With us when the tide turned, the converse was the case, and it was at least a part reason of success against an enemy who fought bravely and often bitterly almost to the end.[1]

From the British Commander-in-Chief, Sir Douglas Haig, dispatch of 20th July, 1918, the following is taken:

Reference has been made more than once in the body of this report to the very valuable work accomplished by Tanks and Tank personnel in the course of the Somme battle. Throughout the whole of this fighting Tanks took part in numerous successful counter-attacks, many of which were instrumental in checking the enemy's progress at critical points. On these occasions Tanks have shown that they possess capabilities in defence little, if at all, less than those which they have already proved in attack. In their first encounter with German Tanks, Officers and men of the Tank Corps displayed with success under conditions new in warfare the same energy and resource which have always characterized their action.

Then, Colonel Seely, M.P., Deputy Minister of Munitions, addressing a meeting on 31st August, 1918, in the East Midlands, of workmen engaged in the manufacture of Tanks, said:

... he spoke the literal truth when he declared that he and hundreds of others with whom he had been in action would certainly have been dead but for the Tanks. Now Tanks were being provided in thousands and would be instrumental in saving thousands of lives. With the Tanks available casualties were relatively small. There was no doubt that on a certain day the Tanks saved Amiens.

Later, Sir Douglas Haig, in his dispatch of 21st December, 1918, observes:

Since the opening of our offensive on 8th August Tanks have been employed in every battle, and the

[1] Introduction. *The Tank Corps*, by Major Clough-Williams Ellis, M.C., and A. Williams Ellis.

TANKS IN ACTION

importance of the part played by them in breaking the resistance of the German infantry can scarcely be exaggerated. The whole scheme of the attack of 8th August was dependent upon Tanks, and ever since that date on numberless occasions the success of our infantry has been powerfully assisted or confirmed by their timely arrival. So great has been the effect produced upon the German infantry by the appearance of British Tanks that in more than one instance, when for various reasons real Tanks were not available in sufficient numbers, valuable results have been obtained by the use of dummy Tanks painted on frames of wood and canvas.

It is no disparagement of the courage of our infantry or of the skill and devotion of our artillery, to say that the achievements of those essential arms would have fallen short of the full measure of success achieved by our Armies had it not been for the very gallant and devoted work of the Tank Corps, under the command of Major-General H. J. Elles.

We are told that:
"Between 1st March and 1st August, 1918, the strength of the Tank Corps increased by 27 per cent. . . ."
"In August, 1918, the Allies had 1572 Tanks, the Germans practically none. . . ."
"The allied workshops were turning out an increased output of Tanks. . . ."[1]

General Fuller has stated: "With the invention of mechanical skirmishing fortresses called Tanks, the attack regains its power and there is deadlock no longer. It was imagination, foresight and enterprise that produced the Tank and won for it due recognition from our Conservative-minded Military Leaders."

In dealing with the final offensive operations on the Western Front, Mr. Lloyd George states:

> Beyond a doubt, one of the most brilliant performances and decisive strokes of this succession of colossal battles was the smashing blow delivered by Haig and his dauntless Army of British and Dominion Troops at the Siegfried line between Marcoing and St. Quentin. . . .

[1] Numbers given by Mr. Lloyd George.

Immense Tank-proof trenches, sunken fields filled with barbed wire entanglements, strong points and machine-gun nests and vast shell-proof dugouts and underground chambers where whole battalions could shelter from a barrage—and the highly fortified line of the Canal du Nord adding a natural and seemingly impassable obstacle in the heart of this network of massive and ingenious defences.

The Tank played a fine part in our final victories and by 28th September, 1918, these massive defences were crossed. Ludendorff and the German General Staff's dream of holding this great fortified line was for ever shattered.

There is no doubt that the moral effect of the Tanks in several of the operations towards the end of the War was sometimes decisive, as disclosed in General Haig's final dispatches, the British official history of the War and many other documents and books that have been written in this Country.

One report that reached me stated that a British General, towards the close of the War, took an enemy's position with the aid of eight Tanks. Next day he made a surprise find and captured the enemy's Brigade Headquarters. In a special message to Divisional Headquarters, a copy of which was found, the German Brigadier referring to the first attack implored help, as he was being attacked by 200 Tanks.

Also this fear of Tanks has been revealed in many books and articles by German writers since the War terminated.

In later war days the mere fact that our great Ally, the French, and ourselves had the industrial resources to develop Tanks in large numbers and the Germans could not, was of paramount importance to the field Armies of our two Nations. It is now undisputed that during the War the Tank saved, as that very gallant and famous General, now Lord Mottistone (better known to the British public as Jack Seely) has more than once publicly stated, thousands and thousands of our comrades' lives at the Front, and that this novel weapon gave our infantrymen greater confidence when their morale was partly undermined through the stress of a long campaign, will not, I think, be challenged.

This opinion is supported by Monsieur Louchier—French Minister of War—when he said in January, 1919:

There are two kinds of infantry: men who have gone into action with Tanks and men who have not; and the former never want to go into action without Tanks again.

Moreover, the Tank crews of both Nations created a great tradition and made their Countrymen proud of their gallant deeds with an untried weapon of war. An invention like the Tank, which in skilful hands tended to shorten hostilities instead of allowing them to drag on for years, would seem to have been of great value to the Allies' cause.

Although many Staff Officers had at first cold-shouldered mechanical weapons, there is abundant proof that the Tank broke up static warfare and restored the war of movement. The series of attacks planned by General Haig towards the close of the War forced Ludendorff to admit that the German Armies could no longer stand up to the British and French Armies that were so well equipped with the latest weapon of war—the Tank.

(2) FRENCH OPINION ON VALUE OF TANKS

"Whoever shall first be able to make land ironclads armed and equipped, roll over heavy, damp ground, will have 'Won the War.' "—COLONEL ESTIENNE, September, 1914.

After considerable delays in appreciating the value of Tanks, the French first designed some heavy caterpillar landships that were constructed by the Schneider Company and St. Chamond Company. Many of these machines had the usual mechanical difficulties, but on the whole they were a big success. Their armament was more formidable than British Tanks, but were necessarily less mobile with their 75 mm. (about 3·3 in.) guns and ammunition. These machines did well at the Battle of Noyan and other engagements. Later, the French developed their famous light Renault Tank Char-Léger of 6½ tons, about half the weight of a British Whippet Tank. This work was done under the guidance of General Estienne, the first French Tank Pioneer.[1] The crew of these small Tanks consisted of two

[1] See page 155.

men, one to manœuvre the machine and the other to work the 37 mm. gun or 8 mm. Hotchkiss machine-guns. They offered a very small target to Enemy's gun-fire and were most mobile. In a few seconds the Char-Léger could be swung round on her tracks like a spinning ball. They were also good climbers and their powers in this respect excited general admiration.

A very large number of small Tanks were built and played an important part in the Battles of the Aisne, where they appeared for the first time. One of the secrets of their great success was to employ them in large numbers with the French infantry. These small Tanks fully justified General Estienne's great faith in them.

By June, 1917, an order had been placed for 3500 light Tanks with the Renault, Schneider and Berliet Firms.

After many more successes with these Tanks the General Commander-in-Chief of the French Armies addressed to the Artillerie d'Assaut, then responsible for Tank development, on 30th July, 1917, the following order of the day:

"Vous avez bien mérité la Patrie."

A special correspondent with the French Army, writing on Saturday, 27th July, 1918, observed:

> The smooth working of this operation is in practice greatly hampered by the daring of our infantry, who advanced accompanied by our light Tanks which, being speedy and tireless, care nothing whatever for machine-guns, and also by our Airmen, who keep the Enemy's infantry constantly under fire from low heights. It is reckoned that each Tank section engaged to-day has put 15 to 20 machine-guns out of action, and it is claimed that the light Tank is doing at least as much for the French in the advance as the German infantry guns do for the Enemy.
>
> In the Montagne de Reims, opposite the British, the Enemy will hold on along the Soissons road until the last moment to save his centre from the enclosing pincers.
>
> Light Tanks advancing with the troops continue to render excellent service in breaking up the machine-gun nests with which the Enemy is seeking to delay our pursuit.

On 28th July, 1918, a French communiqué was issued which stated:

Since July 18, the day of the French counter-offensive between the Aisne and the Marne, our Tanks have taken a glorious part in the battle. After driving in the Enemy lines and facilitating the forward rush of our infantry, they unceasingly accompanied, or preceded, our troops and those of our Allies in their advance, giving proof of great skill in manœuvring and of unparalleled bearing.

The crews drove their Tanks into the centre of the battle, shirking no obstacle and attacking the centres of resistance and Enemy batteries under a terrible machine-gun and anti-Tank gun-fire which the Enemy had concentrated against them. Such heroism obtained the best results.

Each section of Tanks destroyed on an average from fifteen to twenty German machine-guns. A number of them, which attacked some batteries, put the gun crews out of action and assured the capture of material. The losses inflicted on the Enemy by the Tanks are, according to the statements of prisoners, very heavy.

From July 18 to July 23 the Tanks daily participated in attacks, and the greater part of them made two raids, while others were returned to the battle four or five times in the same day. At this date each company had three full days of fighting to its record, and the drivers put in thirty hours on July 18 and July 19.

In a very gallant attack in the autumn of 1918 by French and American troops between Soissons and Château Thierry, French Tanks took an active part, and it was reported from an authoritative source that the fire from these Tanks had a most dire effect on the Germans opposed to them. In several instances Squadrons of Tanks were directed by aeroplanes with great success.

Perhaps few people had a higher opinion of the French Tanks than Mr. Lloyd George, for he writes:[1]

> In another important respect the Entente had a great superiority to aid their march to victory. This was the Tank.

[1] "War Memoirs," The *Daily Telegraph*, 2nd July, 1936.

The Germans surprisingly neglected to develop this new device, even after they had witnessed its effectiveness. Its failure through stupid use at the Somme and Passchendaele and through ineffective exploitation of its success at Cambrai had misled the Germans as to its possibilities. But the tactics of the massed Tank Attack, which proved so successful in breaking the German line at Cambrai in November, 1917, were adopted by the Allies repeatedly in 1918. They were the spear-point of the French thrust on July 18, which was the turn of the tide. Their nimble little Tanks dashed through the German lines and created confusion and dismay. They similarly opened the British attack of August 8, and were largely responsible for that notable victory, and still more for its depressing effect on the German Army.

At the end of the War the opinion of the higher Command in France was that their light Tanks were undoubtedly one of the factors that helped to end hostilities.

(3) German Opinion on Value of Tanks

"More momentous for us is the question of Tanks."—GENERAL VON WRISBERG, Minister of War.[1]

Many German writers, when inditing their Supreme Command, say that they underrated the effectiveness of the British Tanks and that the German Army had not time to develop properly this weapon, otherwise it is often suggested the German offensive in the spring of 1918 would have been successful and the whole course of the War altered. General Kabisch has written an interesting account of the operations of March, 1918; he holds this strong opinion:

> If the Germans had been in possession of a couple of hundred light Tanks the offensive would have been successful.

In support of this opinion the General gives details of some fine work done by four German Tanks near St. Quentin on 21st of March, 1918. After that date German Tanks took no further part in the operations.

[1] Speaking in the Reichstag at the time of the battle of Amiens.

TANKS IN ACTION

There is no question that the Tank did play an important part in the final catastrophe and the mere fact that the British and French could turn their factories into production of Tanks in large numbers, whereas the Germans had left the provision and study of these machines until too late, was one of the determining factors in ending the War.

On the anniversary of the appearance of the British Tank in Flanders some eighteen years ago, and of their first successful attack which made an indent into the German line greater than had been done by many famous Divisions, we are told "a German Artillery Officer in an observation-post in front of Flers rubbed his eyes. He stared in the early morning light at a ridge ahead. A night of horror was behind him, the sort of night that was excuse enough for a man's eyes or nerves to play tricks on him. For days and weeks he had studied that ridge till he knew every fold and shell-hole on it. Even then he was prepared for many queer sights after a vicious barrage, but never such a queer one as this. Wonderingly he stepped along to the post of another German observer. 'Look,' he whispered, 'there is something I cannot make out. It looks like a threshing machine.'"

A threshing machine in front of the British line! But let that other German Officer tell the story as he recalled it to a Reporter.[1]

"It did look something like a threshing machine," he said, "but why should it have arrived there in the middle of a war, and on a most unhealthy sector at that? Should we turn our batteries on it or wait and see what happened next?

"We waited and watched. Then it moved. It actually started to come towards us. But that was not all. Suddenly into view came another. It joined the first one, and side by side they came on, ugly and ungainly, but terribly business-like. Then without warning from both of them came streams of bullets. Next they were on top of us...."

For a moment he was silent, and then he said quietly: "You did surprise us and you did make a mess of us. Those of us who survived will not forget that morning when your

[1] Taken from the *Evening Standard*, 17th September, 1935.

Tanks first came into action. And to think we thought they were threshing machines!"

When Tanks were first used German Prisoners related that models were made of the British Tanks and sent into the first-line trenches so that those who had not seen them would know in future what these grotesque beasts looked like. The respect inspired by these new and unexpected weapons of war was great. Stories were circulated about them in the German trenches which lost nothing in the telling, and it is true to say that amongst the more ignorant German soldiers the sinister power of the new British arm was a real terror to them in the new year of 1917.

In the autumn of that year *The Times* correspondent with the British Army related:[1]

> There are individual Tanks which have run over 400 miles in the battle since August 8th. That the Germans now are thoroughly afraid of the Tanks and fairly have them on the brain we know. It is a fact that for a considerable time before the attack a number of our Tanks were on one side of a village while the Germans were on the other side, and the enemy never guessed their presence. At other places where no Tanks were the Germans had nightmares about them.
>
> Besides fearing and hating the Tank, German Officers consider it most ungentlemanly of us to employ a machine to which they cannot surrender. Some complain bitterly that when the Tanks came along they tried to surrender to them, and chased them as if they had been 'buses, hailing them to stop and take them on board, but the Tanks, having small accommodation for prisoners, merely left them for later comers to round up, and went on to attend to the next machine-gun post. One of these Officers said he had been fighting since 1914, and never thought he would be treated with so much discourtesy when he did us the honour to surrender.
>
> A well-known and much-esteemed constituent of mine was recently on a visit to Germany and at a Dinner Party he sat next to a Military Officer of high rank. The conversation turned to the War. The German Officer said at

[1] 26th August, 1917.

one place near Amiens a British Tank was particularly offensive, and the only way he could get his men to attack it was to spread the tale that the Tank was full of chocolates. His men had been very short of rations and the knowledge that the British Tank contained chocolates spurred them on with renewed energy in trying to knock out the Tank, but they failed and the Tank remained uncaptured much to the annoyance of his men, who were looking forward to a delicacy long untasted.

At the time of the Battle of Amiens, the Prussian Minister of War sent out this message:[1]

> The superiority of the enemy is principally due to the use of Tanks.

And that the German soldiers in the early autumn of 1917 *did* fear the Tanks is shown by a paper captured by the Australians, giving the reasons to which the German Staff attributed the defeat of the Second Army.

It reads:

> August 8th. Reasons reported by Officers detailed by the Higher Command to inquire into the defeat are:
> The fact that the troops lost their heads when the Tanks suddenly appeared behind them through coming up under cover of an artificial fog.
> To the non-existence of any new pattern obstacles either in front or rear.
> Insufficient artillery held with reserve infantry in order to deal with Tanks and troops breaking through.

Among the measures ordered are that troops must overcome their dislike to trench digging, and must construct posts and positions designed to support each other. The document adds:

> It must be made absolutely impossible for Tanks which have broken through to penetrate without meeting obstacles, as far as the headquarters of the Staffs.

The principle that troops, even if employed must, if necessary, fight on for days to the last man, and the last cartridge, appears to have been forgotten.

[1] *Tanks, 1914–18. The Log Book of a Pioneer*, by Sir Albert Stern.

If the Tanks are to be fought, the order concludes, it means mobile artillery, trench mortars, anti-Tank rifles, and obstacles like blown-up bridges, contact mines, and flooded water-channels.

Also General Von Ardenne, commenting in the *Berliner Tageblatt* on the words of German evening communiqué of 8th August:[1]

In the attack of the English between the Ancre and the Avre, the enemy has forced his way into our position, recalls the impression the Tanks made on the German soldiers on 18th July, on the Front at Soissons and Château Thierry.

And adds:

Before the soldiers were able to regain their mental balance the fire roller,[2] which was followed by dense enemy attacking waves, had passed over them. The sequel was the loss of a relatively large number of prisoners and guns. In the fighting on 8th August the beginning of the battle appears to have taken the same course. Losses in ground, guns, and prisoners are painful, especially since the German Army Command has desired in the past, and is especially anxious now, to act on the principle of economizing its forces.[3]

And a German Officer made this interesting statement as to the causes of the German defeat:

Two great mistakes were made. The first was the complete under-rating of the Englishman as a land fighter; the second was the under-rating of America both in her capacity to build ships and to raise an Army.

The troops in the (German) offensive of 1918 attacked in massed formation. As a result we had enormous losses in the first offensive, 180,000 men. There were not enough troops available, and so the break-through via Amiens to the coast could not be made.

The revolution was not the cause but the result of defeat. With us it came when all confidence in General Headquarters was lost, and especially when the American leaflets (really the British propaganda leaflets) under-

[1] 1918.   [2] Tank.   [3] *Morning Post*, 13th August, 1918.

mined this confidence more and more, and the Tanks as a new weapon broke it down altogether.

May I give General Ludendorff's account of the operations around 22nd August, 1918? He says:

During the following days, however, the English, who had but few fresh reserves at their disposal, gained ground towards Bapaume after very severe fighting.

The characteristic of their tactics was narrow but deep penetrations by Tank after short but extremely violent artillery preparation, combined with artificial fog.

Mass attacks by Tanks and artificial fog remained hereafter our most dangerous enemies.

This danger increased in proportion as the *morale* of our troops deteriorated and as our divisions grew weaker and more exhausted.[1]

The German text of the official papers published in Germany regarding the events which preceded the Armistice (Vorgeschichte des Waffenstillstand) contains some interesting particulars of the secret cross-examination of Ludendorff as to the position of the German armies on 17th October, 1918.

Ludendorff admitted that the German troops in the west had lost all power of attack; the "strain on individuals has reached a degree which could not be exceeded; when the Officer gives way privates say: 'Where are you going, Sir?' and take themselves off." He said that "our men are not anxious about the Americans, but they are anxious about the British." He declared that the 41st German Division let the British through the front on 8th August, 1918, in the Battle of Amiens, but that it had suffered severely from influenza and had not received its ration of potatoes.

Of our Tanks he said: "I hope the Tank panic, which at one time was overcome and now has revived again, will be once more overcome. It returned in all its force on August 8th. We cannot keep pace in the construction of Tanks."

The Deputy Chief of the Staff—General Von Freytag

[1] *My War Memories*, 1914-1918, by General Ludendorff, page 692.

Loringhoven—in a lecture given to German Staff Officers in Berlin in September, 1918, said:

We should long since have settled with the French if our troops had not had to perform the Sisyphus labour of encountering the reinforcements which the Allies brought to the French, and their unparalleled technical fighting means including numberless Tanks. Our brave soldiers are more and more learning how to dispose of these monsters. Nevertheless, the abundance of technical fighting means which our enemies employ against us constitutes an essential reason why we cannot adhere to the war of movement which brought us a decision in the East.

Yet our troops can claim the tremendous achievement of, on the whole, having held and occupied this territory for four years. In the East our victory is complete. In the West we are wrestling to preserve what we have won there and in the East. Our field Army will not let this be snatched out of its hands. The most important thing is that the people at home shall hold out morally. We soldiers certainly don't under-estimate our Enemies. We esteem their courage, above all that of the French, very highly. We know, however, also that the infantry of all the Nations allied against us can do nothing without their artillery and their Tanks and that our infantry is absolutely superior to it in hand-to-hand fighting, and is conscious of the fact.

When commenting upon the General's lecture it was noted that ex-Colonel Gaedke, writing to order in the *Vorwärts,* says: "*In view of these conditions the German High Command has decided not to conduct in future a war of offence, but a war of defence.*" The words are italicized. The conditions referred to are those which, he says, arise out of Foch's successful return blows, of the superiority of the French and British Armies in men and material, of the gathering of thousands of new Tanks and countless new aeroplanes to continue the long-planned offensive for months, "the Entente's almost inexhaustible supplies of raw materials, and the American Army."

Finally, it is of great interest to all those who initiated

the Tank and those that brought this weapon to a high stage of efficiency towards the end of the War to know that General Von Zwehl in his interesting book[1] wrote:

> It was not the genius of Marshal Foch that defeated us, but General Tank.

This is, of course, an exaggeration. Nevertheless, it is the opinion of a great German General who has had access to many military documents and reports which no doubt showed from the German side the weapon that was considered to be by high Military Authority one of the determining factors in the defeat of the German Armies on the Western Front in the Great War.

[1] *Die Schlachter im Sommer*, 1918, *an der Oest Front.*

CHAPTER V

TANKS OF TO-DAY

(1) MODERN TANKS REVERT TO ROYAL NAVAL AIR SERVICE TYPE.
(2) FOREIGN NATIONS ANNEX THE TANK INVENTION.

(1) MODERN TANKS REVERT TO ROYAL NAVAL AIR SERVICE TYPE

SOON after the successful demonstration of the Killen Strait Caterpillar Machine before Mr. Lloyd George on 30th June, 1915, I instructed Commander Boothby to unship one of the Turrets of an Austin armoured car and place it on the Killen Strait Caterpillar and run it about for demonstration purposes to show exactly how a small caterpillar landship could be used (Diagram II).[1] This machine was quite good at crossing obstacles and going over rough ground. We were all impressed with this demonstration and after our experience with this machine both Boothby and myself became more convinced that single-unit landships on the general lines of my first caterpillar landship drawing prepared for me by Mr. Diplock were far more preferable than Colonel Crompton's articulated type.

This Turret, mounted on the Killen Strait Caterpillar in 1915, became the godfather of the Whippet and the French light Tanks that were produced in numbers in the last year of the War. On active service Mr. Tritton's and Lieutenant Wilson's Rhomboidal Tank had the usual mechanical defects that always appear when introducing a new weapon of war. We had plenty of them when we introduced Submarines into the Navy.

At first the Tanks suffered from the rollers that had to take the weight, when the machine was fully loaded being too weak. Some of the sprockets were defective and plenty of other mechanical defects occurred which was to be expected.

[1] Page 238.

Many of the Tank experts did not like the sponsons because they were too near the ground. This was a grave defect when operating in soft terrain. Also the gun was too low.

After some experience at the Front with the first Tanks, General Elles sent in a rough design for a new type of Tank. This led to the Whippet and Hornets being introduced. These Tanks were much lighter and faster than the Rhomboidal Tank. The sponsons were done away with and the gun carried in a turret, as I always advocated. The turret is shown, incomplete for secrecy purposes, in my first caterpillar landship drawing[1] prepared for me by Mr. Diplock. In the evidence given before the Royal Commission[2] Mr. James Whitehead, K.C., remarked:

> Your Lordship must have observed that it is mentioned in fact in Commodore Sueter's claim that his description of his weapon of war with its caterpillar track in the form in which they were put, and with its turret, its armament and its armour is almost an exact description of the Whippet Tank, and that in fact when you had the Whippet Tank you had a reversion of type as the biologists call it—you had a reversion to the very suggestion Commodore Sueter made.

In modern designs the Rhomboidal type of Tank has been abandoned and Tanks of to-day have reverted more to the Royal Naval Air Service type of caterpillar landship, that is our revolving turret armoured car body mounted on caterpillars, as I advocated to Mr. Churchill on the Horse Guards Parade on 16th February, 1915, and which is shown clearly in Plates XXXVI, LIV and LV.

Shortly after the War terminated an interesting article[3] appeared in the *Evening News* from which I take the following:

> Whatever size may be the Army which Parliament decides to maintain, it is certain that the Tank arm will play a very big part.
> By developing the Tank we shall prevent the needless shedding of blood. We have kept careful statistics of

---

[1] Diagram I.   [2] Minutes of Proceedings.
[3] *Evening News*, 16th December, 1918.

the life-conserving value of the Tanks. I will give you an instance.

At one point near the Hindenburg Line it was found that a line of 36 Tanks a few yards apart were the means of preventing 1000 casualties in a single day.

New types were shown during the Review of the Army by his late Majesty King George V in Jubilee Year in the Rushmoor area. That display showed how the military forces of this country are becoming mechanized (Plate XXXV). All those fortunate people who saw the march past of the infantry and cavalry thought them as splendid as ever. But the parade of the mechanized units, the motor cars with their wireless masts, the Tanks led by Major-General Sir Ernest Swinton, the Army pioneer of armoured caterpillar vehicles, was a tremendously impressive sight and raised a great cheer from the sightseers, and showed how they appreciated these mechanical additions to the British Army. This should be a good omen for the future.

Many spectators at His Majesty's Review no doubt recalled that some nineteen years had elapsed since the British Tanks made their first appearance on the Somme and later at Cambrai, on being used in large numbers, proved for all time that mechanical weapons, when handled properly and used over terrain where they can operate, will be of great value in helping the infantryman when faced with great difficulties.

It is quite possible that some of the onlookers at this parade of Tanks may have owed their lives to the introduction of these novel weapons of war.

If that is so, I wonder if any of them gave a thought to that little band of Naval Airmen who burnt much midnight oil and worked so hard in small and stuffy rooms at the Admiralty to devise a caterpillar landship that would help their Army comrades in the grim struggle they were up against in the Great War.

They are, I submit, worthy of an occasional thought because they initiated the caterpillar landship under very great difficulties, much ridicule and hostile criticism from their Senior Officers. But never for a moment did they flinch from the task they set themselves which was to see a successful caterpillar landship constructed.

Those of us who received so many kicks for our initiative can now afford to laugh, and I would remind them that my astute colleague on the First War Air Committee, and good friend of all Airmen, the late Lord Montagu of Beaulieu, said in words something like these:

"It is the penalty of all Pioneers to receive bricks and kicks: to be scoffed and jeered at: to be intensely disliked for being right in their anticipation. When their work comes to fruition and they see the good seed sown produce a bumper harvest they can feel they have been of some little use to their Country and the satisfaction comes that none can remove."

The use of Tanks has, of course, been greatly extended in modern war, and they are no longer confined to the assistance of infantry in a set piece attack. Probably their most important use under modern conditions is in the Tank Brigade. This formation consists of one battalion of light Tanks and three battalions each composed of a mixture of light and medium Tanks. The Tank Brigade is intended to be used either independently or in co-operation with mechanized cavalry in mobile operations. By advancing ahead of the normal formations it is hoped these mobile troops will keep operations fluid by attacking the Enemy in flank or rear and so preventing the establishment of strong defensive positions. The light Tanks are used mainly for reconnaissance and as a screen while the medium Tanks advance to strike the main blow.

Mechanized cavalry also need light Tanks for reconnaissance, but as they will often be working in more enclosed country they will also need men carried in suitable mechanical vehicles to co-operate with them. We thus have Tank brigades consisting of light and medium Tanks for use in a more or less open country, where full use can be made of their mobility, and mechanized cavalry with light Tanks and men carried in vehicles for operating in country less suitable to Tank brigades. The mechanized cavalry may often have to open the way through difficult country to enable the Tank brigade to debouch into the open, and later they may have to advance and take over the ground gained by such action.

In addition to the Tanks used for these mobile operations, there is still the necessity for a Tank to co-operate with the infantry in an attack on a strong defensive position. If the operations by the mobile troops should fail, the Enemy may well be able to establish himself on a defensive line which cannot readily be turned. It then becomes necessary for the infantry to be able to penetrate through this line. To assist them in this role it is proposed to use the Infantry Tank. For this work speed and mobility is of less value, for if the Tanks pass at speed over a defensive position they will not see the defenders who will be concealed and dug in. To clear a way through this position it becomes necessary for the Tanks and infantry to co-operate closely on the battle-field as they did during the Great War. But where as special anti-Tank guns hardly existed during the War, all Armies are now equipped with these in considerable numbers. It therefore becomes necessary to provide sufficient armour on an Infantry Tank to resist the lighter types of anti-Tank weapon.

These three classes, Light, Medium and Infantry Tank, comprise our main requirements in fighting vehicles to-day. In light Tanks we are well ahead. Some seven years ago the genius of the late Sir John Carden produced a two-man light Tank which gave us a long lead and was eventually copied by nearly all military Nations. Then about two years ago we again took the lead by the introduction of a third man into this Tank, and the re-design of this small Tank to accommodate a third man was again a stroke of genius. One cannot, of course, gain advantages without some corresponding disadvantages, and the Tank became heavier and more inclined to pitch on rough ground, and the extra weight may shorten the life of the Tank; but within the limitations of a small machine of this nature, it is a thoroughly sound and efficient vehicle.

For medium Tanks we require more armament and a Tank which provides a steadier gun platform in motion, for whereas the main role of the light Tank is reconnaissance and protection, the medium Tank is primarily intended to fulfil a fighting role.

With the Infantry Tank, heavy armour is the main essential. A turn of speed is useful while approaching a

PLATE XXXV

THE ALDERSHOT REVIEW, 1935. KING GEORGE V TAKING THE SALUTE OF HIS TANKS

PLATE XXXVI

THE BRITISH LIGHT TANK MARK V

defensive position, but the Tank must be able to dwell on the enemy position while assisting the infantry to overcome the opposition.

In the debate on the 1937 Army Estimates in the House of Commons,[1] the Secretary of State for War, Mr. Duff Cooper, in a most able speech stated:

So far as Tanks are concerned, we are very satisfied with our new light Tanks. We believe them to be as good if not better than any other light Tank in existence. The position with regard to medium and heavy Tanks is not so satisfactory, but progress is rapidly being made and difficulties are being overcome. So far as we are aware, other Countries are meeting with similar difficulties in this particular development of the medium and heavy Tank. So far as we are aware, no Country at present is very satisfied with such machines as they have been able to produce.

Then Sir Archibald Sinclair, the Leader of the Liberal Party, and firm friend of all Airmen, asked :

"How many of these good light Tanks have you?"

Mr. Duff Cooper replied:

"I cannot give the exact number but the supply is satisfactory. They are being turned out with increasing rapidity. Eight Army field brigades have already been mechanized and the mechanization of the Divisional Artillery is proceeding."

The characteristics of this successful light Tank are of considerable interest.

LIGHT TANK MK. V. (PLATE XXXVI.)

Weight	$4\frac{3}{4}$ tons.
Crew	3.
Armament	1·5-in. M.G. and 1·303-in. M.G.
Engine	30 h.p., developing about 80 h.p.
Dimensions	Length 13 ft.
	Width 6 ft. 8 in.
	Height 7 ft. 3 in.

[1] 16th March, 1937.

Speed   30 m.p.h.
Circuit of action   150 miles.
Trench crossed   5 ft.

In the evidence given before the Arms Enquiry Commission, Mr. Lloyd George said "that Tanks in the last three months of the War played a greater part than any other particular weapon. They were a wonderful invention, but they were crude and clumsy in comparison with their successors of to-day."

Each one of my Officers, Boothby, Briggs, Hetherington, Macfie and myself can be well satisfied that the caterpillar landship seed we sowed has fallen on good soil and Tanks by the thousand proved of value to this Country and our Allies when faced with grave danger in the greatest war the World has ever seen, and the modern type as the Army Council's letter to me states, forms so valuable a part of the armament of the British Army.

(2) Foreign Nations Annex the Tank Invention

No one can now question that the Tank was evolved from ideas germinated in British brains and was built in British workshops. It is a purely British invention.

The question then arises why should so many Foreign Countries annex this British invention without making some kind of slight acknowledgment officially through the British Government to those who were responsible for this invention. Up to date they have not done so.

The Royal Commission said it was my duty as a Naval Officer to contribute to the evolution of the Tank. A weapon not for Navy, but for Army use.

That is a matter for argument.

But it certainly was not my duty to use my brains for the benefit of other Nations. Neither was it the duty of Boothby, Briggs, Hetherington or Macfie to do so.

Let me first take:

France

That great Country has led Europe for many generations in new designs embodying the highest Engineering skill.

In the old maritime days her ships were always better designed than those of other Nations, though perhaps not quite so well handled.

In more recent times the success of the *Normandie* in making a record run which secured for her the Blue Riband of the Atlantic[1] in March, 1937, shows that the high skill of the French Naval Constructors and Marine Engineers has in no way diminished.

She was the first Nation to armour ships and introduce breech-loading guns.

For many years she was in advance of any other Nation in modern submarine construction and had great success with the Belleville and Niclaussé Boilers.

Her successes with motor cars are too well known to need comment.

Blériot's great achievement in being the first man to fly across the Channel and the subsequent work of her Air Pioneers placed France in the front rank with regard to aeronautical development.

It can be truly said that in developing many modern weapons of war, the French have led the way, but the advent of the British Tank, after it had been proved successful, brought about the adoption of this novel weapon of offence by our good French Allies.

One of their great Officers—Colonel Estienne—who possessed a scientific turn of mind, made a speech just before the Battle of the Marne in September, 1914, in which he made this prophetic announcement. "Whoever shall first be able to make land ironclads, armed and equipped, roll over that," pointing to some heavy damp ground they were passing by, "will have won the War."[2]

Without taking away one iota of the credit due and recognized by the French Government to Colonel Estienne, may I submit to him that the British Airmen and British Constructors were the first in the field in developing caterpillar landships, as the evidence produced in this book will show.

It will be remembered that my first proposal to fit caterpillars to our armoured cars was made to Mr. Churchill on 16th February, 1915, and my first caterpillar landship

[1] Wrested the record from the *Queen Mary* by one-third of a knot.
[2] Taken from "The French Tanks," November, 1920, *R.U.S.I. Journal*, by Major J. E. Crompton.

drawing was shown to the Admiralty Landship Committee on 4th March, 1915.

Towards the end of 1915 the French Tank Pioneer addressed the following letter[1] to his Commander-in-Chief:

> MERICOURT-SUR-SOMME,
>
> *1st December,* 1915.
>
> From Colonel Estienne to the General Commander-in-Chief.
>
> Object—Request for an interview.
>
> In the course of the past year I have had the honour to call your attention, on two occasions, to the question of employing mobile armoured constructions for the purpose of assuring the progress of infantry.
>
> During the late attacks the incomparable value of this procedure struck me with increased force, and after a new severe analysis of the technical and tactical conditions of the problem, I consider the realization of vehicles possible with a mechanical traction capable of conveying infantry through or over obstacles, under fire, with arms and baggage and with guns, at the speed of nearly four miles an hour (six kilometres).
>
> I consider that it would take six months and ten millions (of francs) to produce material necessary for the transport of twenty thousand men, force sufficient to capture by surprise successive positions on a front of twenty-five miles (forty kilometres) allowing of the irruption of reserves formed in rear. Such an enterprise necessitates absolute secrecy and the prompt realization of a first vehicle, conditions incompatible with discussions on a Committee of Examination.
>
> In order to succeed I want only one thing, General, your confidence; and this I hope you will give me if you are willing to allow me to share with you my confidence, which is that of a careful technician, as well as my ardent faith (in the efficacy of the invention) as a soldier who has been in contact with the realities of the war since its beginning.
>
> (Signed) ESTIENNE.

---

[1] Taken from *Sous L'armure*, by Pierre Lestringuez, Lieutenant à l'artillerie d'Assaut, page 28.

After Colonel Estienne's famous letter quoted above, we are informed:

An interview with General Janin followed, and 400 cars were ordered in February, 1916, of a design drawn by M. Brillé, one of the Creusot engineers, in collaboration with Colonel Estienne. These cars were the *tracteurs* Estienne of General Galliéni, referred to above.

On December 12th General Janin only gave him (Colonel Estienne) leave to go to Paris, where, however, he saw M. Brillé. Meanwhile, M. Breton was doing good work by demonstrating the advantage of caterpillar traction, and although the invention of the armoured car was clearly due to the soldier, M. Breton's experiments with the American mode of traction for agricultural vehicles over bad and broken ground (which method both soldier and civilian had independently advocated) doubtless tended to obtain the approval of the French authorities for its immediate manufacture.

Colonel Estienne will go down to history as the great French Military Officer whose untiring energy in persuading his Authorities to adopt mechanical weapons of war made it possible to create their Tank Corps. His appointment as delegate to the French Ministry of Munitions ensured the success of the Tanks. Towards the close of the Great War thousands of Tanks were being constructed. This was largely due to the Colonel's fine support. The success of his French Tanks is given on pages 137 to 140.

The French classify their Tanks into three categories:

(1) Char-léger, under 10 tons.
(2) Char-medium, 10 to 30 tons, which can be transported in railway trucks.
(3) Char-lourd, which to be moved by railway would require a special truck.[1]

These mechanical weapons of war now form a very important Branch of the French Army (Plate XXXVII). Even their Metropolitan Army has ten Tank Regiments and three independent Tank Battalions.

An unusual French ceremony took place at Varines when

---

[1] "The French Tanks," by Major T. E. Crompton, *R.U.S.I. Journal*, November, 1920.

a Standard was presented to the 505th Regiment of Tanks in May, 1936.

On that occasion the Tanks with lorries and motor-cyclists were drawn up in perfect alignment to receive this high honour, as shown in Plate XXXVII.[1]

The French Tanks look most efficient and we can feel confident that should emergency unfortunately arise again, the crews of these machines will give just as good account of themselves as their forerunners did in their gallant and most successful efforts on the Western Front in 1918.

AMERICA

In his War Memoirs[2] Mr. Lloyd George lifts the veil and informs the World that whilst the courage of the United States Soldiers and Airmen was superb and second to none, there was a good deal of organization muddle when the Americans first came into the War, which was surprising from a Country so well equipped with men of great business capacity. Their brain-waves seemed to lack the ability to organize home industries with rapidity, and many difficulties arose in providing the latest weapons of war for the use of their troops at the Front in France. We are informed by Mr. Lloyd George:

> When the Armistice was signed on November 11th[3] half the aeroplanes used by the American Army were of French and British make.
>
> The same tale of fussy muddle can be repeated when you come to guns, light and heavy, for the new American Army. The light and medium artillery used up to the end of the war by the American Army were supplied by the French. The heaviest artillery was furnished by the British. No guns of American pattern or manufacture fired a shot in the war. The same thing applies to Tanks. Here one would have thought that the greatest manufacturers of automobiles in the world could have turned out Tanks with the greatest facility and in the largest numbers; but not a single Tank of American manufacture ever rolled into battle in the war.

---

[1] *Illustrated London News*, 16th May, 1936.
[2] *Daily Telegraph*, 26th June, 1936.   [3] 1918.

PLATE XXXVII

(*Above*) PRESENTING THE STANDARD TO THE 505TH REGIMENT OF TANKS AT VARINES, FRANCE, MAY, 1936
(*Below*) FRENCH 6-TON HIGH SPEED RENAULT TANK

PLATE XXXVIII

PLATE XXXIX

(*Above*) THE CONVERTIBLE, WHEEL AND TRACK, MEDIUM TANK, UNITED STATES ARMY

(*Below*) THE LIGHT TANK NOW IN CURRENT USE IN THE UNITED STATES ARMY

(By permission of " The Journal of the Army Ordnance Association," United States.)

The criticism of Mr. Lloyd George is mild compared to the very strong indictment of General Dawes, the United States Ambassador in London, when, speaking at Bush House, he declared that:

> We had 2,000,000 soldiers 3000 miles from their home base, from which came little or no munitions, no horses, few rifles and artillery, and not a single aeroplane. We were badly let down from home. . . . In every instance our requests for supplies or assistance were gladly given (by France and England) even at sacrifice by their own men. We even had to make a request for anæsthetics because our own men were being operated upon without them.

There is no doubt that considerable delays did occur in providing munitions, aeroplanes and Tanks for the Americans, and Mr. Lloyd George is right in his criticisms. It was not until early in 1918 that an agreement was made between America and this Country for the building of some 1500 Tanks. A British Tank was sent to America to have a Liberty Engine installed, and many of the necessary component parts were to be manufactured in America; also a large number of light Renault Tanks were being constructed for the United States Government in France, when the Armistice stopped all building of war material.

During the War the Americans used British and French aeroplanes, and French Tanks assisted the American troops with great success.

One of my former and most able Colleagues, Sir Harry Brittain, who represented Acton for many years in the House of Commons, told me:

> That soon after America joined the Allies the Minister of Information, then Lord Beaverbrook, sent for him and said the Prime Minister, Mr. Lloyd George, has invited the American Labour Leaders numbering 50 or 60 to come over as the guests of England to see what efforts we were making in the War, to go across the Channel and visit the Belgian lines, our lines, and the French lines as far as Verdun, and then on their return to give a series of talks at the great munition centres in

England, to encourage the workers and let them know that the ever-growing American Army was with us and that the millions of munition workers were behind us on the other side of the Atlantic.

Sir Harry Brittain continuing his story in these words:

Lord Beaverbrook said this invitation had been accepted and apparently little else had been done. He told me that this large body of American Labour Leaders, with, I think, four or five women included, were aboard the *Carmania* on the Atlantic, some two days off Liverpool.[1] No arrangements whatsoever had been made to look after them. He, Beaverbrook, had asked his fellow-Canadian, Sir Campbell Stuart, to give a helping hand, and he wanted me, if I could do so, likewise to act as host for the British Government, to meet these good people at Liverpool, take them in charge, show them all we had to show in England and eventually take them along and down the fighting front in France, then let them return to England and speak of their experiences before going back to their native land.

My humble services having been given to the Government, I told Lord Beaverbrook that I would, of course, undertake the task.

Later, I took the party up to Birmingham and from there we went to the works presided over by Mr. Dudley Docker, who duly received us.

We knew nothing of Tanks, the Americans, of course, like myself, had not the faintest conception of what a Tank looked like, and I shall never forget the surprise with which I gazed upon these ungainly iron creatures for the first time. We were taken out to a huge field, the mud probably to a large extent artificial, to show up better the manœuvrings of these unwieldy weapons.

We were received at the entrance of the works by my old friend George Grossmith. G. G. got up in some sort of uniform, I think, if my memory is right, either R.N.R. or R.N.V.R. At any rate, there he was, and amazingly helpful he was in making the inspection go.

---

[1] They arrived 12th April, 1918.

Our immediate host was the great Dudley Docker himself, one of the outstanding manufacturers of the Midlands.

The Tanks were all drawn up in line, and I distributed my guests, who were seething with enthusiasm, particularly when they saw the Stars and Stripes floating over each individual unit. We tucked them up, a Yank in every Tank, and the great ungainly machines rolled forward in procession round this great big muddy field.

At the finish of the manœuvres the Tanks and their possibilities were explained to our guests by various of our hosts, and I well remember Mr. Dudley Docker going in to his office and returning with a huge silver challenge bowl won by him at some event or other, but at that present moment filled with champagne. It was sent round amidst considerable enthusiasm and these formidable new weapons and their success was toasted by our new and virile Allies.

I had these men on my hands for at least five weeks and had the privilege of presenting them to His Majesty the King, and after a most amazingly interesting time spent visiting the fighting front, I saw them back again at Liverpool and on their ship for home.

They returned with innumerable experiences, but of all the experiences which they collected during their stay in England and in Europe, I do not think there was one which affected them as much as their first sight of this amazing new weapon of war, the secret of which had been so well kept that no idea of what they were about to see was in the mind of any of that party which witnessed the first type of Tank and its evolution.

Sir Harry Brittain's account was of great interest to myself. But I could never understand, with all the wonderful industrial resources of the United States and knowing how helpful that Country had been to the Royal Naval Air Service in supplying at short notice aeroplanes and seaplanes for training our Pilots during the early War period, how it came about that no American Tanks were completed before hostilities ceased. Someone must have blundered badly on the production side ! Once the design

L

was approved there should have been no difficulty in turning Tanks out by the hundreds. After the War we were informed by the *Evening Standard*[1] that certain disturbances occurred in the United States between soldiers, police and politicians. To quell these unfortunate disputes a Tank had to be used. A New York communication stated:

> From Cleveland, Ohio, it is reported that many persons were injured yesterday afternoon in street fighting between soldiers in May Day demonstrations and the police. When one of the parades reached the square in the centre of the city, where a meeting had been planned, it was noticed that red flags were being carried by soldiers and sailors. The police then interfered, and fighting became general for a distance of more than a mile in the city's main thoroughfare.
>
> Two men in American Army uniforms were attacked and badly beaten while the fighting was progressing. Eventually the police and military dispersed the other parades by driving trucks and a Tank through the marching lines. A hundred and fifty persons were arrested, including several Socialist leaders.

There is no doubt that a few Tanks well placed are of the greatest value to Authority in all civil disturbances and may be the means of saving much bloodshed.

The characteristics of typical United States Tanks taken from the *Army Ordnance Journal*,[2] January-February, 1937, are as follows:

AMERICAN MEDIUM TANK (CHRISTIE TYPE).
(PLATE XXXVIII)

Weight   11 tons.
Crew   5.
Armament   In turret, one 3·7 cm. and one M.-G.
           In front, one M.-G.
Armour $\frac{3}{4}$ in.

---

[1] 2nd May, 1919.
[2] This United States journal is of great interest to those who study Defence problems and the introduction of New Weapons of War.

Engine   550 h.p.
Dimensions Length 19 ft.
           Width   8 ft.
           Height 7 ft. 6 in.
Speed   75 m.p.h. on wheels.
           35 m.p.h. on tracks.

This is an interesting type of Tank and is convertible to wheel or caterpillar according to the terrain that is being encountered.

AMERICAN TANK. T.5. (PLATE XXXIX)

Weight   8 tons.
Crew   4 men.
Armament   Two ·3 in. M.-G.s, one ·5 in. M.-G. Twin turrets.
Armour   ¾ in.
Engine   260 h.p. radial air-cooled.
Dimensions Length 12 ft. 9 in.
           Width   7 ft.
           Height 6 ft. 6 in.
Speed   50 m.p.h.

This is a lighter Tank and shows clearly the angularized track that was invented in this country by my Armoured Car Officer, Lieutenant Macfie and Mr. Nesfield.

ITALY

Can we learn anything from the Italo-Abyssinian conflict and the collapse which resulted in the fall of the Emperor who represented the focal point of resistance in his Country? The first lesson is that with the advent of Air Power smaller Nations must consider its great possibilities.

The result obtained by the Italians in Abyssinia, the Japanese in Manchuria and Jehol, could not have been achieved in such a short time with so few losses had not aircraft been so effective as to prove, in certain conditions, the decisive arm.

Guerilla warfare that has played such a prominent part in the small wars of the past has now to meet a superior weapon, the bomb-dropping aeroplane of great mobility.

The nerve strain of continual air bombing produced its effect upon the Ethiopian Armies and the knowledge that Tanks were kept in readiness to use, when the terrain was favourable, helped in no small way to shorten the period of hostilities.

In the early days of the campaign several Italian Tanks were captured by the Abyssinians when they fell into traps carefully cut in the road, then covered with brushwood and loose stones. The Tanks being used by the Italians suffered from the great disadvantage of having no revolving turret and no holes cut in the after end of the fixed turret.

This was no doubt due to the necessity for economy when constructing a large number of these machines.

The Abyssinians soon learnt this defect and several Italian Tanks, when in difficulties over rough ground, had their guns smashed with rocks from behind and the crews then speared, shot or beheaded.

On October, 1935, news reached Addis Ababa that the Abyssinians successfully trapped four Italian Tanks in pits in the ground, and it was reported the crews were all killed.

Adapting the method of trapping wild animals in camouflaged holes, the Abyssinians dug a number of wide and deep ditches in the tracks which the Tanks were expected to follow.

Branches of trees, twigs and leaves, and soil were strewn over the top until the surface was practically indistinguishable from the normal track.

The pits were dug deep enough to make it impossible to haul the Tanks out again without very great difficulty.

The Italian Tanks were of the greatest value in the operation described by the military correspondent of *The Times* in their issue of May 14th, 1936:

> Thus, when the New Year opened the Italians' military situation was not an enviable one. But in mid-January the campaign took an ominous turn. Emboldened by Italian passivity, Ras Desta's forces pushed forward to the Somalian border near Dolo. If this was a potential threat to the flank of the Italian line of invasion from the south, it exposed the Ethiopians to a counter-stroke in an

area where the terrain was favourable to Tanks. General Graziani seized the opportunity, temporarily shifting his axis, and struck at the target thus offered. The Tanks appeared in the Ethiopians' rear, their resistance collapsed, and the victory was followed up by a 240-mile pursuit to Negelli. The following week the Italian forces in the north launched an offensive in the Tembien to relieve the pressure on the position at Makale. The Ethiopians met it with a counter-offensive in which particular success was purchased at heavy cost. It provided disquieting evidence of a new tendency—to charge machine-guns. The "memory of Adowa" was asserting itself, dangerously. Marshal Badoglio noted that after the failure of these repeated attacks the Ethiopians "discouraged by their heavy losses, a shortage of ammunition, delay in the arrival of reinforcements, and food supplies," had lapsed in passivity. In consequence he decided that he could safely take the offensive south of Makale, having now straightened out his communications.

And on the same day the *Daily Express* informed us that:

General Starace himself took armoured cars, Tanks, infantry and artillery northwards to Gallabat.
Abyssinians fled before them, many crossing the Sudan border and taking refuge in British territory.
No armed resistance was offered. According to a communiqué sent to Rome last night by Marshal Badoglio, the Italian Commander-in-Chief, the townspeople cheered the invaders as they entered the region.

General Rowan-Robinson describes the Abyssinian as a "gallant fighter," who does not realize that the balance of fire-power is weighted against him far more heavily than in 1896.
"At Wal Wal he is said to have assaulted Tanks with a scimitar, and he believes that aeroplanes can be brought down easily with a rifle."
Primitive people, or those who neglect to study and provide modern weapons of war, cannot stand up to the attacks that can be made by hostile aircraft and Tanks working in close co-operation.

166   THE EVOLUTION OF THE TANK

In their Abyssinian Campaign the Italian Tanks showed many weaknesses, but there is no question that they played an important part when operating in good Tank country. This was brought home to Ras Desta's forces when stupid enough to think they could defeat the Tanks.

War, as we have known it in the past, is becoming completely altered by the introduction of these mechanized forces.

At the end of August, 1936, it was reported from Rome[1] that in the Annual Army Manœuvres:

> An experiment was conducted against a detachment of whippet Tanks, when light solutions of tear gas and asphyxiating gas were used together. The men in the Tanks wore rubber suits and gas-masks, and it is claimed that no one was affected. The gas was thrown from a lorry, manned by "rubber men" belonging to the chemical corps. Thick screens of smoke made operation very exciting. High speed Italian Tanks are shown in Plate XL negotiating perpendicular slope.

Germany

Having captured by force of arms during the Great War some British Tanks, Germany has a perfect right to build Tanks to British designs without making the slightest acknowledgment to those who initiated the Tank weapon.

It may be recalled that the Treaty of Versailles not only limited German arms in general, but Tanks were forbidden. Until 1935 the Germans used in most of their military manœuvres dummy Tanks constructed of thin sheet-iron and pasteboard carefully fitted to motor cars and made to represent gun-turrets, etc.

Now Germany possesses a very large number of war Tanks constructed to give great speed.

Exercises have frequently taken place during the last few months at Döberitz, the old military training camp near Berlin (Plates XLI and XLII).

Most of the new Tanks can attain a speed of 37 miles per hour and are of the two-men type, carrying two machine-guns.

The German Chancellor and Supreme Commander-in-Chief, Herr Hitler, held a review on his forty-seventh birthday[2] in the Tiergarten.

[1] *Morning Post*, 29th August, 1936.   [2] 20th April, 1936.

PLATE XL

NEW ITALIAN HIGH SPEED 3.3-TON LIGHT TANK DESCENDING ALMOST PERPENDICULAR SLOPE DURING MANŒUVRES BEFORE THE KING OF ITALY, 1936

PLATE XLI

PLATE XLII

(*Above*) GERMAN TANKS ADVANCING DURING TACTICAL EXERCISES AT DÖBERITZ, JULY, 1935
(*Below*) GERMAN TANK, SHOWING ANGULARIZED TRACK

The Times informs us that 15,000 officers and men of the Army, Navy and Air Force, with 1000 horses, 1500 armoured cars and Tanks paraded before the Führer.

The light Tanks, each with a crew of two men, passed the saluting base. One cannot judge a Tank by a photograph, but these Tanks gave the impression to all spectators of being very efficient fighting machines.

German Military experts are considering from every angle the "sudden attack" and what part non-combatants will have to play in the next war to produce the war needs of the combatant.

Needless to say aircraft play the most important role, followed by massed armed force with their Tanks, lorries, etc. They argue that lightning attacks from the air will be first made. These will not secure a final victory, but will tend to paralyse the non-combatants and make it extremely difficult to keep factory work going for producing munitions.

BELGIUM

This country has added Tank units to her Army for defence services. From their appearance the Tanks and their crews look most efficient.

At the Fascist attempt to seize the reigns of office on 25th October, 1936, the Government's firmness in parading thousands of National Police and Soldiers with Tanks saved an ugly situation and the *coup d'état* was a fiasco.

The Belgian new light Tank is shown in Plate XLIII.

RUSSIA

For a considerable time the Military experts of the Soviet Government have been mechanizing the Russian Army. This consists of providing a large number of Tanks, lorries, etc. They possess the 10·2 ton Christie fast Tank and the heavy 33-ton Tank.

On May Day, 1936, no less than 300 Tanks were on review in Leningrad. Plate XLIV shows Russian Tanks.

Over such a vast Country as Russia and Siberia Enemy troops would have long lines of communication should they ever be called to undertake military operations against that Country. This fact is well appreciated by the heads of the Soviet Army, and a large number of experiments have been undertaken to transport troops by aeroplane and recently we learn that light Tanks have been sent long distances by air.

This opens up the possibility of operating and feeding a large number of Tanks required to infest any area, with petrol, lubricating oil and general stores at great distances from their base.

All Russia has become very air-minded and these novel experiments are of great interest to all who study the use of modern weapons of war.

During the Soviet's Army manœuvres in the autumn of 1936 near the Polish Frontier, some 1200 parachutists jumped simultaneously from 48 four-engined troop-carrying aeroplanes and captured the aerodrome near Minsk, in the rear of the defending Army.

The parachutists carried 150 machine-guns and their ammunition. Eighteen light field-guns, suspended from automatic parachutes, were also landed safely.

The raiders had come from 100 miles behind the front. Within 7½ minutes of their appearance over the aerodrome the parachutists had routed the defenders, and the troop-carriers were landing safely on the captured aerodrome. The aeroplanes carried a complete mechanized unit, including lorries and light Tanks, swung under their fuselages. This manœuvre is one of the Soviet's most formidable schemes for creating panic in the enemy's rear. It is especially adapted for the kind of warfare likely to be waged in the great open stretches of Eastern Europe and Asia.

Major-General A. P. Wavell,[1] the head of the British Military Mission, attended these Soviet Russian manœuvres and, when addressing Marshal Voroshilov at the dinner given at Minsk in honour of the foreign delegations, bestowed (according to report) marked praise on the "Brilliant Red Army," and said that "Its tremendous achievements . . . have greatly astonished us. We particularly admire the fighting spirit and pertinacity of all your Red Army men and Commanders." Like many other experts, he expressed surprise at the extent of the Red Army's mechanized resources, especially in Tanks and armoured cars.

It is common knowledge that Russia aims at possessing an Air Force equal to the combined Air Forces of the

[1] The General in command of the 2nd Division at Aldershot.

PLATE XLIII

THE BELGIAN NEW LIGHT TANK

PLATE XLIV

(*Above*) RUSSIAN TANKS IN RED SQUARE DURING A MILITARY PARADE, 1936
(*Below*) RUSSIAN 10·2-TON CHRISTIE FAST TANK NEGOTIATING OBSTACLES DURING RED ARMY MANŒUVRES NEAR MOSCOW

World,[1] and desires to take the foremost place with her Tanks and resources for Tank production.

JAPAN

Looking away from Europe to the Far East we find that soon after the successes with the Tanks on the Western Front in the Great War, Japan turned her attention to mechanization for her Army.

Tanks were built in considerable numbers, and ever since have formed part of her military equipment. But some of the great Japanese Generals are no believers in Tanks,[2] and found them of little use in their Manchuria and Jehol campaigns, largely because of the difficult country, with their enemy scattered over wide areas. Whereas they soon found that the aeroplane was of the greatest use for reconnaissance, bombing and for conveying stores to their front line troops.

But the Tanks have been used to quell a military revolt that occurred in Tokyo in the spring of 1936, when it was reported falsely that Admiral Okada, the Premier, had been shot by the rebels. He had been mistaken for his brother-in-law, who was shot. In these disturbances three Statesmen were killed. The Military Governor of Tokyo, General Kashii, first appealed to the rebels in the sacred name of the Emperor to lay down their arms.

His words carried great weight, and all but a few desperate men laid down their arms. Even then—and nothing could indicate the changes taking place in Japan more than this—some of the rebels refused to obey! His Majesty, the rebels were informed, had given orders that they were to lay down their arms and return to barracks under arrest. The rebels still held out until the Governor gave orders to close in upon them with Tanks.

On seeing the Tanks being manœuvred into position to

[1] The non-stop flight of 5,400 miles from Moscow to Vancouver in June, 1937, by three Russian Airmen in a low wing monoplane, is one of the most important Air efforts of recent years and shows that the Soviet Pilots lack nothing in courage in flying over the North Pole. It is a fine piece of Arctic Pioneering. The second non-stop Polar flight of 6,750 miles is a fine triumph for Mikhail Gromoff and gives Russia great prestige throughout the whole world.

[2] In the Sino-Japanese clash outside Pekin near Marco Polo Bridge and Lungwangmiao in July 1937 it was reported that twelve Japanese Tanks, eight field guns and a number of lorries laden with troops were rushed up from Tientsin to the disturbed area. Also Tanks were called out to patrol the town of Tientsin.

encircle them, the rebels gave in, and the revolt collapsed. A very dangerous position was saved by the Tanks because much sympathy was entertained for the rebels by the rest of the Japanese Army.

General Kashii has visited Europe many times, and is known to be a most resolute, courageous and efficient Officer.

When he started to move the Tanks the rebels knew exactly what General Kashii meant. Japanese Tanks are shown in Plate XLV.

The characteristics of the latest Japanese Medium Tank are:

Weight	14 tons.
Crew	5.
Armament	One 37 mm. gun and one M.G. in turret, one M.G. in front.
Armour	$\frac{3}{4}$ in.
Dimensions	Length, 21 ft.
	Width, 8 ft. 6 in.
	Height, 8 ft. 6 in.
Speed	25 m.p.h.

Turning back to Europe we find Poland, Czechoslovakia and Sweden all possessing most efficient Tanks (Plates XLVI, XLVII and XLVIII). The characteristics of these Tanks are given in table on page 173.

Spain

Some of my Colleagues in the House of Commons who have visited Spain recently inform me that the mechanization used by the Government and anti-Government Forces in the 1936–1937 Civil War is mostly foreign. General Franco possesses nearly one hundred Tanks, partly the two-man Italian Army Midget Tanks, Fiat-Ansaldo type, and partly the two-man German Army model.

On the Government side they possess a considerable number of the Russian three-man Tanks fitted with a quick-firing automatic light gun, and some are provided with flame-throwers. Although the Tanks on both sides have had many breakdowns, due to mechanical defects, and are often badly handled, they are playing their part in this unfortunate war. In the fall of Bilbao Tanks were used.[1]

[1] 19th June, 1937.

PLATE XLV

JAPANESE TANKS

PLATE XLVI

(*Above*) POLAND SMOKE-SCREEN GENERATOR MOUNTED ON RENAULT TANK FRAME

(*Below*) POLAND 6-TON VICKERS-ARMSTRONG TANK

When one remembers that paid foreign mercenaries are using these new weapons of war, it would be unwise to attach too much importance to their failures.

In his most interesting book, *Red, White and Spain*, that gallant Airman, Nigel Tangye, tells the story of one of General Franco's Moorish soldiers who captured a Tank and insisted on regarding it as his own perquisite.

"Not so long ago the Russians made a Tank attack, before which the opposing Moors fled. Not so one Moor, who remained alone behind a tree. After the Tanks had advanced some way they discovered that their infantry were not following them up, so they turned round and retired towards their own lines.

"One of them got stuck in the mud, and the crew of three, observing no enemy about, cautiously stepped out to try to rectify matters. This was the solitary Moor's opportunity. He pipped them off—one, two, three—like that, and then got into the Tank and sat in it till the whites approached again.

"An Officer, seeing this Tank standing alone with three dead Russians in the mud outside, jumped in and found the Moor in the driver's seat. A few words, and the situation was explained. The Officer congratulated the Moor, and ordered him to get out and a trained crew to drive the Tank into captivity.

"But oh, no. The Moor was not going to have that. 'This is mine,' he said. 'I captured it. And what is mine you pay for!'

"Before the Tank could be driven away the Officer had to agree that its price was 1500 pesetas. With a signed agreement the incident was closed."

SWITZERLAND

Recently the Federal Council of Switzerland have been looking into the reorganization of the Swiss Army.

Switzerland has no standing Army, but three new Corps have now been created—the Grenzshutz—for protection of the frontier and to prevent a surprise invasion.

The Grenzshutz is recruited from those who live in the neighbourhood of the frontier. Under its protection divisions will be recruited from the regions round Berne and the Lake of Lucerne, and kept as a reserve for reinforcing the points of danger.

The whole idea of the new organization of the Swiss Army is based on the principle—fewer soldiers, more mechanized weapons.

In 1935, for the first time, Swiss Tanks, similar to those in the British Army, have been used during their Army manœuvres. For many years the Swiss General Staff have not been in favour of Tanks, but recently the great success of the British Light Tank has so impressed the Military mind in Switzerland that these mechanized units are now being attached to the Army in Switzerland.

Austria

The Chancellor of Austria, Dr. Kurt Schuschnigg, writing in the *Morning Post*,[1] states:

> The Defensive forces of our Country do not only ensure the peace of Austria but also that of Central Europe.

And then observed that

> the whole Austrian people welcomed with the greatest enthusiasm and the greatest satisfaction the Government's Bill for re-establishment of Compulsory Military Service.

Although conscription has been decreed in Austria, it is contrary to the Treaty of Saint Germain, which appears to have been torn up. Young Austrians have been called up and the whole Country is rearming. Until recently Austria possessed very few Tanks, but last year[2] in a parade in Vienna during the spring some thirty small Tanks took part. These Tanks are very similar to the Italian Tanks (Plate XLIX).

Afghanistan

The *Illustrated London News* is the first to inform us that Afghanistan has acquired Tanks which have been constructed for her in America (Plate L), with the view of

[1] 24th April, 1936.   [2] 1936.

PLATE XLVII

PLATE XLVIII

(*Above*) CZECHOSLOVAKIA TANKS DURING MILITARY REVIEW BEFORE KING CAROL, PRINCE MICHAEL AND PRESIDENT BENES AT PRAGUE, 1936

(*Below*) SWEDEN 11-TON MEDIUM TANK, LANDVERK

PLATE XLIX

PLATE L

(*Above*) AUSTRIAN LIGHT TANKS DURING MANŒUVRES
(*Below*) AFGHANISTAN TANKS

In the February, 1937, issue of *Völkerbund*, the journal of the German Association for League of Nations questions, the following interesting list of European Nations who possess Tanks is given:

Country	Tank	Width m.	Length m.	Height m.	Moves km. per hour	Climbs cm.	Slopes at angle of deg.	Crosses trenches with width of m.	Number of crew	Armament
France	11-ton Renault Tank, D1 1935	2·18	5·30	2·40	18	120	35	2·00	2	1 gun 4·7 cm. and 1 or 2 machine-guns.
,,	6-ton Renault Tank, AMR 1934	1·65	3·40	1·55	37	50	40	1·70	2	1 machine-gun 7·6 mm. in pivot turret.
,,	74-ton break-through Tank, 3 C.	2·92	12.00	4·04	13	170	45	5·30	14	1 howitzer 15·5 cm., 2 guns 7·5 cm., 9 machine-guns.
England	3·1-ton Carden-Lloyd fast Tank	2·08	3·96	1·83	64	50	45	1·53	2	1 machine-gun 7·69 mm.
,,	12-ton Vickers, Mk. II 1927–29	2·74	5·31	3·08	26	80	45	2·00	5	1 gun 4·7 mm. and 6 machine-guns.
,,	16-ton Vickers, M 1935	2·65	6·60	2·49	50	96	40	2·75	6	1 gun 4·7 cm., 1 machine-gun, 2 twin machine-guns.
U.S.S.R.	10·2-ton Christie fast Tank, M 1934	2·15	5·76	2·31	62	75	40	2·10	3	1 gun 4·7 cm. and 1 machine-gun.
,,	33-ton heavy Soviet Tank, M II	3·20	9·30	2·75	30	120	40	4·57	12	2 machine-guns or 1 gun 3·7 cm.
Italy	5·6-ton light Tank, Fiat, 3000 B	1·67	4·29	2·20	22	60	51	1·80	2	1 light machine-gun.
,,	3·3-ton Fiat-Ansaldo, M 1933	1·40	3·03	1·20	42	60	40	1·50	2	2 machine-guns 7·69 mm.
Poland	6-ton Vickers-Armstrong	2·41	4·88	2·41	35	75	45	1·80	3	1 heavy machine-gun, 1 light machine-gun.
Czecho-slovakia	2·48-ton small Tank, TK 3 1932	1·78	2·58	1·31	45	45	45	1·50	2	
Sweden	6-ton light Adamov Tank AH 43	2·00	4·00	1·80	45	80	45	1·90	? 3	
,,	11-ton medium Tank, Landsverk, 10	2·15	5·20	2·22	35	75	40	1·80	4	
Belgium	Latest type of Tank Light Tank	—	—	—	35	—	—	—	3	1 machine-big gun, 1 machine-gun.

bringing her Army of some 72,000 men up to date by the provision of a mechanized contingent. In addition, Afghanistan boasts of a small Air Force for working with the Tanks.

Now it is estimated[1] that the chief European Nations possess:

    France, 5000 Tanks.
    Germany, 5000 Tanks.
    Russia, 6000 Tanks.
    Great Britain, 500 Tanks.
    Italy, 400 Tanks.

Having briefly reviewed the Nations that have annexed the Tank invention and shown their Tanks in several plates, may I ask this question. Was it the duty of Boothby, Briggs, Hetherington, Macfie and myself to initiate a weapon of war so that some of the firms of the great Nations should build these machines and sell them for profit to the smaller Nations?[2] It would seem that the Admiralty did indeed neglect our interests by not taking out Foreign Patents for the Tank invention. Being only Naval Airmen we smile. But always remember that it is the Royal Naval Air Service type of Tank that has been copied throughout the World and not Mr. Tritton's and Lieutenant Wilson's rhomboidal type.

After such a lapse of time it is too late for any of my Airmen to benefit financially for initiating caterpillar landships. But a letter of thanks, on the lines of our Army Council's appreciative letter, would cost little more than the postage, and be much appreciated, from those Nations who have without acknowledgment annexed the Tank invention.

[1] International News Service.
[2] Even the British Government is reported by Reuter to have informed the Egyptian War Minister that Britain is ready to supply the Egyptian Army with the required Tanks according to the Anglo-Egyptian Treaty (Cairo, 23rd June, 1937).

PART II

CHAPTER I

TO WHOM THE CREDIT?

> "Here's Freedom to him that wad read!
> Here's Freedom to him that wad write!
> There's nane ever feared that the truth should
>   be heard
> But they wham the truth wad indite."
>
> ROBERT BURNS.

ONE of the most notorious claimants for the Tank invention was Captain Bede Bentley.

Many of my old Air Officers and myself were much amused at the Kitchener Tank film that was shown at the Pavilion Theatre, London, in November, 1921. Invitations were sent to prominent public people, such as Members of the House of Commons, and many others. I accepted, and saw to my amazement depicted on the film Captain Bede Bentley presenting to Lord Kitchener a drawing of the famous Tank.

A large audience witnessed the film and appeared greatly interested. At the end I stood up and protested most strongly "that the film was contrary to the true facts, as we had them in official papers and photographs of the Naval Airmen's caterpillar experimental work at the Admiralty. The film did not depict the accurate story of the evolution of the Tank." That was the last I ever heard of Captain Bede Bentley's Tank film.

Letters from several of my old Armoured Car Officers, who were familiar with our caterpillar work, came from all over the Country congratulating me on making this public protest.

At a later date, towards the end of 1925, Captain Bede Bentley claimed, under a Petition of Right, that he was the originator of the War Tank. He claimed £300,000 from the Crown, and stated that he had brought the War

Tank Scheme to the notice of Lord Kitchener. At the Admiralty we never heard of Captain Bede Bentley, and had no knowledge of any discussion he may have had with Lord Kitchener. It is well known that Lord Kitchener, with so many pressing matters on his mind, was rather sceptical about mechanical weapons of war being of much value, until they were tried out in 1916. In any case, Captain Bede Bentley was not in the chain of causation that led to the construction of the Tank, and his Petition of Right accordingly failed.

Whilst Captain Bede Bentley's claim was being heard, the Solicitor-General stated: "In addition to letters and telegrams, I have been rung up twice by a gentleman from America who wanted me to take notice of what happened in Minneapolis in 1883." Whereupon Mr. Justice McCardie said: "I have received a document relating to the invention of an armoured car in 1855."

Then we were informed that a suggestion for an armoured vehicle or land ironclad was submitted to the First Lord of the Admiralty in 1911. Another proposal we heard of was made in October, 1914, suggesting a travelling motor fortification and charging device constructed with a front and rear plough for charging earthworks, the whole to skip over trenches 10 or 12 ft. wide. Neither of these proposals ever reached the Air Department.

When calling upon the Third Sea Lord in November, 1917, he informed me that in all probability a Lieutenant in the Grand Fleet had invented the Tank in his proposals for building a land battleship using steam. On hearing this statement I at once claimed priority. We had no proposals in the Air Department from this Lieutenant all the time I was at the Admiralty.

Neither did we have any suggestions from a Marine Lieutenant who, I was informed, invented the Tank, because he demonstrated with a pedrail machine at one of the Naval and Military tournaments held before the War.

During the War I begged our very able Press Censor, Admiral Sir Douglas Brownrigg, to check the articles about the Tanks appearing in the Press, and to suppress as far as he could the claimants for the Tank invention having too big an innings, whilst we serving Naval Airmen were not allowed to say one word or publish any denial of inaccurate statements. Press communications by serving Officers were not allowed by Article 14 of the King's Regulations then in force. It was no fault of the Press that misleading statements were made about the Tank, as no official account had been issued, and naturally the public were interested in such a novel weapon of war.

Sir Douglas Brownrigg did his best, and at that time stopped a good many inaccurate statements from appearing in the newspapers.

One interesting communication came from the Press Censor to me marked "Do what you like with this!" So I left the article in my file of interesting papers, hoping the Tank controversy would rapidly die down and some sort of official statement before long would be made by the Admiralty or Mr. Winston Churchill, who was the First Lord during the inception of the caterpillar landship. Even now I do not know if this communication ever appeared in the Press. If not, my apologies are due to the writer with initials S. W., and the date is 3rd October, 1916.

It is not within my knowledge which newspaper this article was written for, so I am unable to ask permission to publish this account of War events. After such a great lapse of time, over twenty years, I feel certain the writer will not mind me using his communication to sum up so admirably a situation which then arose and could not possibly be improved upon.

THE TANK MYSTERY

In Sir Douglas Haig's communiqué of Sunday, 1st October, 1916, mention is again made of the valuable work done by the new type of armoured cars, commonly known as Tanks.

It will be recalled that the construction of these latest war-engines had been a secret so well guarded that their first appearance in the field came as a complete surprise to both parties of belligerents, with the exception of the favoured few who had necessarily to be led into the secret.

Their entry marked a welcome departure from the ding-dong methods of modern trench warfare, and invested it with an interest wholly new. Each subsequent despatch brought fresh tales of wonder, and there seemed to be no limit to the prodigies these waddling monsters might achieve.

In successive communiqués dealing with the great push on the Somme, full credit has been given them for crossing trenches, negotiating shell-holes, ripping asunder the most formidable of wire entanglements, and, where necessary, of even nosing their way through houses and other impedimenta that opposed them. In the open, their favourite method was to lie athwart an enemy trench and enfilade it with machine-gun fire, thereby inflicting heavy loss upon the enemy, and demoralizing him with indescribable confusion.

The work carried out by the Tanks at Combles, Fourneaux Wood, Flers, Bouleaux Wood, Wedge Wood, and Thiepval, has been magnificent; and the highest praise is due to the respective crews.

At Gueudecourt alone a Tank is credited with killing 300 Germans; while it has been definitely proved that our own casualties have been far fewer on those fronts where the Tanks have been employed than on those from which they have been absent.

Such being the admitted service of the Tanks, it is not surprising that we await with unusual interest some official account of their origin.

Our contemporary, the *Morning Post*, in its issue of 21st September, states: "other people have no doubt rendered great assistance, but to Colonel Swinton and to Colonel Swinton alone is the credit due as the originator and the persistent elaborator of the idea of the Tanks." Elsewhere it further states: "The idea of the Tanks in the form in which they now are is entirely the work of Lieutenant-Colonel Swinton, D.S.O."

We challenge the *Morning Post* to prove these statements or to produce any evidence that Colonel Swinton either originated the idea of a Tank, assisted with the early designs, or was in any way instrumental in carrying out the long series of experiments that culminated in the building of the first Tanks.

That some mystery still shrouds the origin of these machines, and that much idle chatter has operated to divert public opinion into false channels, is sufficiently evidenced by the following statement which was recently issued by the Ministry of Munitions:

In view of the many statements, more or less erroneous, which have appeared in the Press, the Ministry of Munitions desires to deprecate the circulation of statements regarding the origination and construction of the new armoured cars, commonly designated Tanks. In due course an official statement will be issued giving the history and development of these machines, when credit will be given to whom credit is due.

It is only fair, however, to state that the design and construction of the first Tank are due to Officers working under the Admiralty. The Ministry of Munitions subsequently undertook to provide facilities for further experimentation, and for the construction and supply of these machines.

It would thus appear that the entire credit for the conception of the Tanks, no less than for the early stages of design and subsequent period of experimentation, lies with certain Officers working under the Admiralty, and to them alone; Officers, it may be remarked, who by virtue of their very positions are precluded from voicing their claims to a measure of the recognition and appreciation which a grateful public are only too eager to bestow.

What the Nation wants to know is: "Did Colonel Swinton carry out the experiments that led to the creation of the Tanks, or did he not?" Tanks, we understand, do not grow on trees. They have to be evolved and developed by men highly trained in mechanical science; men possessed of a high degree of imagination and of many other attributes that go to make a master mind.

One contemporary gaily suggests that Mr. Winston Churchill is the real inventor because he suggested using steam-rollers for flattening out the enemy's trenches. Mr. Churchill has come into his own over "hornets," but while praise is due to him for encouraging the inventive genius of his department we absolve him from any inventive genius in producing Tanks.

Mr. Lloyd George even claims the invention for the

ex-First Lord, but omits all mention of the grounds on which he bases the claim.

Our contemporary, the *Daily Express*, in the issue of 22nd September, suggests that a "Tank be shown on the Horse Guards Parade, so as to let the people see it." An excellent suggestion which we fully support; nor can we think of any better way of impressing the people with the wonder and the importance of these new machines.

The Nation desires to pay tribute to the real inventor of the Tanks. Secondly, the Nation desires to pay tribute to those through whose indefatigable labours the visionings of the inventors took ultimate visible shape. Lastly, the Nation desires to honour Mr. H. G. Wells, whose concept of a land battleship first formed a fitting subject for literary endeavour.

We have been promised the full story of the Tanks, and record the hope that Mr. Balfour may be prevailed upon to let us have it before the "caterpillars" have had time to sink into the comfortable obscurity of their chrysalides.

S. W.
3.10.16.

The writer (S. W.) of this very interesting article shared my hope that the Admiralty would issue an official statement giving credit to those who initiated the Admiralty's caterpillar landship. But the stocks of the Naval Airmen, who had been pressing for Naval air development against much hostility from some of the Sea Lords, were then very low indeed, and had Janus given them some deadly instrument to create for stopping the War, or had they invented a wondrous weapon from ideas received straight from Mars, most of the Sea Lords at that time would have endeavoured to smother them in the same way as they tried, and partly succeeded, in smothering some of the Naval air effort, as several of the official papers dealt with by the late Marquis Curzon,[1] if published, could disclose.

In dealing with this memorandum I am quite certain that Colonel Swinton, R.E., never claimed to have invented the caterpillar landship that was initiated, as the official papers at the Admiralty clearly show, by the Naval Airmen

---

[1] President of the First Air Board.

then serving in their Air Department. His many admirers may have made this claim for Colonel Swinton, but it is on record that during the hearing of the Tank claims before the Royal Commission it was clearly brought out by the Attorney-General that General Sir Scott-Moncrieff's Committee turned down all caterpillar tractor proposals made by Army Officers after some practical trials with caterpillars at Aldershot on 17th January, 1915, in these notable words that I repeat from page 50:

> The result of that preliminary trial was not such as to satisfy the War Office Committee that the scheme was practicable and the members of the Committee being unable to suggest any Engineer competent to work out a fresh design, that project appears to have been abandoned on the 26th February, 1915.[1]

That deals with Colonel Swinton's supposed claim to have invented the Admiralty caterpillar landship.

We must repeat again that the War Office side of Whitehall turned down the efforts of all their Army Officers to introduce caterpillar landships for military purposes.

In his evidence before the Arms Enquiry on 22nd May, 1936, Sir Tennyson D'Eyncourt, in dealing with great inventions and improvements, mentioned Tanks and stated:

> This particular form of mechanized weapon, which did so much in the latter years of the War, was definitely given up as impossible by the War Office.

Now let us look on the other side of Whitehall where Mr. Churchill was First Lord of the Admiralty, and ask this simple question: Did Mr. Churchill invent the Tank or did one of his Air Officers?

During the debate on Defence in the House of Commons in November, 1936, Mr. Winston Churchill stated:[2]

> Look at the Tank Corps. The Tank was a British invention. This idea, which has revolutionized the

---

[1] From Minutes of Proceedings dated 7th October, 1919, before the Royal Commission on Awards to Inventors, page 3.   [2] Hansard, 12th November, 1936.

conditions of modern war, was a British idea forced upon the War Office by outsiders. Let me say they would have just as hard work to-day to force a new idea on it. I speak from what I know.

I am quite certain this view of the War Office under the present very efficient administration of the Army Council is quite incorrect from what I know.

The War Office are now full out to encourage new ideas, no matter who they come from.

The Tank is obviously a British invention, for did not His Majesty, the late King George V, say so in his message to Lord Haig?[1]

At the hearing of the Tank claim by the Royal Commission in cross-examination Mr. Churchill seemed to the Naval Airmen, who were listening with much attention to his evidence, to become a little perturbed when he snapped out on the 7th October, 1917: "I know nothing whatever about mechanical matters."[2] That is quite correct; Mr. Churchill's political training would scarcely embrace much in the way of mechanical knowledge, and all the years I served under him as his Director of the Admiralty Air Department he never once imparted to me a single mechanical idea or suggestion of any value with the exception of his steam-roller proposals for crushing in enemy's trenches, as explained in Chapter I, Part I. This suggestion was of the utmost value, but in the exact opposite way to that intended by Mr. Churchill.

After Lieutenant Barry and myself carried out practical experiments with steam-rollers coupled together at Wormwood Scrubs, we saw how they stuck in soft ground and became very difficult to dislodge. Then I became convinced that we were on wrong lines, and what was required was a lightly loaded machine to better distribute the load, and not a heavily loaded machine like a steam-roller.

The failure of Mr. Churchill's steam-roller proposals led directly to my giving him the first demonstration of a caterpillar machine before many witnesses on the Horse Guards Parade on 16th February, 1915.

[1] Page 308.
[2] Minutes of Proceedings of Royal Commission on Awards to Inventors, page 27.

TO WHOM THE CREDIT?

This was the first caterpillar demonstration given to Authority, namely the First Lord of the Admiralty, that was proved before the Royal Commission to be in the direct line of causation that led to the building of the first Royal Naval Air Service caterpillar landship (Plate XXV).

This caterpillar landship experimental work was initiated by myself when serving as the Director of the Admiralty Air Department, as the official papers at the Admiralty can show—and nobody else. Even the first caterpillar truck was procured by myself.[1]

Mr. Diplock got out for me the first drawing of a caterpillar landship.[2] This drawing was placed before the Admiralty Landship Committee by my instructions on the 4th March, 1915, and I reported to Mr. Churchill that I had done so.

May we examine the question of who was responsible for initiating the Admiralty caterpillar landship experiments in some detail, producing evidence, as it deals with a novel weapon of war that has become historic.

Serving at the Admiralty during the time I was called upon to create the Royal Naval Air Service was Mr. W. J. Evans,[3] one of the heads of the Department of the Secretary usually known as M Branch. He was very much liked and respected by all his Naval colleagues who had the good fortune to work with him before and during the War.

Mr. Evans had a wide experience of Admiralty Administration and could bring a broad mind to bear on the big problems that were constantly arising, particularly during the period of hostilities. I was indebted to him muchly for sound advice in my difficult task of creating a Naval Air Service, then the first Anti-Aircraft Corps for defence of London and the Armoured Car Force. This kindly Civil Servant would always put himself to any amount of trouble in assisting myself and those Naval Airmen associated with me in solving our novel air problems that had no precedent in Naval law or in the Admiralty Office. In our turn we Airmen would do anything for this likeable man who represented the finest type in our great Civil Service and was one of the

[1] Page 45.   [2] Diagram I.
[3] W. J. Evans, Esq., C.B., C.B.E., late Director of Establishments, Admiralty.

few men in a higher position at the Admiralty who went out of his way to help and not to hinder air development.

Mr. Evans was far-seeing enough to know that there was real purpose in the efforts of the Airmen to develop air-craft for Naval work. Whereas most of the Sea Lords at that time were not very helpful to air advance and thought everything to do with air matters an infernal nuisance. With their other great responsibilities they did not seem to be able to grasp the enormous possibilities of the air and how air development could be applied with much advantage to Naval purposes. Mr. Evans was very interested in our caterpillar experiments and seemed to like the novel ideas of the Naval Airmen.

One day I received the following letter from Mr. Evans:

BRACKSOME,
MILFORD-ON-SEA,
26th September, 1916.

MY DEAR SUETER,

I saw Murray on Sunday about the Tanks and expressed my views at length. As chance would have it I have also had some conversation with Dale Bussell, who came to me about passports for the Committee's visit to Paris. So far as I can make out, it seems likely that credit will be given to D'Eyncourt and some Engineer at Coventry whose name has slipped my mind, and as there are other people who also want to receive credit but to whom little is really due, it seems extremely likely that the latter may belittle the Committee and as a consequence attention will be entirely drawn from the originators of the scheme—yourself and those you mention in your report. This result will be extremely unfair, but you see Colonel Swinton is already claiming to be *the man*. Churchill's share in the matter will also, I have no doubt, have to be acknowledged, and very properly so, too. It seems to me that when this is done he should acknowledge the share you had in shaping the invention up to the point when the Committee took charge.

The Admiralty, of course, ought to make use of your memorandum which is extremely interesting and very clear. I should suppose, however, that any statement on

PLATE LI

PLATE LII

(*Above*) ADMIRAL BACON'S TRENCH-BRIDGING MACHINE
(*Below*) SQUADRON OF ROYAL NAVAL AIR SERVICE ARMOURED CARS. REVOLVING TURRET, ROLLS-ROYCE CHASSIS, 1915

PLATE LIII

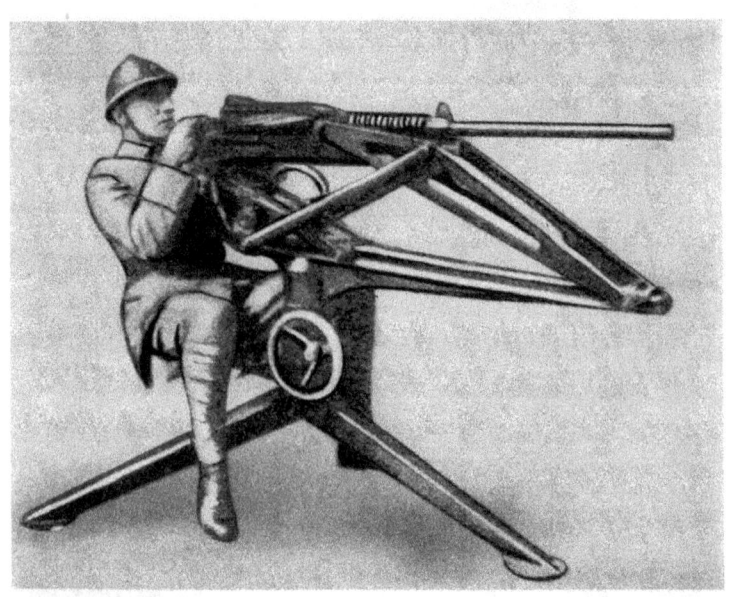

FRENCH 13·2-MM. ANTI-TANK MACHINE-GUN

the subject in future will be made by the Ministry of Munitions. Major Stern is employed under the Ministry I think, and I suppose he may have something to say in the matter. I don't know whether he was in the armoured cars when you were in charge of them. But the old Officers of that Force should certainly see to it that credit is given where credit is due.

I sincerely hope that your share in the matter will be fully recognized, as is your due, and I will gladly do anything in my power in that direction.

I have just come down here for a few days' holiday—the first real holiday I have had since the War started.

Yours very sincerely,
(Sgd.) W. J. EVANS.

In perusing this letter it may be noted that Mr. Evans' opinion is that Mr. Churchill will acknowledge my share in the Tank invention. But he did not in his evidence before the Royal Commission. One wonders why.

May I take this a step further?

Mr. Churchill wrote with his usual charm one of the great books of the War entitled *The World Crisis* 1911–1915. On page 318 this kindly reference to myself occurs:

> The formation of the Armoured Car Squadrons was entrusted to Commodore Sueter. In this task this Officer displayed great energy.

To the amazement and amusement of many Naval Airmen who served with me at the Admiralty, and myself, at the bottom of the next page[1] Mr. Churchill places this extraordinary note:

> The first design of the Tank made at my request by Admiral Bacon in September, 1914, carried a bridge in front, which on arriving at a trench it dropped, passed over and automatically raised behind it.

Admiral Bacon's bridging device was a Foster-Daimler 105 h.p. tractor belonging to a 15-inch howitzer equipment. It had 8 ft. diameter driving wheels and was fitted with an

---

[1] *The World Crisis*, page 319.

11 ft. bridging apparatus. *No caterpillars were used in its construction* (Plate LI).

This bridge consisted of girders which could, on reaching an obstacle such as a trench, be lowered to the ground. The machine then passed over the girders and could pull them clear of the trench or obstacle.

On 19th May, 1915, this machine, without the bridging device, was tried over the special course prepared at Aldershot. It successfully crushed the wire entanglement but stuck in the first trench and had to be hauled out by a 120 h.p. Holt caterpillar. It could not face the double trench. Consequently, General von Donop and General Scott-Moncrieff did not consider this bridging machine to be of the slightest use for service in the field, and turned it down in exactly the same way as the War Office officials turned down, two months previously, Colonel Swinton's and Major Tulloch's caterpillar proposals.[1]

I am quite certain one of the greatest brain-waves the Navy ever produced, my ingenious, mechanically-minded, and most courageous old submarine chief, Admiral Sir Reginald Bacon, would be the very last man to claim that his bridging device machine bore a shadow of resemblance to the caterpillar landship. Admiral Bacon had nothing whatsoever to do with creating the armoured cars, my Diplock caterpillar experiments, or the series of experiments with caterpillars at Wormwood Scrubs or the experiments with the Bullock caterpillar tractors and the first caterpillar landship at Lincoln that were conducted by Naval Air and Armoured Car Officers under my direction, as Director of the Admiralty Air Department.

Admiral Bacon's bridging device was not considered by the members of the Royal Commission to be in any way in the chain of causation that led to the evolution of the successful Tank, whereas the Royal Commission found that my Diplock caterpillar experiments were a very important link in the chain. The Admiralty's letter, given in full on page 232, and the Army Council's letter on page 235 show quite clearly the part played by my Naval Airmen and myself in initiating the caterpillar landship experiments and our part in developing this new weapon of war.

[1] Page 50.

TO WHOM THE CREDIT? 189

Mr. Churchill's statement in his book has no relation whatsoever to the true facts, and does not he give his whole case away that—the first design of the Tank was made at his request by Admiral Bacon in September, 1914—when he so eloquently writes in his abridged and revised edition of his book *The World Crisis*, page 308, these words:

> The armoured car was the child of the Air and the Tank its grandchild.

Mr. Winston Churchill knows perfectly well Admiral Bacon had nothing to do with developing our armoured cars because he wrote in the first issue of *The World Crisis*, page 318, which I repeat:

> The formation of the Armoured Car Squadrons was entrusted to Commodore Sueter.

Moreover, the Reader's imagination would be taxed very heavily if asked to consider that Admiral Bacon's bridging machine (Plate LI) looked like a caterpillar Tank.

Plenty of people had talked about caterpillars. No one person had a monopoly of the subject. Some caterpillar knowledge was fairly general. From my experience with Captain Robert Scott's caterpillar sleighs,[1] I had talked about caterpillars to Mr. Churchill at a very early date. But no Service man took any real action until 16th February, 1915, when I gave Mr. Churchill the first practical demonstration on the Horse Guards Parade before plenty of witnesses how caterpillar tracks could be used to replace the wheels of our turret and 3-pounder armoured cars that were giving us so much trouble with their springs, back axles and tyres failing to support the heavy load of armour, armament, ammunition and crew.

These armoured cars were only successful on flat roads, but on bad roads they were a constant source of anxiety to all my armoured car Officers.

Attending this caterpillar demonstration on the Horse Guards Parade on 16th February, 1915, apart from members of my Staff in the Air Department and my Armoured Car Officers, were two civilians, Mr. Diplock and Mr. Brackenbury, who were Directors of the Pedrail Transport

---
[1] Page 61.

Company. I invited these two experts, as I thought they would be able with their great knowledge of caterpillar machines to convince the First Lord that my caterpillar landship of moderate dimensions was a more practical proposition than Flight-Commander Hetherington's giant wheel battleship, or his steam-roller proposals, and could easily be developed by efficient constructors. Although the Diplock Company were not in a position to build long track caterpillars at that time, both these Directors became full out to develop caterpillar landships, and Mr. Diplock got out for me the drawing of my caterpillar landship that was laid before the Admiralty Landship Committee on 4th March, 1915.

From Mr. Brackenbury's letter to me, dated 30th May, 1919,[1] I extract the following:

> It was your Department[2] that arranged for the demonstration before Mr. Churchill and, on the other hand, Mr. Churchill will no doubt remember your conversation with him in reference to Pedrail[3] armoured cars.

It is so very strange that Mr. Brackenbury remembered the conversation with me that Mr. Churchill entirely forgot in giving his evidence before the Royal Commission or in his books.

Later, at the Killen Strait caterpillar experiments that I arranged for Mr. Lloyd George, when Minister of Munitions, to see at our armoured car station at Wormwood Scrubs on 30th June, 1915, Mr. Churchill was only a spectator. He had no position at the Admiralty, as he had ceased to be First Lord in the previous May, and had nothing to do with the experiments being carried out under my direction. Neither did I ask Mr. Churchill's support in the struggle I had to retain No. 20 Squadron that I formed for caterpillar work, and continue the experiments for the Landship Committee with the Bullock Creeping Grip Caterpillar tractors and the first Royal Naval Air Service landship mounted on the specially lengthened Bullock tracts that we had obtained from America.

After Mr. Churchill ceased to be First Lord of the Admiralty I did not consult him in any way in connection

---

[1] Page 85.   [2] Air Department, Admiralty.   [3] Caterpillar.

with ordering caterpillar machines for experimental purposes or the construction of the first caterpillar landship. I dealt direct with D'Eyncourt, the Chairman of our Landship Committee, as explained in my memorandum, page 70.

As I have previously remarked, the Tank is a purely mechanical weapon. Experiments with caterpillars had to be carried out under all sorts of conditions, and one of the chief and by no means the least achievement was to establish confidence and show Authority that caterpillar landships were worth developing. This the Naval Airmen accomplished. All torpedoists know that the present locomotive Whitehead torpedo was developed from the crude ideas of Captain Lupuis, an Austrian Officer. The late Admiral Sir John Durnford, when he left the battleship *Jupiter* to become Fourth Sea Lord of the Admiralty, turned over to me all his torpedo papers. Amongst them is a copy of the original report of the Admiralty Committee that was set up to develop the Whitehead torpedo in 1870.

I asked Mr. Churchill to set up the Landship Committee to develop my caterpillar landship in exactly the same way as the Whitehead torpedo was developed for the British Navy. The Royal Commission in their finding stated I was the main cause of the appointment of the D.N.C. Committee. You cannot build a caterpillar landship by talking about it.

From much experience of experimental work in so many directions I knew only too well that there were many difficulties to be overcome in introducing a weapon of war of such a novel type. There was, for instance, very little knowledge of caterpillar tracks in our road haulage firms, and the two long-track caterpillars I wanted for my first landship were unobtainable at that time in this Country. A good deal of expenditure is necessary in experimental work. Results of trials have to be closely examined and, above all, confidence has to be kept up often over a long period until success is in sight.

This sort of work is performed always more efficiently under the supervision of a Committee appointed by Authority for that particular purpose. But a guiding hand is also advisable to see the Committee press on with the job entrusted to them, and who can question delay, otherwise there is often a tendency in experimental work to go on for ever, and sometimes it takes a direction not likely to lead to success.

There will be general agreement that Mr. Churchill deserves the greatest credit for encouraging his Air Officers, when he was First Lord of the Admiralty, to pursue novel lines of thought, and backing them when they produced new ideas for constructing a suitable weapon for trench warfare, and the pages of this book show his confidence was not misplaced. But he must not, in common fairness to his former Airmen, give the credit for their work to Admiral Bacon.

Should Mr. Churchill in his calmer moments of contemplation ever refresh his memory by glancing at these pages, which give an accurate account of my Diplock, Killen Strait and Bullock caterpillar experiments, which can be checked by official Admiralty documents, in addition to the Admiralty letter on page 232, and the Army Council's letter on page 235, all of which can be seen at the Admiralty Office, he may recall that the Royal Commission pointed out that his former Director of the Admiralty Air Department (myself) had something to do with impressing upon his mind the importance of caterpillar traction, and that the note in his book, "The first design of the Tank was made at his request by Admiral Bacon," is incorrect, as it is contrary to fact.

We had all worked very hard for Mr. Churchill in creating the Royal Naval Air Service, the first anti-aircraft corps for the defence of London, and the Armoured Car Force. A public statement by himself as our former First Lord with Admiralty approval, apportioning the proper share of credit for the Tank invention to my little team of Airmen who conducted under my direction the Diplock, Killen Strait and Bullock caterpillar and first landship experiments, was so simple, and all that was needed to check some of the claimants to be sole inventors of the Tank having it all their own way for so many years. But we waited in vain. Even at the inquiry by the Royal Commission the Naval Airmen expected Mr. Churchill to make a fair and generous statement based upon the Admiralty documents which, as Secretary of State for War, he could naturally have had full access to for the asking.

But nothing was forthcoming from the War Minister. We waited again in vain.

In making my simple protest at Mr. Churchill's lack of generosity to my Airmen and myself, his former Director of the Admiralty Air Department, when giving evidence before the Royal Commission, and in his books, I do so with great reluctance, but I am quite certain, had Shakespeare been alive, he would have expressed the view that

> "Bad cricket in the great ones
> Must not unchallenged go."

From time to time considerable feeling was being aroused by various people claiming the sole invention of the Tank.

This even annoyed Mrs. Hetherington, the Mother of my gallant driver of the first caterpillar machine, for she sent a strong letter of protest to my Wife, as can be seen by its perusal:

BERECHURCH HALL,
COLCHESTER.
Thursday.[1]

MY DEAR MRS. SUETER,

Don't you think your husband should really take a very firm and determined stand about the naval part of the Tank business? I know lots of people who think so, and there is much feeling. If he does not, the ground will be cut from under the feet of the Admiralty lot.

Mr. Churchill knows the truth; can't he see him about it? I really think he is very unwise if he does not.

Wing-Commander Longcroft and Colonel Maitland have just written me *very strong* letters on the subject, as they both know the whole thing from the beginning and think Tommy is being purposely ignored because he is a soldier attached to the Navy.

Of course, nothing can be done while he remains in the service by his civilian friends, but as it must all come out some day, it seems a thousand pities time is being wasted. Don't you yourself think so?

Are you still hard packing up garments?[2]

Yours very sincerely,
(Sgd.) F. A. HETHERINGTON.

[1] Undated.
[2] For the Royal Naval Air Service Comforts Fund that Lady Sueter was running at that time.

The action I took is given on page 257, and for me had some extraordinary results.

The claim of Mrs. Capron to have invented the Tank can be dealt with in a few words.

Seventeen years is a long time to wait before any person's claim is finally disposed of, and in all this long period I have felt very sorry for Mrs. Capron. She seemed to strike a line for developing a mechanical weapon of war which led nowhere.

If she had brought her suggestion to myself, and I was always approachable as Director of the Admiralty Air Department and in charge of the Armoured Car Force, I would have had her proposals taken before the Landship Committee in exactly the same way as was done with the Macfie-Nesfield model, and the first drawing of a caterpillar landship that Mr. Diplock prepared for me.

Instead of that she took her ideas, I understand, to an Army Officer, and it is now common knowledge that mechanical weapons were not then in favour at the War Office.

Whether Mrs. Capron's ideas were of value is not within my knowledge, as I have never seen any of her drawings. Since the War Mrs. Capron has more than once written to me, but I have always referred her to the Admiralty, as they possess all the official papers to show who initiated the Tank.

In any case, Mrs. Capron was never remotely in the chain of causation of our experimental work, which led to the building of the first R.N.A.S. caterpillar landship.

Early in 1935 the Admiralty informed me by official letter that Mrs. Capron's claim had been turned down, after which I received the Army Council's gracious letter given on page 235. I think Mrs. Capron is the very latest claimant for the Tank invention.

There is a good deal of evidence in the official papers at the Admiralty to show that I initiated the Diplock caterpillar experiments that led to the construction of the first R.N.A.S. caterpillar landship. In that department they have a complete set of photographs that I left behind, before proceeding on active service in 1917 to Southern Italy, with the official papers dealing with the Diplock, Killen

Strait, Bullock Tractor and first landship experiments carried out whilst I was Director of the Admiralty Air Department by my Air and Armoured Car Officers. They have also the first drawing of the caterpillar landship prepared by Mr. Diplock for me, and laid before the Admiralty Landship Committee by my instructions on 4th March, 1915. Moreover, the original brief history of how the Tank was initiated is signed by three Air Officers. Unfortunately for some of these kind people who sought to reap where they did not sow, the Civil Servants at the Admiralty have kept their own complete dossier of all the important documents, orders placed and photographs of our caterpillar experiments, and have kept my name in the Tank picture. For their kindly action I thank them.

The members of the Admiralty Civil Service who have handled the Tank papers have lived up to their great traditions. Their vigorous code of impartiality in controversial cases is of a very high standard, and on more than one occasion in my now fairly long life I have admired the fine cricket played by the members of our great Civil Service. Good cricket in public life is just as important as on the playing-field. Cricket has entered all our lives since my great-great-grandfather, Tom Sueter, a pioneer of British cricket and famous wicket-keeper, played on Broad-halfpenny Green, 1769–1791, and is it not true that

> "... on a Hampshire hill top
> Beside the 'Bat and Ball'
> Old Richard Nyren nurtured
> The noblest game of all."

No better example of good cricket in public life could be given than the action of the Prime Minister, Mr. Ramsay MacDonald, in the crisis of 1929.

To part with most of his lifelong political friends and supporters must have been a great wrench and difficult undertaking that needed some courage of the four o'clock in the morning order.

But Ramsay MacDonald, being a true Scotsman, did not fail the Nation in her hour of need. After most of his old Colleagues refused to follow him, he called upon a new crew to man the "Ship of State," and with their help and that of the few stalwarts who loyally stood by their leader, the Prime Minister steered the good ship, that was then being buffeted about in a full gale, on a lee shore into calmer waters and safety.

For the rest of his life Ramsay MacDonald will be honoured by the majority of his Countrymen for his very fine cricket during a great economic disturbance in our Country's history.

Whilst serving at the Admiralty many of the Civil Staff used to bring me in cuttings from the Press and say:
"Here you are, Commodore. This is another. Who in the devil is——?"

"What about this one? He says he told you how to build the Tank. We have never heard of him. Put him in the dock."

This was an Admiralty docket; on the outside some wag had written—

> "Now who shall we thank?
> Who invented the Tank?
> Was he man of the People or person of Rank?
> Was he broke to the wide or with cash at the Bank?
> .   .   .   .   .
> Much has been written but here is a new blow,
> Who is Mr. —— of —— & Co.?"

As each claimant came forward we put him in the docket. How we did laugh at some of these scramblers for credit for the Tank invention, and nobody enjoyed the joke more than the Civil Servants at the Admiralty and myself, because we had retained all the reports, which showed quite clearly that the caterpillar landship experiments were initiated by Admiralty Air Officers and nobody else.

The Royal Commission on Awards to Inventors

After the War a Royal Commission was set up to investigate the claims of all those inventors who had introduced a new weapon of war, such as a gun or mortar, new scientific instruments, improvements in machinery or munitions, etc. Amongst many reports that the Commission issued is the following:

CLAIMS IN RESPECT OF "INVENTION OF TANKS"
By the following claimants, namely:
Major-General E. D. Swinton.
Lieutenant-Colonel F. L. M. Boothby.
Commodore F. M. Sueter.
Lieutenant R. F. Macfie.
Mr. A. C. Nesfield.
Major T. G. Hetherington.
Sir Eustace H. Tennyson D'Eyncourt.
Colonel Crompton and Mr. Le Gros.
Sir William Tritton and Major Wilson.
Mr. L. E. de Mole.

The Commission have examined all the above claims in immediate succession, and consider it advisable to embody their recommendations in a single document.

In the first place, the Commission desire to record their view that it was primarily due to the receptivity, courage, and driving force of the Rt. Hon. Winston Spencer Churchill that the general idea of the use of such an instrument of warfare as the "Tank" was converted into a practical shape. Mr. Winston Churchill has very properly taken the view that all his thought and time belonged to the State, and that he was not entitled to make any claim for an award, even had he wished to do so. But it seems proper that the above view should be recorded by way of tribute to Mr. Winston Churchill.

MAJOR-GENERAL SWINTON'S CLAIM

This Officer, acting outside the scope of his general duties, made an important contribution to the invention and adoption of the Tank. This contribution included first the conception in October, 1914, of a machine-gun destroyer of the general character of the Tank; secondly, the persistent, energetic, and successful advocacy from then onwards of the value and feasibility of the employment of such an instrument of warfare; and, thirdly, the specific definition in June, 1915, of the necessary characteristics of the weapon, the conditions of its use and the tests which it must be required to satisfy.

We conceive that the terms of reference to us do not contemplate the recommendation of awards for general services such as those secondly above mentioned, but limit us to those which contributed to the invention and design of the actual weapon of warfare in question; and in respect of these latter services we recommend an award of £1000.

But beyond this we desire expressly to recognize the still greater value of that part of Major-General Swinton's work for which a pecuniary reward is not appropriate.

Commodore Sueter's Claim

This Officer contributed in a definite degree to the evolution and adoption of the Tanks. He appreciated at an early date and urged on Mr. Winston Churchill the importance of caterpillar traction for attack across country; he organized the Diplock trials in February, 1915, and he was the main cause of the appointment of the D.N.C. Committee in the same month. We think that his services were of great value. But, on the other hand, he was acting throughout within the scope of the duties assigned to him, and no specific invention of great merit is attributable to him.

We consider that the case of this distinguished Officer falls within the general rule to which we have given effect on previous occasions that (unless in quite exceptional circumstances) no award should be made to a servant of the Crown for the efficient discharge of duties definitely assigned to him.

Claims of Lieutenant-Colonel Boothby and Major Hetherington

In each of these cases we consider that valuable services were rendered by the Officer in question, for which he deserves high credit. But inasmuch as in each case these services were rendered within the scope of the employment of the Officer, and there was not any such exceptional invention or discovery as might possibly justify an award even under these circumstances, we are unable to recommend an award to either claimant.

Claims of Mr. Macfie and Mr. Nesfield

These are separate claims, but we deal with them together because they are in effect rival claims to the merit attaching to the conception, embodiment, and communication of the same set of ideas. These ideas were of considerable value, but on a careful review of the evidence there is no conclusive proof that they were brought to the notice of, or communicated either directly or indirectly to, the actual designers of the Tank, so as necessarily to form a link in the chain of causation resulting in the evolution of the Tank. In view, however, of the general similarity of these ideas, as evidenced by Mr. Nesfield's provisional specification with those embodied in the Tanks, we have given these claimants the benefit of the doubt and credited them with some share in the evolution of the weapon, and we estimate the value of this share at £1000. As between the two claimants, we think the credit should be divided equally and accordingly we recommend the award to each of them of a sum of £500.

Sir E. Tennyson D'Eyncourt's Claim

This is a claim with regard to which we have found much difficulty. This claimant undoubtedly rendered exceptional services as chairman of what has been called the "D.N.C." Committee in the selection and elimination of the various forms of design proposed, and particularly in the determination of those features of the Tank which were concerned with armament; and he was acting outside his duties as Director of Naval Construction. On the other hand, he was acting within the general scope of his duties as chairman of the committee in question, and further it was mobility rather than armament which formed the principal inventive feature of the Tanks. On the whole, we recommend the award of a sum of £1000 to this claimant.

Joint Claim of Colonel Crompton and Mr. Le Gros

These claimants were employed for some six months as consulting engineers to the D.N.C. Committee at a substantial agreed remuneration. In the discharge of their duties they worked loyally and very hard, and no doubt supplied the Committee with useful data and sound advice. But they did not, in the result, invent or discover the special features subsequently incorporated in the Tanks, and we cannot consider their services as of such an exceptional or extraordinary character as could alone justify an award in addition to their agreed salaries.

Joint Claim of Sir William Tritton and Major Wilson

It is to these two claimants that we attribute the credit of designing and producing in a concrete practical shape the novel and efficient engine of warfare known as the "Tank"; and it is to them that in our judgment by far the largest award should be made, though allowance has to be made for the special opportunities afforded to Major Wilson by his official position.

It was objected on behalf of the Crown that Sir William Tritton at any rate had been sufficiently remunerated by the contracts placed with his company. But it is to be observed, in answer to this, that the principal contracts were placed with another company, who were supplied with the working drawings of Sir William Tritton and Major Wilson without any separate payment, and who fixed a price which was subsequently accepted without any addition by Sir William Tritton's Company. It was also objected on behalf of the Crown that some considerable defects in design were discovered when the Tanks were originally used in the course of the Battle of the Somme. But it would seem that the conditions of actual use of the machines were much more stringent and protracted than those stipulated for by the Government when ordering them. And, further, the defects in question appear to us to have been no greater than those ordinarily discovered in course of putting into actual use and service any novel mechanical contrivances. Indeed, the fact that within a few weeks of the first use of the Tanks on the Somme the Government ordered a very large additional number of the machines is the best proof of their generally satisfactory character.

We recommend that there be awarded to these claimants jointly the sum of £15,000.

CLAIM OF MR. L. E. DE MOLE

The case of this claimant was heard a few days after the conclusion of the other cases. We consider that he is entitled to the greatest credit for having made and reduced to practical shape, as far back as the year 1912, a very brilliant invention which anticipated and in some respects surpassed that actually put into use in the year 1916. It was this claimant's misfortune and not his fault that his invention was in advance of his time, and failed to be appreciated and was put aside because the occasion for its use had not then arisen. We regret exceedingly that we are unable to recommend any award to him. But we are bound to adhere to the general rule in such cases as these that a claimant must show a casual connection between the making of his invention and the use of any similar invention by the Government.

In estimating the value of the invention of the Tanks for the purpose of the above recommendations, we have taken into account not merely the precise class of Tanks which went into action at the Battle of the Somme, but also any modified or improved classes of Tanks which may fairly be considered to result from the normal development of the inherent potentialities of the original invention. But we have not taken into account any special or exceptional inventions which may subsequently have been applied and have resulted in substantial extra utility.

(Signed) CHARLES H. SARJANT (Chairman),
JAMES J. DOBBIE,
W. TEMPLE FRANKS,
A. C. COLE,
H. J. MACKINDER,
ROBERT YOUNG.

P. TINDAL ROBERTSON, Secretary.
Date: 17th November, 1919.

The foregoing is perhaps the most singular finding a Royal Commission ever made.

In referring briefly to those Naval Airmen ,who were responsible for initiating the caterpillar experiments, may I recall once more that I started the caterpillar landship idea in the Admiralty Air Department and showed Mr. Winston Churchill, then First Lord of the Admiralty, on the Horse Guards Parade, how we could utilize with advantage a caterpillar for replacing the wheels of our turret armoured cars and heavy armoured lorries. Then Mr. Diplock got out for me the first caterpillar landship drawing that I had placed before the Admiralty Landship Committee on 4th March, 1915 (Diagram I).

A very learned patent authority, the late Mr. James Whitehead, K.C., in giving evidence before the Royal Commission said that I had something patentable.

The Royal Commission state I was acting within the duties assigned to me. In the name of common sense how can an Officer be directed to attempt to invent or invent a weapon of war, as part of his duty, when Authority, in the person of Mr. Churchill, then First Lord, did not know what was required, as can be seen by the instructions he issued to me about his steam-roller idea, page 53. Nor did any other Officer senior to me, Admiral or General, know what weapon was required to be developed for trench warfare.

Certainly none of the Admirals who were then Sea Lords knew. They made no creative suggestions. Apart from the third Sea Lord, Admiral Sir Frederick Tudor-Tudor, who invented a very good armoured shield[1] for infantry protection, no other Sea Lord took the faintest interest in our armoured car work, on the contrary they did their utmost to block my armoured car and caterpillar landship efforts.

Most of the Sea Lords, at that time, considered the Navy should have nothing to do with armoured cars or caterpillar landships. Certainly the Generals at the War Office had no idea in which path the development of a weapon for trench warfare should proceed, as they turned down all caterpillar proposals that had been put forward officially to them by Hankey, Tulloch and Swinton.

There is nothing in the printed document outlining my duties as Director of the Admiralty Air Department—before me—to say I had to attempt to invent or invent a caterpillar landship for use of the Army.

[1] Page 46.

My duty was clearly to see that air machines were created for the Navy. This I did, and with Admiralty approval I turned over in the early days of the War a very large number of aeroplanes, hundreds of aero engines, many sections of kite-balloons and a large number of armoured cars to the Army, in addition to my naval air work. This practical assistance to the Army during their most difficult time was much appreciated by many Senior Military Officers, as the documents in my possession clearly show.

My complaint is that the Admiralty were not helpful to their Naval Airmen whilst the Royal Commission enquired into the claims for the Tank invention. I am quite confident the Chairman of the Royal Commission was never shown a copy of my orders as Director of their Air Department, and they gave no guidance to the Chairman which was most unfair.

I had to listen to this during the enquiry—*Re* the date, 30th June, 1915:[1]

The Chairman: Of course by that time Commodore Sueter had dropped out as an efficient agent in the matter, had he not?

Mr. Caradoc Rees: If your Lordship pleases.

The Chairman: He had dropped out of the chain.

Mr. Caradoc Rees: However, we showed it to him!

At this date, the 30th June, 1915, I was very much in the chain, as it was the very date I gave my big caterpillar demonstration and had all the obstacles prepared with Commander Boothby's good help for Mr. Lloyd George and many Military Officers and others to see at Wormwood Scrubs. The demonstration is fully described on page 75.

I had taken a great deal of trouble with Commander Boothby in having many good obstacles constructed out of railway sleepers, railway metals, barbed wire, fitting up the pioneer net cutters to the Killen Strait Machine, etc., to make this demonstration the complete success it was.

Then to hear it stated I had nothing whatever to do with these experiments, and had dropped out of the chain, was approaching the limit. Under the Board of Admiralty I was the responsible Authority. The Armoured Car force was under my orders.

[1] Page 79, Minutes of Proceedings, Royal Commission on Awards to Inventors.

I appealed to Mr. Whitehead, K.C., but he said nothing could be done.

It always seemed to me a little unfair that the Admiralty could not have given some guidance to the Chairman over such simple matters, as to what their Officers' precise duties were and when each Officer ceased to help with the Tank experiments.

All through the hearing of the Tank claims the Admiralty never offered to place any official papers or give any help to their Naval Airmen in pressing their claim before the Royal Commission. The Naval Airmen had to rely on their memories and any copies of official documents that they may have retained. Commander Boothby and myself had to listen to certain persons giving evidence, saying they sent my Armoured Car Officers to France, to America, to dash here and to dash there.

Neither D'Eyncourt nor Crompton or anybody else had any executive authority over my Armoured Car Officers all the time I was the Director of the Admiralty Air Department. No one could order any of my Officers to move one inch without my approval. The Board of Admiralty gave their orders through me, their executive Officer.

The Landship Committee was purely advisory and had no executive powers over any of my Air or Armoured Car Officers. Moreover, I had to purchase all material for our early experimental work, as is shown by my memorandum dated 30th March, 1915, given on page 70, and issued with the concurrence of the Director of Naval Construction and Director of Contracts to Commander Boothby, Flight-Commander Hetherington and Colonel Crompton, R.E.

I arranged with D'Eyncourt, the Chairman of the Landship Committee, that my Air and Armoured Car Officers, Boothby, Briggs, Hetherington, Stern, McGrath, Field and Wilson, with the necessary Ratings, were at his disposal whenever he wanted them. Also I placed all our resources at the Armoured Car Depot and Experimental Ground at the disposal of the Landship Committee.

I was in exactly the same position as the Captain of *Excellent* with his gunnery experiments, or the Captain of *Vernon* with his torpedo experiments, or the Admiral (S) with his submarine experiments, but in addition, being the

Director of the Admiralty Air Department, I had direct access to the Members of the Board of Admiralty whenever necessary.

I am the last person in the Naval Service who desired to make money out of the War. But to present my claim before the Royal Commission and live in London during the whole of the Tank Claims cost me in legal expenses[1] in having my case presented by a K.C. and hotel bills the sum of £490 4s. 8d.

The Reader will agree that it is expensive work to be a "Pioneer," and in addition there are the kicks which are described in Chapter III, Part II.

More than one of my Airmen represented to me that we were promised fair treatment by the Third Sea Lord.

Up to the time of writing these pages this has not been forthcoming, and the promise was made through the Director of Air Services, Admiral Vaughan Lee.

Other Naval inventors seemed to have had a sort of "favoured person" treatment—at least that is what Squadron Commander Briggs called it when, to the amazement of many of us, whilst the claimants for the Paravane—the well-known anti-mine device—were being heard before the Royal Commission, it was disclosed that Commander Burney received from Messrs. Vickers £300,000 for his part of the Paravane invention, whilst another Naval Officer, Captain Usborne, sold his part of the Paravane invention in so far as they related to merchant ships for £4,800.

These seemed to the Naval Airmen to be nice little sums for the inventors of the Paravane to receive in pursuance of their Naval duty. I have no doubt these two Officers richly deserved every penny of the sum they were fortunate enough to receive.

But what did those Naval Airmen who initiated the caterpillar experiments that led to the Tank receive—nothing.

---

[1] Messrs. Cooke, Bristow and Carpmael's account was:

	£	s.	d.
Professional charges	325	0	0
Counsels' Fees	125	8	6
Payments for Copy Correspondence and Sundries	19	16	2
	470	4	8

+ Hotel Bill, £20.

Whereas those who assisted in the evolution of the Tank received:

> Sir Tennyson D'Eyncourt, £1000.
> Colonel Swinton, £1000.
> Mr. Nesfield and Lieutenant Macfie between them, £1000.
> Sir William Tritton and Major Wilson between them, £15,000.

That is, the Government obtained the Tank invention for £18,000, whereas Messrs. Vickers paid Commander Burney and Captain Usborne £304,800 for the Paravane invention.

No wonder one of the Chief Law Officers of the Crown at the completion of the Royal Commission's investigation of the Tank claims was heard to remark:

> The Government came very well out of the Tank enquiry.

They most certainly did at the expense of my Naval Airmen and myself.

May we now turn to a pleasanter side of Tank work.

Not only did the Tanks help the interests of the State on Active Service in the Field, but much help was given to this Country on the financial side.

As previously stated[1] the *Daily Express* was the first to suggest that the Tanks should be shown, as can be seen from the following extract taken from their paper dated 22nd September, 1916:

> The Ministry of Munitions issue the following:
>
> In view of the statements, more or less erroneous, which have appeared in the Press, the Ministry of Munitions desire to deprecate the circulation of statements regarding the organization and construction of the new armoured cars commonly designated "Tanks."
>
> *In due course an official statement* will be issued giving the history and development of these machines, when credit will be given to whom credit is due.

[1] Page 182.

It is only fair, however, to state that the design and construction of the first "Tank" are due to Officers working under the Admiralty. The Ministry of Munitions subsequently undertook to provide facilities for further experimentation and for the construction and supply of these machines.

MEANWHILE, WHY NOT SHOW ONE OF THE "TANKS" ON THE HORSE GUARDS PARADE? LET THE PEOPLE SEE THEM.

This idea caught on well and at the end of the War the Tanks toured not only many places in this country but throughout the EMPIRE.

A War Bond Tank did good work in Trafalgar Square in November, 1917, and at Portsmouth during the Tank week in Town Hall Square at Christmas in the same year a fine effort was made which yielded £165,644.

On the 16th September, 1918, the following report was received in this country from Melbourne:

> Tremendous enthusiasm marked the inauguration of the seventh War Loan campaign. After a Naval and Military procession, including three Tanks, and aeroplanes overhead dropping leaflets, Mr. Watt sold the Lord Mayor of Melbourne the first Bond.
>
> Then Mr. Watt, from the top of a Tank, was kept busy meeting the public requirements, the Tanks making a tour of the populated areas. The whole of Australia has been divided into areas and a quota allotted to each, honour flags being raised on reaching the amount. It is expected that forty millions will be raised easily within a month.—*Exchange Telegraph.*

And the *Morning Post* of 25th September, 1918, stated:

> The Tanks which are touring the country districts in Australia in support of the War Loan report much enthusiasm among country people, many of whom are driving miles to buy War Bonds.

In all a great many millions must have been subscribed in War Bonds to assist the finances of the War, and I feel quite certain the Naval Air and Armoured Car Officers and Ratings who were associated with our caterpillar work must have felt no little pride even in this side of the Tank activities in helping to finance the Great War.

Tank Patents

New weapons of war are not evolved daily either at the Admiralty or War Office and it is open to question whether the Naval Airmen who initiated the Tank experiments were treated quite fairly by the Admiralty over the Tank patents. After perusing the following the Reader can judge.

When the D.N.C.'s Landship Committee was set up, I placed all the information I had collected before Colonel Crompton firstly, and afterwards Mr. Tennyson D'Eyncourt, and in a minute the latter wrote, when I challenged the question of patents:

> If therefore it is desired to recognize the preliminary proposals made by Commodore Sueter and the other Officers of the Air Service, it is hardly seen how this could be done by adding their names to the patent specification of a machine with the actual production of which they did not deal. *The mention of their names in Parliament appears to recognize the pioneer work which they actually did*, and the patenting of the actual machine in detail appears to be entirely another consideration.

The extract referred to by Sir Tennyson D'Eyncourt is a reply to Captain Burgoyne[1] (U.), North Kensington, in the House of Commons on 18th October, 1916, in which Mr. Macnamara (Secretary to the Admiralty) said:

> There was no doubt that the idea of employing armoured cars for trench warfare occurred independently to several people. All the Admiralty could do was to take what appeared in Admiralty official records. According to them the idea was suggested to Officers of the Royal Naval Air Service by their experience of the Naval armoured cars in Flanders in the early days of the War. After various experiments by Officers of the Royal Naval

---

[1] Afterwards Sir Alan Burgoyne, M.P.

Air Service, Mr. Churchill (then First Lord of the Admiralty) instructed Mr. D'Eyncourt, the Director of Naval Construction, to undertake the design of a Tank or landship, capable of carrying out certain definite operations. The Officers of the Air Department of the Admiralty primarily concerned were Commodore Sueter, Wing-Commander W. Briggs and Squadron-Commander T. G. Hetherington, while the principal credit for the Tanks rests with Mr. D'Eyncourt.

The Admiralty, in their letter of 8th November, 1917, to the Commodore Commanding British Adriatic Force when I raised the question of Patents for the Tank invention whilst serving in Southern Italy, stated:

With reference to your submission of the 23rd September last No. 91/84, enclosing a report from Commodore Murray F. Sueter, C.B., R.N., on the subject of the origin of Tanks, I am to acquaint you for Commodore Sueter's information that they are advised that the Tank and its various features are not patentable.

On 4th December, 1916, I answered their Lordships, letter and submitted that "their letter concerning the Tank patents has been shown to the Officers mentioned therein and we beg to be permitted to thank their Lordships for their letter. Whilst fully realizing that it is now too late to take out patents, we most respectfully submit to point out that general covering patents could easily have been taken out before the Tank was handed over by the Navy to the Army.

The Officers concerned in bringing the Tank scheme to notice fully realize that 'Their Lordships' will now safeguard their interests. . . ."

For years and years the Board of Admiralty have used the late Lieutenant-Commander Hyde Thomson's and my secret patent for the Torpedo Aeroplane and Seaplane. If we could take out a patent for Torpedo aircraft, why not Tanks? Now, what does a great patent law expert, the late Mr. James Whitehead, K.C., say about it? Before the Royal Commission he stated:

As your Lordship knows, in many phases of invention the first step is the conception of the general idea. When the matter was really crystallized out of Commodore Sueter's mind, what did it amount to? It amounted to a concrete notion of a weapon of war having certain well-defined qualities. Those qualities were to involve a particular method of steering and a particular shape; they were to involve a particular method of driving and the various other features which I need not enumerate. I venture to say that there can be no question that, had an application been made at that time for a patent for what has been described in the box, such a patent could have been obtained. There would have been nothing in the Patent Office to have prevented the grant of the patent. Of course I know that that, perhaps, would not carry me very far. It might well be said at once that such a patent, if granted, would be invalid.

May I just look at that for a single moment and endeavour to see what this amounted to? I venture to suggest that there is not only a possibility, but a probability that such a patent, if granted, would have been a valid patent and would, in fact, have conferred a monopoly. If that is so, there is a definite answer in favour of my client as to the step he took being in the nature of an invention.

Chairman: There is nothing in the suggestions that he made, that were embodied to some extent in Mr. Diplock's drawing, sufficiently definite to be the subject of a patent in favour of Commodore Sueter.

Mr. James Whitehead: May I deal with that first of all, my Lord?

Chairman: I do not say that that is fatal to your case. You seem to me to be putting it too narrowly in trying to make out that Commodore Sueter had something which was patentable.

Mr. James Whitehead: I think I can make that out, my Lord. I am going to suggest in a moment or two that it would not be necessary for me to make that out in order to succeed, but I am proceeding to test my submission on that footing. . . .

Your Lordship raises the point and suggests that a valid patent could not have been obtained. I only want to deal with that for a moment or two in order to apply the test for the first time. There would have been brought into our specification a description of a vehicle on broad lines, armoured, protected in itself and carrying armament, and driven in a particular way. It is quite true that the method of driving was old as applied to other vehicles, but it was not old as applied to a weapon of war. It was to be steered in a particular way and it was to be capable of doing something and of solving a problem which had never been propounded. I submit that it is one of the first principles of Patent Law that, had we had a patent with a claim of that sort, it could not have been upset by bringing against it a mosaic of a number of things where you had separate items shown in vehicles of other kinds. I cannot contend that it would have been the easiest of cases to have established, but I do venture to say there is a strong ground for suggesting that had a patent been applied for that patent would have been sustained under the circumstances. Be that as it may, I have recited the actual proposals and so far as they went I venture to suggest that you really had described there the essence of the Tank.[1]

In a well-known book on how to take out Patents we are informed that:

> Letters Patent for Invention are practically in the nature of a bargain between the Inventor of any new manufacture and the State, by which in consideration of the former disclosing clearly and distinctly what his invention is, the latter restrains others from using or practising it for a certain number of years (usually fourteen) during which time the Inventor retains the sole monopoly.[2]

Officers serving in important administrative posts at home or abroad during the War had no time to protect their own interests. Surely the Admiralty might have seen that their Officers' interests were protected. It is no use

---

[1] Attention is drawn to Mr. Harris Booth's Memorandum, page 224.
[2] *How to take out Patents*, by E. and A. E. Edwards, Fellows of Chartered Institute of Patent Agents.

the Admiralty saying the Tank invention was not patentable, and so wriggling out of their responsibilities. As I have previously mentioned they allowed the late Lieutenant-Commander Hyde Thomson and myself to take out a secret patent for the torpedo-dropping seaplane, which they retained. This was permitted because it was an entirely new weapon of war.

Major Bumpus, in his lecture on the development of torpedo-carrying aircraft, before the Royal Aeronautical Society, on 15th December, 1927, said:

> Carrying ourselves back therefore to the year 1914, to the elementary stage of development of aircraft and to the relative lack of operational facilities at that time, we must feel the profoundest admiration for the vision and faith of Rear-Admiral Murray Sueter and the late Colonel Hyde Thomson, who in that year took out a patent for the means of carrying a torpedo on a seaplane. The scheme devised by these Officers of the Royal Naval Air Service was undoubtedly the germ of all torpedo plane development in this country and, at any rate, preceded such developments abroad.

In the first place, to take out a patent, the invention must be new, that is the inventor must be able to declare that he is the first inventor and that to the best of his knowledge and belief, it has not been previously used by any other persons.

Now, was the caterpillar landship invention that I gave Mr. Churchill a demonstration of, and of which Mr. Diplock prepared a drawing for me, new. This drawing was laid before responsible Authority, the Admiralty Landship Committee, presided over by Sir Tennyson D'Eyncourt.

Nobody else had laid a caterpillar landship drawing before this Committee prior to 4th March, 1915. I claim it was new, and I claim priority. Nobody else had done it before, nobody else had produced a single drawing before that date and laid it before a responsible Authority. Suggestions had been made at the War Office, but they had been turned down by General Sir Scott-Moncrieff's Committee, who had no use for caterpillar armoured vehicles, whereas the Admiralty Air Officers pressed on, and we gave to Mr.

Lloyd George the demonstration of what a caterpillar machine could do at my armoured car station at Wormwood Scrubs on 30th June, 1915.

One of the conditions of grant of a patent is that the inventor hands to the Officer appointed by the State a clear description of his invention. My Diplock drawing lacked nothing in clarity. It had all the dimensions, weight, horse-power, armament, etc., clearly marked upon it. I had it laid before the Admiralty Landship Committee. Another condition is that the invention must be useful. My opinion on the value of Tanks would be useless. The German Generals say the Tank was one of the deciding factors of the War. The Army Council in their letter to me state they "are glad to take this opportunity of expressing their appreciative thanks for your contribution towards the perfecting of a weapon which had so weighty an effect on the fortunes of the Great War, and the modern type of which now forms so valuable a part of the armament of the British Army."

Most of the chief Nations have adopted Tanks, so I think my claim that Tanks are useful weapons of war could not be challenged.

I fulfilled every requirement, and asked the Admiralty permission to patent, and that my Air Officers and my name should be included in the patent. This was my usual custom when Director of the Air Department. There are in existence many patents in the name of several of my Air Officers and myself, in connection with aircraft, wireless telegraphy, etc. Why this permission was withheld in the case of the caterpillar landship and granted in the case of the torpedo aircraft, wireless telegraphy, etc., is difficult to understand.

It may be said the caterpillar system was not unknown in England, but I could not obtain any long caterpillar tracks in England. The Diplock Company could not manufacture them. We had to send to America, on Colonel Crompton's advice, to obtain the long Bullock tracks. These were what our first R.N.A.S. landship was mounted on. They were specially built for experimental purposes.

Therefore they were new as far as this country was concerned. Nothing like them had ever been produced in America. They were the forerunners of long caterpillar track work in this Country. Nothing like it or approaching them had ever been produced in this Country before, as far as this Country is concerned they were built for a new purpose. It is common knowledge that a well-known apparatus, however modified and altered so as to render it applicable to a new purpose, is patentable so far as the modifications and improvements are concerned.[1]

This means that long-track caterpillars for landships would be patentable. Now the question arises, would the patent be granted to a Turret Armoured Car? The Turret principle is old as far as Naval guns are concerned, but a turret holding a gun and mounting had never been mounted on the chassis of a car and the whole armoured before.

So many modifications and improvements were necessary, all new, that the Turret Armoured Car, as we built it for R.N.A.S. use, was patentable. Nothing like it had ever been produced in this Country before.

In my official letter to the Director of Contracts of 16th January, 1917, I stated:

> That some special steps should be taken to allow me to take out a Master Patent for Caterpillar Armoured Cars in this Country and Foreign countries, and if this is allowed I desire that the names of my two assistants, Squadron Commander Hetherington and Wing-Commander Briggs, be associated with me.
>
> Messrs. Fosters could then take out patents for any details they like. It would seem to me to be grossly unfair to allow any firm to take out any Master Patent for Tanks without including my name, as they are bound to bring in the general principles I demonstrated.

In my humble opinion, the Admiralty in respect of the Tank patents failed to protect the work of the Naval Air Officers serving in their own department.

Why we should, and I repeat it, give the United States of America the Tanks for hunting down their disturbers of the peace without making that great Country pay or

---

[1] *How to take out Patents*, by E. and A. E. Edwards, Fellows of the Chartered Institute of Patent Agents.

TO WHOM THE CREDIT? 215

acknowledge that they have acquired this weapon of war in some appreciable way, quite passes my comprehension.

To give such a very rich Country a new weapon of war, or a weapon for dealing with civic disturbances, was surely outside the duty of my Naval Airmen and myself.

Also, we learn on 8th April, 1936, in answer to a question in the House of Commons, Mr. Runciman, President of the Board of Trade, stated twenty-five licences for the export of 179 Tanks were issued in 1935. Neither myself nor those Naval Airmen[1] associated with me in initiating the caterpillar landship, worked to enable firms to export, at a later date, Tanks at no doubt a good profit, and the natural question for some of us to ask is, Where do those who initiated the Tank come in?

The late Mr. James Whitehead, K.C., stated we could have obtained a Master Tank Patent, and our names should have been associated with the general specification.

After the finding of the Royal Commission has been perused it will have been noticed under Sir Tennyson D'Eyncourt's claim that the Commissioners state,[2] "and further it was mobility rather than armament which formed the principal inventive feature of the Tanks."

From the evidence produced in this Book and the Royal Commission's own finding that I "urged on Mr. Churchill the importance of caterpillar traction for attack across country," and that caterpillars are shown on my Diplock drawing, it would seem that I introduced the principal inventive feature of the Tank.

Being Airmen, the Admiralty failed to look after our interests when on Active Service abroad, and when challenged say that they are advised that the Tank and its variable features are not patentable!

But the late Mr. James Whitehead, K.C., the celebrated Patent Law Expert, said it was, and he reminded the Chairman of the Royal Commission that "in many phases of invention the step is the conception of the general idea."

If my caterpillar landship drawing got out for me by Mr. Diplock as shown before the Admiralty Landship

---

[1] These Officers were Commander Boothby, Squadron-Commander Briggs, Flight-Commander Hetherington and Lieutenant Macfie.
[2] Page 199.

Committee on 4th March, 1915, giving the length, diameter, armament, horse-power, type of engine, turning radius, loading on tracks, etc. (Diagram I), was not the conception of the general idea of a caterpillar landship, what was it?

His late Majesty King George V alluded to the Tank being a British invention in his famous message to General Haig.[1] Surely, then, this novel British invention was patentable.

A natural question for me to ask is: Was Commander Burney allowed to take out Patents for his Paravane Inventions. If not, how did he manage to obtain £300,000 from Messrs. Vickers?

[1] Page 308.

CHAPTER II

THE CLAIMS OF THE ROYAL NAVAL AIR SERVICE

"Truth cannot die. It can only be injured for a time."
                                          CANON DICK SHEPPARD.

OUR great War Prime Minister, Mr. Lloyd George, informed us recently in the House of Commons:

When the War came the Services had been thinking departmentally, and not one of them was equipped with the things which turned out to be vital in the War. . . .

They had not even given consideration to some kind of appliance or mechanism to enable troops to advance in a battle against rifle and gun fire. The impetus for that came not from the Army, which was responsible to the soldiers, but from the Navy. . . .

The Tanks, which were a war weapon, were never thought about.[1]

No doubt it was natural for many claimants to come forward after the War as the sole inventors of the Tank. Many sought to reap where they had not sown. But fortunately I kept a copy of every paper, every minute, every photograph, and these show the part the Naval Airmen played in evolving a quite novel type of weapon for use by our Army in the Great War.

In ʽSeptember, 1916, on reading one of our London journals I felt it my duty to my Air Officers to put forward the following memorandum to the Board of Admiralty although it repeats in some respects what I have previously said. It is a concise statement of the case, and as the Tank has become an historic weapon, it would be as well that the history of this product of evolution, with the official papers,

[1] Hansard, 10th March, 1936.

be recorded and available to those who study the evolution of new weapons and new methods of warfare:

History of Armoured Cars, Juggernauts, Land Battleships, Tanks

With reference to a leading article in the *Daily Mail* on the 18th[1] instant (copy attached) and to other reports in the Press on the invention of the armoured cars now being used at the Front, I submit that in justice to those who really conceived the idea, I may be permitted to place on record the history of their inception.

When instructions were received by the Air Department from the First Lord that the R.N.A.S.[2] was to establish an aeroplane base at Dunkirk and temporary bases as far inland as possible, it became necessary to develop an armoured car support to rescue aeroplanes which had to make forced landings in territory which at that time was overrun by bands of Uhlans (*vide* Air Department reports on 1st September to 31st October, 1914, copy attached).

As a first start Commander Samson was instructed to obtain some ordinary steel plating from the firm of Chauteurs de France, Dunkirk, and to bolt it to the bodies and in front of the radiator, etc., to form some slight protection.

This plating was found, unless the thickness and weight were excessive, not to be of much real protection, so a form of wagon was produced, mounted on a touring chassis and covered with flat armour plating, which after a series of experiments, was obtained .3 in. thick and which would resist the German bullets at point-blank range.

At this point the War Office were asked if they possessed any details of the necessary thickness of armour plating to resist rifle-fire at short range and were found to possess no information, either with regard to this or to the penetrative qualities of various rifle-bullets. Nor did they appear to have any information of what was considered desirable in an armoured car. From this point the War Office were not consulted in any way regarding the design.

These cars had to be made in such a form that protection

---

[1] 18th September, 1916. [2] Royal Naval Air Service.

could only be given with flat plates, since at this time the art of bending these plates had not been acquired and was only later attained as the result of further experiments.

On returning from Antwerp the evening before its fall, and having seen the work of the armoured cars in the villages between Antwerp and Dunkirk, I became convinced that both Lord Wimborne and myself were on the wrong lines with armoured cars. Our cars suffered from the lack of overhead protection and the crew were open to fire from snipers at the upper windows of houses and in the arms of trees.

After discussing several possible forms of cars with Lord Wimborne, Squadron-Commander W. Briggs and Squadron-Commander T. Hetherington, a revolving turret, completely covered, was decided to be the only real solution, and accordingly a model car was made on these lines in three-ply wood.

The weights were carefully worked out, and it was found possible to carry them on either a standard Rolls-Royce or Lanchester chassis. The work of making this car in armour plate then commenced and after a certain amount of experimental work, these cars were satisfactorily produced, and subsequently a large number of Squadrons were fitted out, which have given uniformly good service wherever employed under conditions at all suitable for their use. At the same time, it was realized that such cars carrying only machine-guns required to be backed by some heavier weapon, and the question was approached of providing a motor-lorry which could carry a three-pounder or even a twelve-pounder and the Vickers 1-in. Pom-Pom. Lorries were accordingly built protected by shields and armour plate to resist machine-gun fire.

These were none too satisfactory, as the three-pounder was not well protected, and the weight was almost too much for the wheels, although it may be added that these three-pounder lorries did useful work with the Army around Ypres.

About this time Squadron-Commander Hetherington brought to me an idea for mounting a 12-inch gun on a large land battleship running on wheels, and I subsequently discussed this idea with Squadron-Commander Briggs, instructing him to go into the matter in conjunction with Mr. Booth, the technical adviser to the Air Department, and to obtain all the information available regarding agricultural tractors and similar forms of machinery.

Finally, it was found possible roughly to design a land battleship which was protected as regards its vital parts by approximately 4-in. armour, and which mounted six 4-in. guns. It was considered that such a vehicle would traverse practically any country at a speed of about 4 miles per hour, and that it would be invulnerable to rifle and machine-gun fire, and also to that of ordinary field guns. Of course, heavy artillery would wreck it with a direct hit.

Several schemes were worked out, and eventually Squadron-Commander Hetherington, Squadron-Commander Briggs, and myself drew up a paper for the First Lord, proposing to build land battleships. The First Lord approved of the scheme and invited the First Sea Lord, Lord Fisher, to look into the matter. The First Sea Lord agreed and asked Sir Percy Scott also to go into the question.

The first R.N.A.S. design was to be a land battleship with the following rough data:

Armament	3 twin 4-in. turrets with 300 rounds per gun.
Horse-power	800, with 24 hours' fuel or more if desired.
Total weight	300 tons.
Armour	3 in.
Diameter of wheels	40 ft.
Tread of main wheels	13 ft. 4 in.
Overall length	100 ft.
Height	46 ft.
Top speed	8 m.p.h. on good roads.
,, ,,	4 m.p.h. on bad roads.

After discussion at a conference, Sir Percy Scott dissented from the idea of land battleships on the ground that heavy artillery would probably wreck them before they could be brought into use.

It was agreed that the original design afforded too large a target, and attention was then turned to reducing the diameter of the wheels.

At this point it occurred to me that we should abolish wheels and try some form of Pedrail system. Acting on this idea, particulars were obtained of caterpillars as used in the United States. Catalogues were collected and Squadron-Commander Hetherington was instructed to visit the Pedrail Company at Fulham and obtain the loan of Mr. Diplock's Pedrail, and a demonstration was subsequently arranged before Mr. Churchill on the Horse Guards Parade.

The Air Department obtained more data from America and discussed various systems and designs. Squadron-Commander Hetherington obtained a small caterpillar (Killen Strait[1]) and demonstrations were given in forcing wire entanglements, surmounting obstacles, etc., before Mr. Lloyd George, Mr. Churchill and various officials from the War Office.

I suggested to Mr. Churchill that the D.N.C. should be invited to assist us with the proposal. Mr. Churchill then instructed the D.N.C. and myself to build and organize a force of eighteen land battleships.

I had a private conversation with Mr. D'Eyncourt, the D.N.C., and for reasons irrelevant to the subject asked him to take over the work.

He readily agreed, our models were turned over to him and a Committee was appointed, consisting of:

> The Director of Naval Construction.
> Colonel Crompton, C.B.
> Colonel Dumbell.
> Squadron-Commander Hetherington.
> Mr. Dale-Bussell (of Contract Department).

The organization of personnel was commenced by Wing-Commander F. L. M. Boothby and Squadron-Commander Hetherington, and as a preliminary measure a landship squadron was formed under Squadron-Commander Hetherington, it being known as No. 20 Squadron of the Armoured Car Force.

Various experiments were tried with caterpillars bought in America, much useful information gained, and the original designs modified owing to the results of these experiments.

[1] This machine was procured on the advice of Colonel Crompton.

It may perhaps be remembered that the papers dealing with this subject were known as the "Juggernaut"[1] papers.

It will thus be seen that the Air Service was responsible for:
1. Producing the idea of the so-called Tanks or land battleships.
2. Demonstrating their possibilities;

after which the First Lord approved the building of eighteen of these land battleships.

The Third Sea Lord[2] inspected the Armoured Car Force at Wormwood Scrubs, invented a shield which was tried against other types, and encouraged the Air Department to use armour.

This encouragement had much to do with the determination to produce a land battleship.

Satisfactory trials were carried out in Hatfield Park in the presence of several Cabinet Ministers and the Naval and Military Authorities. The machine was accepted and the whole project handed over by the Admiralty to the War Office. It was at these trials it was suggested to General Sir Scott-Moncrieff, Sir Maurice Hankey, and other Army Officers, that orders should be placed for a large number of machines.

In view of the large amount of pioneer work carried out by Officers of the R.N.A.S., there is a feeling of disappointment that so much credit should have been taken by the Military Authorities without any being given to the Admiralty for starting and evolving the scheme of land battleships which has proved of value to the State.

This submission is naturally only intended briefly to recapitulate for their Lordships' information the history of the machines in question up to the time when the Director of Naval Construction took them over, and to bring to their Lordships' notice the names of the Officers primarily responsible for the idea and its evolution.

Acting-Wing-Commander W. Briggs and Squadron-Commander T. G. Hetherington are the two Officers concerned.

[1] Called juggernaut for secrecy purposes.
[2] Admiral Sir Frederick Tudor-Tudor, K.C.B., a very able scientific gunnery Officer, and most capable Controller of the Navy.

THE CLAIMS OF THE ROYAL NAVAL AIR SERVICE 223

A series of photographs, showing the first experiments and gradually leading up to what is now known as the Tank, is attached.

(Signed) MURRAY F. SUETER.

20th September, 1916.

On reading my memorandum, the Third Sea Lord, Admiral Sir Frederick Tudor-Tudor, sent me by hand the following minute, dated 29th September, 1916, with a verbal message by Admiral Vaughan Lee, then Director of the Air Services, that he would see justice done to the Air Officers:

S.A.C.[1] (Commodore Sueter).

I shall be glad if you will furnish me with a copy of your "History of the Tanks" for retention.

Your account exactly fits on to that of D.N.C. without overlapping or contradiction.

I have always realized that the conception and initiation of the idea was due to the R.N.A.S. and that you carried out the early pioneer work.

(Initialled) F. C. T. T.
(Admiral Sir Frederick Tudor-Tudor)
(Third Sea Lord).

29th September, 1916.

Even the very hard-working Assistant Secretary of the Admiralty at that time managed to spare a few moments and sent me the following letter:

ADMIRALTY,
26th September, 1916.

MY DEAR SUETER,

I have read the interesting paper about the early history of the Tanks and had talk with Evans as you suggested. In one way and another I have come into contact with the matter at various stages, and I am sure there can be no question that you are right in your narrative. I understand that there has already been a certain amount of talk at the War Committee about the

[1] The Air Department had then been reorganized, and I had been appointed Superintendent of Aircraft Construction.

cool way in which credit has been claimed in the Press in connexion with this invention by persons who had nothing whatever to do with its inception and the First Lord recently directed D'Eyncourt to draw up a narrative as from the time when he came in contact with the matter. Your narrative supplies the earlier history and seems to make the story quite complete. I have given it to the Secretary who, I understand, will probably send it on to the First Lord along with D'Eyncourt's paper.

Believe me,
Yours sincerely,
(Signed) O. A. R. MURRAY.

The courtesy of the late Sir Oswyn Murray in writing me that kindly letter was at that particular time of Naval Air Eclipse very much appreciated.

May I give what an independent person, not an Air Officer, not even an Admiralty Civil Servant, says with regard to the initiation of the Tanks.

In a report made by a very able Technician, Mr. Harris Booth, B.A., A.M.I.C.E., F.R.A.C.S., who was specially selected on account of his professional attainments by the Admiralty to assist the Air Department in technical mattters relating to the design of aircraft, stressing machines, investigating causes of accident, designing aircraft propellers, training a new staff in the technique of air work, etc., he states that:

> In February, 1915, Commodore Sueter sent Squadron-Commander Hetherington to me and I learnt from him of the new scheme.[1] This consisted in the construction of a much smaller petrol-driven vehicle, mounted on caterpillar tracks with an upturned bow and roller underneath, protected only by bullet-proof armour and mounted in a turret, a 12-pounder gun or a large number of machine-guns. For turning, the caterpillar tracks were to be worked independently, ahead or astern, and were to be driven by separate engines. He took me to the Horse Guards Parade to look over a caterpillar truck

[1] A different scheme from Major Hetherington's giant wheel landship proposals in which Mr. Harris Booth had assisted whilst working out the weights for me.

which had been brought there. He introduced me to the Director of Naval Construction with whom I examined and discussed the caterpillar truck. We agreed that the method of design and the materials of construction that would have to be used in the development of the proposed vehicle were very different from the methods and materials with which I was familiar, but fell reasonably within his Department.

I therefore reported to that effect to Commodore Sueter. The Commodore quite agreed that this was work for the Department of Naval Construction and said he would see the First Lord (Mr. Churchill) about it.

From that time I took no further part in the development of these machines. I wish to point out that the above scheme as discussed with Commodore Sueter and Squadron-Commander Hetherington at that date contained all the ideas necessary for the development of Tanks up to the date of their first appearance in action.

The following is extracted from Squadron-Commander Hetherington's evidence before the Royal Commission on Awards to Inventors, as I want to make it quite clear that a Naval Airman was the first to obtain the caterpillar machine for Mr. Churchill to see on the Horse Guards Parade, and that he gave to him the first practical demonstration in the War of how caterpillar tracks could be fitted to our turret armoured cars:

1802. Chairman to Major Hetherington: "You were sent by Commodore Sueter to see the Diplock Pedrail?" "Yes."

1803. "And you reported on it to him?"—"Yes, I think it had to do with these shields. I was sent down to simply look at it and I did not know what it was for."

1804. Mr. Gordon: "You knew about this Pedrail?"— "Yes, I made a report to Commodore Sueter, which satisfied him it was all right."[1]

In addition to this evidence, I have Squadron-Commander Hetherington's letter, dated 29th May, 1919, from

[1] Fourth day hearing, "Claim in respect of Tank Inventions," page 100, 10th October, 1919.

which I extract the following: "The caterpillar truck was introduced by yourself (Commodore Sueter) and not Lord Tollemache."

Also, in his letter dated 8th December, 1918, to me, Colonel Crompton writes: "I know you saw the Diplock before the date I joined the Admiralty Committee."

In these pages and in my Air Book I have paid the highest tribute and always shall to Mr. Churchill for his share in the evolution of the Tank. But, Reader, where can I go for a better opinion on how the Tank originated than to Mr. Churchill's very own friend "Ephesian." He is quite well known as being a man of high integrity with a great reputation amongst those who have the best knowledge of his work.

In his book, *Winston Churchill*,[1] on page 198, I find these very interesting words:

> The original practical conception, however, of the Tanks arises from a conversation between Churchill and Admiral Murray Sueter, the able head of the Naval Air Service, to whom the existence of Naval aeroplanes is largely due.

A very large number of Tanks were constructed with great rapidity during the War. Many Officers have claimed credit for this quick output and I am certain they deserve much of the Nation's gratitude for their share. But who was really responsible for this rapid development?

In many books on the War that I have read some are written by Admirals and some by Generals, but mighty few of these contain a single good word for Mr. Lloyd George. In my opinion, when many men were failing through fear, he was the one man who had more "guts" in him than any other politician in the War. It is largely due to Mr. Lloyd George, when Minister of Munitions, backing the Naval Airmen's landship ideas after witnessing the caterpillar experiments that I arranged with Commander Boothby for him to see at Wormwood Scrubs on 30th June, 1915, that led to the Tank being evolved and afterwards being put into production in quantity by his creation, the Ministry of Munitions.

---

[1] Being an account of the life of the Right Hon. Winston Lionel Spencer Churchill, P.C., C.H., T.D., M.P.

Mr. Lloyd George, with that clarity of vision which he was so remarkable for in the Great War, rendered a service to thousands and thousands of his Countrymen whose lives were undoubtedly saved by the development of the Tank and its production in large numbers for use by our Army in the Great War. Had he turned down the Naval Airmen's caterpillar landship proposals on that eventful day at Wormwood Scrubs, there would have been NO TANKS. Consequently, everlasting credit is due to Mr. Lloyd George for shouldering the responsibility for developing caterpillar landships, and those Service and ex-Service men who gained by the introduction of these mechanical weapons of war into the British Army will, I feel certain, join me in paying high tribute to this great Statesman for his foresight.

None of my Readers will, I think, dispute that Mr. Lloyd George has served his Country mighty well whilst holding many important positions.

For three years he was President of the Board of Trade, for seven years Chancellor of the Exchequer, for six years Prime Minister, and as Minister of Munitions he saved this Country from dire disaster.

On this count alone I submit all Service and ex-Service men should always salute this keen-eyed Welshman.

In support of my opinion may I quote the niece[1] of Lord Balfour. Writing some most interesting articles that recently appeared in the *Daily Telegraph*, she states in relation to Mr. Lloyd George becoming Prime Minister, A. J. B.[2] said:

> Personally I am sorry Asquith is not P.M. That is what I wanted. But I was all for Lloyd George being given a free hand. Since the war began he has done two big things—far the biggest things that have been done—and he alone could do them. The first was the creation of that Department for Munitions—a vast thing—a vitally important thing—we couldn't win without it. You may say he didn't run it, that such and such a great business Director undertook this part; such and such a Manufacturer undertook that part. But who

[1] Mrs. Blanche E. C. Dugdale. [2] Lord Balfour.

chose those men and overrode routine, and gave them the chance of working? Lloyd George, and Lloyd George alone.

When occupying his many high offices of State, Mr. Lloyd George has had to shoulder great responsibilities and give big decisions. But I much doubt if he ever spent a couple of hours to greater advantage in his Country's interests than he did at Wormwood Scrubs when witnessing our caterpillar experiments. His decision to continue caterpillar landship work that day meant much to the British Army, for are we not told by many German Generals who are, or have been, in a position to know, that the "Tank" was a determining factor in ending the Great War.

Having examined in some detail in the earlier chapters of this volume the foreshadowings of a weapon, suitable for trench warfare, the armoured car, armoured shields, the caterpillar experiments, the building of the first R.N.A.S. caterpillar landship, then Mr. Tritton's and Major Wilson's successful Tank, and those who made contributions to its success, also the value of Tanks in the late War as expressed by British, French and German opinion, we are now in a good position to survey the various proposals that were brought forward in 1914-15 and judge who came nearest to the successful Tank as finally produced by the experts, i.e. Mr. Tritton and his skilled staff of designers and constructors at Messrs. Fosters' Works, Lincoln, assisted by my Armoured Car Officer, Lieutenant Wilson.

Committee of Imperial Defence

Captain Maurice Hankey's proposal put forward on 28th December, 1914, to the Committee of Imperial Defence, that a weapon for Trench warfare should be developed and consist of heavy rollers driven from behind by engines mounted on caterpillar tracks was not adopted, and no action was taken on this suggestion by the Committee of Imperial Defence.

War Office

On 19th January, 1915, Major Tulloch put forward a Memorandum suggesting that land cruisers and lighter land destroyers to carry ordnance and machine-guns mounted on caterpillar carriages should be constructed.

I understand these suggestions embodied some of the ideas of Colonel Swinton for a trench-warfare machine mounted on caterpillars.

These caterpillar proposals of Major Tulloch and Colonel Swinton were turned down by General Sir Scott-Moncrieff on 26th February, 1915, as stated by the Attorney-General before the Royal Commission on Awards to Inventors.

ADMIRALTY

Lieutenant Macfie's proposals for hauling 12-in. Naval guns by caterpillar tractors, dated 5th November, 1914, were impracticable.

Major Hetherington's Giant Wheel Battleship proposals put forward in December, 1914, and as modified in January, 1915, were turned down by Admiral Sir Percy Scott.

Mr. Winston Churchill's suggestions for coupling up two heavy steam-rollers stuck in the heavy ground during practical experiments in January, 1915, and showed no promise if developed.

Squadron-Commander Briggs' Giant Single Steam-Roller proposal, put forward in January, 1915, was not taken up.

Lieutenant Barry's suggestions put forward in January 1915, were:

(1) Harnessing two Caterpillar Tractors to a heavy Roller for rolling in Trenches.
(2) Giant machines towing a large plough with a roller behind.

Neither of these proposals was tried.

Admiral Bacon's bridging device was turned down in practical experiments by General von Donop on 16th June, 1915.

Colonel Crompton's landship was cancelled before construction was completed.

Mr. Tritton's 16-ft. wheel landship was cancelled.

Lieutenant Macfie's caterpillar landship had to be stopped because of acute differences that arose between this

Officer and Mr. Nesfield, as disclosed before the Royal Commission.

The demonstration I gave Mr. Churchill on the Horse Guards Parade with a Diplock Caterpillar on 16th February, 1915, led to Mr. Diplock getting out for me a caterpillar landship drawing (Diagram I). This was the first caterpillar landship drawing made in the War, and taken before responsible Authority, which was the Admiralty Landship Committee. This was done on 4th March, 1915.

The dimensions of my caterpillar landship proposal when compared with the dimensions of Mr. Tritton's and Lieutenant Wilson's successful Tank are not without interest.

The drawing was shown at the investigation on Tank Awards held by the Royal Commission and is at the Admiralty with the Landship Committee papers.

Commodore Sueter, Director of Admiralty Air Department, proposed Caterpillar Landship. Drawing[1] laid before Landship Committee on 4th March, 1915, and now in Admiralty Office.

Mr. Tritton's and Lieutenant Wilson's successful Tank. Designed August, 1915. Completed January, 1916, for trials at Hatfield Park.

Approximate Dimensions on Drawing, Diagram I
Length, 38 ft.
Width overall, 12 ft. 6 in.
Height to top of turret, 10 ft. 6 in.
Height to top of body, 7 ft. 3 in.
(Crew, 8 men.)[2]
Horse-power, 92.
Bow and stern upturned. (Armament, 1 twelve-pounder.[3])
Total weight, with armour, armament, ammunition, crew, etc., mounted on caterpillars, 25 tons.
Will turn on a radius of 65 ft.
Pressure per square inch on ground, 12 lb.

Dimensions
Length, 31 ft. 3 in.
Width with sponsons, 13 ft. 8 in.
Height, 8 ft.

Crew, 8 men.
Horse-power, 105.
Bow upturned. Armament, 2 six-pounders.
Total weight, with armour, armament, ammunition, crew, etc., mounted on caterpillars, 28 tons 8 cwt.

---

[1] This drawing, with its sectional drawing, was laid before the Royal Commission on Awards to Inventors.

[2] and [3] not shown on drawing for secrecy purposes.

My submarine experience came in well in working out the approximate dimensions of a caterpillar landship for the consideration of the expert designers and constructors to build in exactly the same way as they constructed our first submarine boats at Messrs. Vickers' Works at Barrow-in-Furness.

As I am not a constructor or designer I could not take the job any further, and could only show by demonstration that Authority should have confidence in developing caterpillar landships for the use of the Army at the Front.

The efforts of one individual are of no avail unless with them can be coupled the skill like we had in the submarine designing office at Messrs. Vickers and their constructors to contribute to eventual success that we obtained with the submarines.

In producing a caterpillar landship I recognized from the first that there would be a score or more of different factors that would have to be considered by engineering experts. There is no more finality in a Tank than there is in the Whitehead Torpedo, submarine or seaplane.

Scientific discoveries may at any time alter the means of providing power for working the tracks.

Every type of Tank produced is usually an advance on previous types.

No person could produce the perfect caterpillar landship in one step.

There were many problems that presented themselves for solution. Some were not unlike those we had in introducing the first submarines into the Navy.

All submarine boat experts who have intimate knowledge of men working weapons of war in confined spaces will agree with me when I say my first effort was not a bad forecast of what the dimensions of a caterpillar landship should be.

Mr. Winston Churchill has had much experience of war. Also he has had greater experience as an Administrator in many public Departments. In the course of his official duties he has had to set his subordinates many difficult problems to solve. But I doubt if any of them ever made a better shot than I did in drawing his attention to the Diplock Caterpillar on the Horse Guards Parade that led the way to the dimensions I gave in my Diplock Caterpillar Landship drawing, which I claim was the first caterpillar landship drawing got out in the War to be placed before responsible Authority—the Admiralty Landship Committee—on 4th March, 1915.

It was almost a "Bull's Eye."

After leaving the Admiralty, and whilst serving in Southern Italy, in command of the Royal Naval Air units, I made again a protest to the Admiralty in connection with Tank claims that were once more appearing in the Press, and Commodore Heneage, in forwarding my submission, did so with this covering minute, dated 23rd September, 1917:

H.M.S. "QUEEN,"
TARANTO.

Submitted.

I have read with much interest Commodore Sueter's paper dealing with the origin of "The Tanks"; as these machines have now become historic, his request that the Officers who pioneered the idea should receive recognition appears to me fair and reasonable.

(Sgd.) A. W. HENEAGE,
Commodore, First Class,
Senior Naval Officer,
Taranto, Southern Italy.

And the Admiralty, in reply, sent to Commodore Heneage the following letter, which they have given me permission to make public:

C. Sec. 043/17/6608. ADMIRALTY,
Confidential. *8th November*, 1917.
The Commodore Commanding
British Adriatic Force.

With reference to your submission of the 23rd September last, No. 91/84, enclosing a report by Commodore Murray F. Sueter, C.B., R.N., on the subject of the origin of Tanks, I am to acquaint you, for Commodore Sueter's information, that they are advised that the Tank and its various features are not patentable, and that it would not appear that any useful purpose could now be served by the establishment of a special tribunal to adjudicate on the relative validity of claims which have been made to the discovery of the idea of the Tank and its development as a fighting machine.

Their Lordships desire me to take this opportunity of stating that, in their judgment, the idea of the Tank was the outcome of the suggestions and proposals put forward by Commodore Sueter and by the two officers, Wing-Commander W. Briggs and Squadron-Commander T. G. Hetherington, who were associated with him in this matter; and that whatever recognition may be due to those who were responsible for the development and improvement of the idea in detail, these three officers are entitled to the credit of having brought the scheme to notice.

By Command of Their Lordships,

(Sgd.) R. R. SCOTT.

I submit to my Readers that sufficient evidence has been produced in this book to show that my demonstration on Horse Guards Parade with a caterpillar machine on the 16th February, 1915, showing how a caterpillar could be fitted to our turret and three-pounder armoured cars, was the first practical step in bringing my caterpillar landship idea before responsible Authority, then Mr. Churchill, the First Lord of the Admiralty.

The second step was the Diplock Caterpillar Landship drawing got out for me, with the approximate dimensions on it, by Mr. Diplock and which by my instructions was placed before the Admiralty Landship Committee on 4th March, 1915. In this drawing I limited the weight[1] of my caterpillar landship with armament, ammunition, armour and crew to 25 tons, which was only 2 tons 12 cwt. less than the first successful Tank that carried out experiments at Hatfield on 26th January, 1916.

The third step was my demonstration with caterpillar machines, arranged in conjunction with Commander Boothby, the Officer commanding the Armoured Car

[1] Page 68.

Force, under my orders at Wormwood Scrubs, to show Mr. Lloyd George, the Minister of Munitions, that caterpillar landships were a practical proposition and well worth backing. The skilful driving of the caterpillar machine over many difficult obstructions by Flight-Commander Hetherington convinced Mr. Lloyd George that there was something in the Naval Airmen's caterpillar landship proposals.

The fourth step was the order placed by the Admiralty on 29th July, 1915, for the first Royal Naval Air Service landship to be built on the special lengthened Bullock tracks I sent Lieutenant Field to obtain in America.

The fifth step was the design and construction of Mr. Tritton's and Lieutenant Wilson's Rhomboidal type of caterpillar landship with sponsons designed by Mr. Tennyson D'Eyncourt, and angularized track on somewhat similar lines to that invented by Lieutenant Macfie, of my Armoured Car Force, and Mr. Nesfield.

The sixth step was the construction in 1917 of the Whippet Tank which reverted to the original type of Royal Naval Air Service caterpillar landship which had a turret instead of sponsons and it had modified angularized tracks as invented by Lieutenant Macfie and Mr. Nesfield.

In connection with this step it is interesting to note that a small caterpillar landship was shown at Wormwood Scrubs in July, 1915. It consisted of the turret and armour I gave instructions to Commander Boothby to take from one of our Austin Armoured Cars and place upon the Killen Strait Caterpillar tracks. The demonstration with this machine showed that light Tanks might have some value (Diagram II).[1]

In the course of my work as Chairman of the Conservative Party's Parliamentary Air Committee, I was accompanying some dozen of my Colleagues on a visit to Messrs. Vickers' Aircraft Factory; just before we left Palace Yard, Westminster, I went up to the Lobby for my letters.

One was from the War Office that I thought was a pension case.

On reading it I could scarcely believe my eyes, or was I

[1] Page 238.

dreaming? For in my hand was a letter from the Army Council that I had been waiting for nearly twenty years to receive. A quick glance and I put it in my inner pocket, and we were off to Weybridge.

This is the letter:

THE WAR OFFICE,
LONDON, S.W.1.

84 Claims 1905 (C.1.)   *10th April,* 1935.

SIR,

I am commanded by the Army Council to state that they have recently had occasion to take cognisance of the various stages in the evolution of the Tank[1] and they have observed with interest and gratitude the prominent part taken by you, and those Officers of the Royal Naval Air Service associated with you therein. Although, therefore, as recorded by Royal Commission on the Awards to Inventors, you were acting throughout within the scope of the official duties assigned to you, the Council are glad to take this opportunity of expressing their appreciative thanks for your contributions towards the perfecting of a weapon which had so weighty an effect on the fortunes of the Great War and the modern type of which now forms so valuable a part of the armament of the British Army.

           I am, Sir,
                 Your obedient Servant,
                     (Sgd.) H. J. CREEDY.

Rear-Admiral
    Sir Murray Sueter, C.B., M.P.,
       House of Commons.

I have no hesitation in admitting that through a fairly long career of ups and downs, this was the proudest moment of my whole life. And if it was the proudest, it was also the humblest. My humble self to be told that I and the Naval Airmen associated with me had earned the Army Council's gratitude and appreciative thanks for our contributions towards the perfecting of a weapon which had so weighty

---

[1] Mrs. Capron's claim to have invented the Tank was turned down finally by the War Office shortly before this letter from the Army Council was sent to me, p. 194.

an effect on the fortunes of the War. This was a great moment and indeed a big thrill.

For years and years I felt that this letter would one day come.

With my Colleagues we inspected Messrs. Vickers' interesting Aeroplane Works, and we found one of my old R.N.A.S. Officers had got out a most original design of an aeroplane on the Geodetic system.

This machine, with such a weight-saving form of construction, gave a good performance in her trials and is now in production.[1] Such a radical departure from the ordinary aeroplane design took my fancy very much. Whilst congratulating my former Officer on his work, I should have liked him to see the Army Council's letter in my pocket. I felt he would be as interested in his old Chief's caterpillar landship effort, as I was in his new aeroplane design, but scarcely believed it was true. After finishing our inspection of Messrs. Vickers' works, my Colleague, Mr. Oliver Simmonds, M.P. then the very efficient Secretary of my Air Committee, took me to his home.

As we commenced tea I told him I was the happiest man in the whole World. Anyhow, I thought I was. He wanted to know why?

I read out the letter and my Colleague jumped up and shook my hand most warmly, saying: "My hearty congratulations; Admiral, after all these years, you have come into your own at last." Later, Mrs. Simmonds came into the room and her Husband insisted on again reading the letter. Her remark was: "Isn't it splendid? You mustn't lose that letter. It is historic."

At dinner my very kind Colleague and his charming Wife insisted on drinking the Army Council's health, my health and wished good luck to every crew of any Tank in all parts of the world! This I thought uncommonly nice of them and showed a feeling of real comradeship which on that day was much appreciated by one who had received so many rebuffs in trying to develop caterpillar landships for the Army in their time of greatest need.

The Army Council's fine tribute to my work and those

---

[1] The "Wellesley" is the first Service aeroplane to be built on the Vickers-Wallis geordetic system which makes use of curved diagonal members.

Air Officers who were associated with me is the highest honour any man could wish for.

I am indeed proud of their gracious letter, and with great respect I submit my grateful thanks to them. Now my Reader must judge for himself who will fill the niche in the Temple of Fame for initiating the caterpillar landship experiments.

On receiving many requests from my former Royal Naval Air Service Armoured Car Officers to make public the Army Council's most appreciative letter for our caterpillar landship work that developed into the successful Tank, and having obtained the permission of the War Office to do so, I published it in the Press and, when doing so, sent a copy of this letter to the Admiralty. In my covering letter to their Lordships I referred to "my" scheme for fitting caterpillars to our armoured cars, as demonstrated to Mr. Churchill with a Diplock Caterpillar on 16th February, 1915, on Horse Guards Parade, still holding the field and that modern types of Tanks now used in the British Army are on the lines of my proposals and not those of Sir William Tritton's and Lieutenant Wilson's Rhomboidal type. I also pointed out that my claim to have initiated the caterpillar experiments that led to the construction of the Tank, as used in the War, is still watertight and has stood the test of many investigations of several claimants.

In my letter I expressed the hope that their Lordships will be satisfied that a Naval Officer serving at the Admiralty initiated a weapon that in the Army Council's words, "had so weighty an effect on the fortunes of the Great War and the modern type of which now forms so valuable a part of the armament of the British Army, and in this creative effort he gained the gratitude and appreciative thanks of the Army Council." In reply, the Admiralty sent me this kindly letter:

C.P. Patents.   ADMIRALTY, S.W.1.
7713/1935.   14*th May*, 1935.

SIR,

With reference to your letter of the 24th April concerning the question of evolution of the Tank, I am commanded by my Lords Commissioners of the

Admiralty to inform you that they note with pleasure the terms of the letter which you have received from the War Office.

I am, Sir,
Your obedient Servant,
(Sgd.) V. M. BADDELEY.

Rear-Admiral Sir Murray F. Sueter, C.B., M.P.,
The Howe,
Watlington, Oxon.

After the rather extraordinary treatment, described in the next chapter, that was meted out to me by a former Board of Admiralty because I appealed, on being rebuffed by the Third Sea Lord, to the Highest Authority for the recognition the Army Council now so generously give me in their gracious letter, and which treatment—I am certain —has no precedent in the great Service for which I toiled in much pioneer work on the surface of the sea, under the surface of the sea and in the air for some thirty-five years, I feel no one would expect me to do more than acknowledge the 1935 Board of Admiralty's kind action in answering my letter and sending me such a courteous reply.

DIAGRAM II.

THE BODY OF A REVOLVING TURRET ARMOURED CAR WAS PLACED UPON THE KILLEN STRAIT CATERPILLAR MACHINE AT WORMWOOD SCRUBS, JULY, 1915, AND USED BY OFFICERS OF THE ROYAL NAVAL AIR SERVICE ARMOURED CAR FORCE TO DEMONSTRATE HOW A LIGHT TANK COULD BE DEVELOPED. *(See page 234.)*

CHAPTER III

MAINLY PERSONAL

There are two sorts of people in this world,
Two sorts only that matter,
Those who build up and achieve,
And those who drag down and shatter,
And the "Noahs" belong to the latter.[1]

MANY Naval Officers and others are quite familiar with the words over the door of the Canadian Parliament House, which read:

"Where there is no vision the people perish."

If these words could be engraved over the doors of some of our Public Departments, much benefit to the State I am certain would accrue.

At each entrance to the Admiralty, in Whitehall and on the Park side, we should place this inscription in large letters of gold and have it illuminated at night, because I believe quite honestly that there is not enough vision in that great Department. Red tape always seems to strangle new ideas. To support that opinion it can be truthfully said the Admiralty showed no vision in not developing efficient means to cope with the Submarine menace that their Submarine experts warned them to expect before the War.[2]

They had no vision in not supplying Zeppelins, aeroplanes and seaplanes with aircraft carriers in sufficient numbers to act as the eyes of the Fleet before the War, as advised by their Naval Airmen.

They showed no vision in not developing Lieutenant Hyde Thomson's and my Torpedo-dropping aircraft that I showed to Admiral Lord Fisher and Mr. Churchill at

---

[1] With apologies to "Historius," *The Saturday Review*, 2nd May, 1936.
[2] *The Evolution of the Submarine Boat, Mine and Torpedo*, 1907. By the Author.

Calshot Air Station before the War. Admiral Beatty, towards the end of the War, pressed for our Torpedo-dropping aeroplane to be provided. Then hundreds were ordered, but their delivery was too late! Some of the Sea Lords had no vision in their destructive criticisms and open hostility to the Naval Airmen's armoured car and caterpillar landship activities.

On the 12th September, 1914, with Mr. Churchill's approval, I sent from the Admiralty Air Department the following orders for the Dunkerque Aircraft Patrol:

The object of this expedition is to establish an aerial control over an area within a radius of 100 miles from Dunkerque with a view to attacking any German Airships on their way to England, and preventing any temporary Airship base being established within the area defined.

The control will be established by means of an Aerial reconnaissance using Dunkerque as a main base, and will be supported by a force of armed and armoured motor cars with the necessary personnel and stores to enable advanced subsidiary aeroplane bases to be established 30, 40 and 50 miles inland. The whole area under control should be kept clear of small raiding parties of the enemy in order to secure any aeroplanes, which may have landed, from being captured, etc. The Force will consist of aeroplanes, armed motor cars with the necessary personnel and transport for the aeroplanes, and an armed force of 200 marines.

It is important to take any opportunity to attack the Zeppelin sheds at Dusseldorf and Cologne. Officers achieving this will render exceptional service.

Steps are to be taken as soon as possible after receipt of these orders, to establish the advance bases mentioned in paragraph 1, and a report is to be forwarded as to the arrangements carried out.

As related in Chapter I,[1] we sent out to the Dunkerque Air Station, armoured cars as soon as they could be completed.

During this early War period the majority of the Sea Lords were always a little hostile in their attitude towards

[1] Part I.

the Armoured Car Force that I asked Mr. Churchill to create in my minute of 1st September, 1914.[1]

Some people may consider it was most natural that the Sea Lords should not have taken kindly to the new ideas of their Naval Airmen.

Many in Authority at that time seemed to be influenced in all air matters, armoured car work, anti-aircraft defence of London, etc., by what Walter Bagehot so aptly expressed: "The instinctive hatred with which we are wont to meet a new idea and the terror with which we approach the mere contemplation of one." The Naval Airmen were confident that if aircraft were developed they would be for all future time of great benefit as eyes to the Fleet and did not take kindly to the many criticisms of those Sea Lords, however learned they may have been in everything appertaining to Sea warfare, who were not likely at their age to master the technics of Air warfare.

When hostilities broke out the Naval Pilots were quite new to air warfare and our first aero-engines were none too reliable, but the knowledge in those early days that Armoured Cars were kept in readiness and whose crews would have made the utmost endeavour to bring them and their engines back to safety if they had to make a forced landing in near hostile territory, gave my Pilots additional confidence in carrying out the completely novel and dangerous war work of attacking Zeppelins not only in the air, but in their sheds at Dusseldorf, Friedrichshafen, Evere, etc. Their successes are well known and have made air history.

The Pilots and engines at that time were most valuable. We could not afford to lose any of them as we had none to spare, and it was becoming increasingly difficult to meet the demand from so many quarters.

All this air warfare, with its new requirements that were entirely without precedent, was very naturally not absorbed readily by some of the Sea Lords then at the Admiralty.

The creation of the Royal Naval Air Service was bad enough, with its Airmen who were considered by some persons in Authority to be such an infernal nuisance, and

[1] Page 29.

who would not keep quiet with their new and awkward ideas.

The first anti-aircraft defence of London had to be recognized in its creation because at that time the Army had no one they could spare to undertake the work, and even the Zeppelins or aeroplanes might drop a bomb upon the sacred Admiralty. After one of the German air raids on London the Chief of the Naval Staff sent for me and told me to suggest to Mr. Churchill that the Flag flying over the Admiralty should be hauled down, as it might give guidance to an enemy's aeroplane in making an attack.

Mr. Churchill very rightly scoffed at this suggestion.[1] Although cordially disliked by many, as being outside the province of the Admiralty, the necessity for creating this anti-aircraft Corps for the defence of London was obvious to everyone in the Admiralty except the then Fourth Sea Lord, who waited until Mr. Churchill ceased to be First Lord and at that difficult time left no stone unturned to discredit the Air Department and everything we did.

One of his priceless Minutes taken from my good collection dated 8th June, 1915, has these helpful words:

> The searchlights in London and elsewhere are the most foolish contrivance it is possible to imagine.

To describe a Searchlight as a foolish contrivance gave me, a Torpedoist, no little amusement.

The Fourth Sea Lord's hostility was nothing unusual. But to have a Minute like the above circulated round the Air Department, for all the Staff who were working night and day to get the first Anti-Aircraft Corps for defence of London really efficient, was not helpful and almost heart-breaking.

The great mistake the Board of Admiralty made, in the early days, was to place the Air Services under the Fourth Sea Lord, who was I believe a great Sailor. But not being a gunnery or torpedo Specialist he could not absorb much of the technics of the Air Service.

In spite of the Fourth Sea Lord's absurd hostility the Anti-Aircraft Corps for London came to stay and became

---

[1] The Admiralty Flag is never lowered except on the death of the Sovereign.

a most efficient force. Being a real necessity it had to be tolerated by the other Sea Lords. But this awful Armoured Car Force which nobody at the Admiralty wanted except the Naval Airmen—what did the Noahs say about it? Most of them argued:

"The whole principal of armoured cars is wrong, or at least it is wrong that the Navy or anyone connected with the Admiralty should organize and run an Armoured Car Force. This is a job for Soldiers not Sailors. If the War Office wanted this Force they could have got it going themselves, or at least they would have asked officially that the Navy should create it."

In any case, and this to many critics appeared to be almost the worst crime—all these subsidiary services, as the Armoured Car Force, the armoured trains,[1] the Kite-balloon Sections and the first Anti-Aircraft Defence of London, are contrary to all precedent. They have nothing to do with the Navy. With the greatest delicacy I used to point out that all really successful ventures, from the construction of the Ark to the manufacture of an aeroplane, have been "contrary to all precedent," and further they were successful because they have represented unforeseen ways of overcoming difficulties and meeting requirements at that time. But the Noahs were adamant, everything to do with armoured cars was wrong. Just fancy seeing armoured cars in the courtyard of the Whitehall side of the Admiralty and flying the much-honoured White Ensign. "Send for the Director of the Air Department," quoth the Second Sea Lord in his wrath.

When I appeared before that august presence he was literally bubbling over with annoyance, and I was met with "D.A.D.,[2] what do you mean by allowing these awful armoured cars of yours with their objectionable smells to fly the White Ensign?" (Plate LII). "Nothing to do with me, Sir. The First Lord (Mr. Churchill) gave the order. He is inspecting the Armoured Cars to-morrow morning

---

[1] These Armoured Trains that we had operating in Belgium were run by Naval crews under a very gallant Officer, Commander A. Scott Littlejohns, R.N.; they were most successful in the early days of the War, and won considerable praise from our Army Chiefs. He was assisted by Lieutenant G. Muirhead-Gould, an Officer of outstanding merit, who was never perturbed, no matter what difficulty or unforeseen occurrence arose on active service. He was a splendid example to his men, who would follow him anywhere.

[2] Director of Air Department.

at eleven o'clock. I hope you will be able to find time to come and see them. We have some of the smartest mechanics in London, and they turn out really well."

The Second Sea Lord declined, saying he was not interested in the Armoured Cars or those stupid Caterpillar landships, and it was not the business of the Navy to run Land Forces.

"That is quite true," I replied, "but we cannot very well leave our Pilots who may have to make a forced landing through engine trouble in Enemy's country when patrolling for Zeppelins from Dunkirk, without trying to make some attempt to bring them and their engine in, and the landships may some day be useful."

After Mr. Churchill left the Admiralty towards the end of May, 1915, the ill-concealed hostility to all the Subsidiary Services that had become part of the Royal Naval Air Service grew and grew. All the Naval Airmen much regretted the unfortunate differences with Admiral Lord Fisher, which led to Mr. Churchill ceasing to be First Lord. Then I was left in a most difficult position by him and, single-handed, had to defend the Air and Subsidiary Services policy he had laid down, against the hostility of most of the Sea Lords. They were more or less silent when Mr. Churchill was First Lord and only became openly hostile to everything connected with the Air Services, after he had left the Admiralty. Then the criticisms of the Anti-Aircraft Corps for defence of London, and the Armoured Car Force were growing daily. Nothing was right with them. The Fourth Sea Lord said: "Look at No. 20 Squadron, they have been idle for months and months. Caterpillar landships are idiotic and useless. Nobody has asked for them and nobody wants them. These Officers and men are wasting their time and are not pulling their proper weight in the War. If I had my way I would disband the whole lot of them. Anyhow I am going to do my best to see that this is done and stop all this armoured car and caterpillar landship nonsense." Remarkable to record, these views of the Fourth Sea Lord were not expressed openly to Mr. Churchill whilst he was First Lord, and only after he left did they become so vocal and so very hostile.

In June, 1915, the First Sea Lord informed me in the presence of the other three Sea Lords, that I had ordered too many aeroplanes to please Mr. Churchill, spent too much money, and in fact the Royal Naval Air Service, armoured cars and caterpillar experiments were scarcely wanted.

I smiled and said many more aeroplanes, many more armoured cars and probably caterpillar landships would be required before the War ended, and this cutting down of the Royal Naval Air Service[1] would be regretted. For this daring impudence in challenging all the Sea Lords I became a marked man. I had the audacity to differ from Authority. In war time, too!

On 30th June, 1915, in an official paper dealing with air and armoured car matters, the Fourth Sea Lord wrote:

"Motor cars have nothing to do with the Naval Service."

I retaliated by putting rather a stiff minute on this paper that was so obviously just, it caused the First Sea Lord to rebuke the Fourth Sea Lord, but to get a dig at me he said my minute was not happily worded. I did not mean it to be.

Mr. Arthur Balfour, the new First Lord, was very kind to me about all the destructive criticism that was going on and said most of the Sea Lords were so much against the Subsidiary Services we had built up under Mr. Churchill's administration, that I had better make the best of it and turn over what was possible to the Army.

In conversation with the new First Lord I said that all these Subsidiary Services had justified themselves. Each one had proved to be necessary so far as proof was possible, and it was merely quibbling, in the face of the fact that they are necessary, to say that they ought to have been prepared by somebody else. I explained that the War Office had been so fully occupied with more important matters in many theatres of the War, that the Army could not take on this creative work; but the Army Council had proved their gratitude to the Admiralty by thankfully accepting a good many Aircraft, Aero Engines, Kite-balloons, and for developing these Subsidiary Services that they accepted with gratitude as soon as they had been completed. I gave Mr. Balfour, by way of illustration, what had happened

[1] The Royal Naval Air Service was then being reduced.

with our so-called useless Kite-balloon[1] Sections that I had created at Roehampton. When Lord Kitchener visited the Admiralty and interviewed me in Mr. Churchill's office, he asked if I could let him have some Kite-balloon Sections, as he wanted them most urgently at the Front.

With Mr. Churchill's permission I complied with this request at once, and when Lord Kitchener came over to the Admiralty again and asked for more Sections, he thanked me personally for this small service I was able to do for the Army. My Roehampton Air Officers and Ratings worked under very great pressure, and we soon complied with Lord Kitchener's wishes and sent over more and more Kite-balloon Sections to the Front. The mere fact that they were working at the express desire of the great Lord "K." inspired them with much additional keenness.

Mr. Balfour was quite interested and said that in his opinion this was the proper way for the Navy and Army to work together. He wished in all cases this could be so well done.

But Mr. Balfour said he was afraid he could not prevent the Sea Lords from breaking up the Armoured Car Force and stopping caterpillar landship experiments, as most of them were so much against the Navy having anything to do with this land work.

I explained how the Armoured Car Force was brought into being and how it was persisted in for many months in the face of many criticisms from some of the Sea Lords, but oddly enough the War Office were then asking officially for more units, as the Force had a definite effect in assisting the Army in certain places where they had been most needed, and had performed really useful service.

On several evenings Mr. Balfour sent for me and he appreciated my rather novel views on a good many matters connected with the air that we discussed. Airship technique always seemed to interest him, and our small Airships had done well. He was very much impressed with my caterpillar landship ideas. I begged him hard to save these landships from the wreckage, and told him that these machines, if we could make a success of them, would be most helpful to

---

[1] At a later date kite-balloons and kite-balloon ships were developed for working with the Grand Fleet, and at many places of strategic importance such as the Adriatic.

our hard-pressed Army at the Front. Our Landship Committee had, I knew, been some time in getting out a caterpillar landship for No. 20 Squadron to handle; but to make no mistakes it is necessary to make nothing at all.

While to make sure in the new circumstances that had arisen at the Front, we must develop some quite new weapon for trench warfare. Consequently, it became necessary to have two or three alternative Caterpillar Landship Schemes either in hand or in mind, such as outlined in my Diplock Caterpillar Landship drawing, Lieutenant Macfie's caterpillar machine I gave him permission to construct, Colonel Crompton's articulated machines and the Bullock Caterpillar tracks we were obtaining from America, one of which, if the work continued, might become an experimental success, and it did.

After many discussions with Mr. Balfour on the question of the future of the Naval Air Service, the retention of the Anti-Aircraft Corps of London, the Armoured Car Force and the caterpillar landship work, he said he would carefully examine the air service papers and he agreed with many of my views, but not quite all. To chaff me, Mr. Balfour said: "After all, you did put the Admiralty Librarian in charge of a gun for the Anti-Aircraft defence of London." This action of mine he always regarded as priceless, and it caused him much amusement. I told him the Librarian, the late Lieutenant-Commander J. T. Perrin, had made an excellent Officer, and one night his gun had damaged the propeller of a Zeppelin, which alone justified my action.

As soon as Mr. Balfour had studied the whole position he sent for me and said the Armoured Car Force would have to be disbanded and the Caterpillar landship experiments carried out by my Armoured Car Officers would have to be discontinued as most of the Sea Lords were obdurate and so very hostile to all this land work. They were of the opinion that these Services should be taken over by the Army, that is if they would be of any value to them.

Once more I begged Mr. Balfour, if the armoured cars had to go, to retain the caterpillar side of our armoured car work and let me keep No. 20 Squadron for caterpillar experiments, as I had arranged to do with Mr. Tennyson D'Eyncourt, and I did not want to let him down.

This, after some further rather lengthy conversations and more enquiries, the First Lord approved, and I asked him if he would talk the whole matter over with D'Eyncourt, as I was certain that a caterpillar landship if developed would be of enormous use to the Army at the Front.

Mr. Balfour's Naval Secretary, one of our great gunnery brain-waves, Commodore Charles de Bartolomé,[1] listened with much interest to my caterpillar landship ideas, and was in favour of using armoured mechanical weapons at the Front. He was responsible for advising Mr. Balfour to retain No. 20 Squadron for experimental purposes until my caterpillar landship idea was thoroughly tried out.

We were most fortunate at that critical time in obtaining Commodore de Bartolomé's good support in saving No. 20 Squadron and the caterpillar experiments from the scrap-heap.

If No. 20 Squadron had been disbanded, it is most likely the whole of the caterpillar landship work would have collapsed. It was indeed a hard fight between the Fourth Sea Lord and myself; but thanks to Mr. Balfour's and Commodore de Bartolomé's great support I won. In this way No. 20 Squadron was saved for Mr. Tennyson D'Eyncourt; but all the Armoured Car Force and other subsidiary Services were to be placed under review.

After a conference had been held between Admiralty and War Office representatives, a letter dated 3rd July, 1915, was sent to the War Office, laying out the whole position and the way the Admiralty desired to get rid of most of the Subsidiary Services.

In August and September, 1915, the armoured cars were turned over to the Army and the Royal Naval Armoured Car Force was disbanded. Many of the Officers and ratings joined up with the Army's Armoured Car and other units. Whilst this Force was being discarded the Fourth Sea Lord showed me, with a good deal of unnecessary arrogance, the draft-orders that he had been largely instrumental in getting drawn up to disband No. 20 Squadron that I had saved previously for our landship work. But I saw Mr. Balfour once more about it and

---

[1] Now Admiral Sir Charles de Bartolomé, former Controller of the Navy, one of the most level-headed and highly efficient Officers the Gunnery School *Excellent* ever produced. He possessed exceptional talent of a high order.

through the good assistance of Commodore de Bartolomé, the order was rescinded promptly. Later my No. 20 Squadron did well in experimental Tank work and received the thanks of the Army Council for their good services (page 94).

In one of his most petty moods, the Fourth Sea Lord said he would not touch my caterpillar landship with a barge pole, and the Director of the Air Services, to get in a good dig at me as he thought, once came out with this priceless remark: "I suppose you have heard your Tank, or any damned thing you like to call it, has been a complete failure at the Front, as one of them has gone over a wounded man's leg and squashed it flat."

Whether this was fiction or the truth, I was not able at the time to ascertain, but these sort of pin-pricks left me cold, as they were made by Senior Brother Officers who in the opinion of many Naval Airmen possessed very limited brain capacity. It was mighty difficult for me to conceal from them that I shared this view of their capabilities.

On looking back at the hostile criticisms hurled at my unfortunate Armoured Car Force that was composed of the finest mechanics in London, how very stupid and unnecessary it all was, when we consider that the development of the armoured car led to the Tank, which was the first stepping-stone towards the mechanization of our Army and thereby commencing the greatest change that has ever been known in the long history of our Military Force.

During many years of pioneer work in the Navy I came across two distinct types of critics.

The first were my old Torpedo chiefs—Admirals Durnford, Bacon, Bethell, Currey and Stuart Nicholson. They were true critics of my work when we were introducing Wireless Telegraphy, Gyroscope Torpedoes, Submarines, Dynamo-firing for guns, and gun-fire control into the Navy. The scientific attainments and great ability of each of them commanded my sincere admiration and respect. For me, all the time I was working for these distinguished Torpedoists will stand out in my memory most prominently, because I profited by every moment of our close association.

They did not look for only faults in our experimental work, but took the good points in what we did or tried to do. They never tore down unless they could replace with something better. No destructive criticism ever came from the lips of any one of them. They would have despised themselves for taking that line. It was always the most helpful criticism—well-informed and constructive. Whenever a little extra help was required, or perhaps a kindly word of encouragement, it was always forthcoming. Any error was always pointed out in a nice way. These men inspired one's greatest endeavour and were Chiefs well worth slaving for.

How could we have ever succeeded with our first submarines if Captain Bacon, holding the position of Inspecting Captain of Submarines, had always been nagging and making destructive criticisms of all our underwater experiments in developing periscopes, proper diving rudder surfaces, efficient electrical storage batteries, torpedo discharge arrangements, air service for blowing water-ballast-tanks, perfecting air, water and petrol joints, efficient propeller blades for underwater and surface work, etc.

These details had to be attended to with very great care in our new designs and experiments following on after the Holland type, otherwise it might have meant the loss of a submarine with her whole crew.

Captain Bacon was simply splendid. Never once did I ever hear him make any destructive criticism unless he had something infinitely better to suggest. He was far too big a man to indulge in petty fault-finding over piffle.

Neither did I ever hear any of the other great Torpedoists I have mentioned descend to the stupid and destructive criticism I had to put up with at the Admiralty from the second type of critic, when discharging the duty I was called upon to perform in creating the Royal Naval Air Service, the first Anti-Aircraft Corps for the defence of London and the Armoured Car Force—the perpetual ignorant, ill-informed fault-finder, nothing was ever right with my Naval Air Service Pilots in the eyes of some of the Sea Lords I served under. It requires mighty little ability to find fault. Many of the incidents are recorded in my book *Airmen or Noahs* and need not be mentioned here.

The Lord Charles Beresford incident,[1] when he attacked

---

[1] "House of Lords Debates," Volumes XXI and XXII, 1916.

our air work and armoured cars in the House of Lords at the instigation of one of the Sea Lords, showed objectionable hostility to the Naval Airmen that cannot be forgotten.

Some of the Sea Lords in the early war period tried to use their Authority to bully me. I told Mr. Balfour quite plainly before Commodore de Bartolomé I did not care overmuch for their destructive criticism of my Air Service, Armoured Car Force or Caterpillar Landship work, as I found at their age they had considerable difficulty in assimilating new ideas. Mr. Balfour had, in addition to his political acumen, a well-balanced scientific mind and could talk on technical matters with a sound understanding. He laughed heartily at my candour and expressed the view that he was not at all sure my opinion was not right.

The mechanical demands of a new age make it necessary for the Admiralty to create the apparatus for a balanced judgment on new ideas that are put before them by their brain-waves with creative faculties.

To down Officers who may think differently from those who may at any time be in temporary Authority is merely stupid and shows that the "Crab Everything" type of Noah is in the ascendancy. He is the man the Pioneer of the future has to fight with every fibre of his being. If the vagaries of Noahs, whether they are on the Admiralty or War Office side of Whitehall, in opposing the creation of new weapons of war, lent themselves only to comedy, one could afford to dismiss them without serious notice.

Unfortunately their hostile attitude to the creative efforts of their own Officers, as instanced by Colonel Swinton's and Major Tullock's caterpillar proposals being turned down on the War Office side, and my armoured car and caterpillar landship experiments being ridiculed and contemptuously treated by more than one Sea Lord—lend themselves to dire tragedy. That is what was threatening the Nation when the Tank made its appearance at the Front in the War.

Fortunately, the Naval Airmen laughed at the hostile criticisms of the Noahs in connection with caterpillar landships.

They stuck to their belief in this new weapon of war in the most difficult times and through the most difficult circumstances. The Tank was developed from their caterpillar experiments and, when placed on service in adequate numbers, as the Naval Airmen always advocated, swept all before it.

No new weapon of war throughout the ages has had such a great success in such a short time as the Tank, and the laugh is on the side of my handful of Naval Airmen and Armoured Car Officers, who have been justified of their faith in caterpillar landships, and not on the side of the Admiralty Noahs with their stupid, unnecessary, ill-informed and piffling criticisms of their Airmen's creative effort, the caterpillar landship that, in the very skilful hands of their gallant Army crews, led the way to victory in the Great War.

As the Admiralty did not make an official announcement giving credit to those Officers who were responsible for caterpillar landships being brought into being, some persons started a wordy warfare in the Press to whom the credit should go. This irritated Flight-Commander Hetherington, who had played such a prominent part in advocating giant landships, helping so well in the development of our first armoured cars, our caterpillar and first landship experiments.

On 1st December, 1916, he sent a letter to the Editor of *The World*, protesting at some of the statements that had appeared in his paper.

For doing so this Officer was called upon to send in his reasons in writing for communicating with the Press.

Hetherington informed me later that in his reply he stated:

> A personal attack had been made on his good name in an article that appeared in *The World*, and as the caterpillar landships were turned over by Commodore Sueter to a Committee working under the Ministry of Munitions and they were now nothing to do with the Naval Air Service, he did not think he was infringing Article 14 of the King's Regulations.

A short time afterwards the Director of Air Services informed me that Hetherington had been severely scrubbed by "Their Lordships." I asked what for? The reply was for daring to write to the Press about those stupid caterpillar landships of yours, which everybody says are quite useless and a waste of time and money. The new Director of Air Services was merely repeating the brief he had received from the Fourth Sea Lord to discourage everything in connection with caterpillar landships. I took no notice of this unnecessary attack on my landship efforts by an ill-informed Chief who, when visiting an Airship Station, much to the amusement of the Airmen, did not know the difference between a blower and the engine of the Airship.

At the time I made a special note of this conversation in connection with an Air Officer who had worked so hard and done so much to make caterpillar landships a success. Hetherington, a young Army Officer, had won the respect and admiration of all the Senior Naval Air Officers he had worked with.

This hostility to an Air Officer seemed to me so unnecessary and such a waste of valuable time that should have been made available in an attempt to solve the many difficult problems we were up against on sea, land and in the air, rather than used to chide a Military Officer who had volunteered to work with the Naval Air Service in war-time.

Fortunately the displeasure of "Their Lordships" did not worry Hetherington overmuch, and he has had a further distinguished career in the Royal Air Force.

But nothing he has done before or since will come up to his valuable services and big part he played in helping to create the caterpillar landship that was one of the great mechanical successes of the War.

At one of the very last War Cabinet Meetings held by Mr. Asquith in Downing Street before he ceased to be Prime Minister[1] I was summoned to attend. On entering the Conference Room, a piece of paper was handed to me on which was written the Sea Lords' views on air matters which were to be discussed. On glancing at the paper, and not concurring in what was going to be said, I tore it up.

After many Officers of high rank had spoken, Mr. Asquith asked if anybody else had anything to say. Then he gave me permission to speak, and I begged him to lay

[1] End of 1916.

down a proper air policy and place a Statesman like Lord Curzon at the head of all air administration to enable us to get on with air developments. I told Mr. Asquith, the Airmen had waited many years for a forward air policy, but up to the present little or nothing had been done. There was dead silence in the Prime Minister's Room, the Naval Noahs all glared at me and the meeting broke up.

This action of mine might be regarded by Noahs as a breach of discipline. But a well-known Admiral used to define discipline as the intelligent obedience to reasonable orders. Most of the Sea Lords' attitude to Air development at that time was not reasonable. This was not only my opinion, but was also held by the late Marquis Curzon[1] as official papers could disclose.

Outside the Prime Minister's Room, Lord Sydenham came up to me and said: "Commodore, they will Court Martial you for that." So I replied: "I can't help it, Sir; my considered opinion must be expressed, no matter what the consequences may be to myself."

Having nailed my colours to the mast for a separate Air Service free from all Admiralty and War Office control, I was prepared for the worst. But that fine old Statesman, Mr. Balfour, would not let me be strangled by the Noahs, who wanted my blood so badly.

Relations between the Admiralty and the Air Board became exceedingly strained and all this friction was one of the factors that led to a separate Air Service being set up, largely on the advice of Lord Curzon, some time later by Mr. Lloyd George, then Prime Minister. Having expressed my views with considerable force to Mr. Asquith, I was delighted shortly afterwards to find myself appointed in Command of No. 6 Wing of the Royal Naval Air Service and instructed to hunt submarines in the Lower Adriatic with aircraft. The submarine sinkings at that time were very heavy in the Mediterranean. Consequently I was able to escape from the battles on the Whitehall Front early in 1917 and get clean away from the mud that sometimes accumulates in the vicinity of the Admiralty Archway.

Having initiated, as I have shown by the official correspondence set out in these pages, the caterpillar experiments

[1] President of First Air Board.

that led to the construction of the first Royal Naval Air Service caterpillar landship from which the first successful Tank was evolved, I was amazed when on board H.M.S. *Queen*, at Taranto, to be shown by Commodore Heneage an article in a magazine by somebody again claiming the Tank invention.

I submitted promptly through Commodore Heneage, the Senior British Naval Officer at Taranto, a letter of protest to Their Lordships, and the reply quoted on page 232 gave my Officers and myself full credit for initiating the Tanks experiments.

Having been recalled in November, 1917, from Southern Italy to London to give evidence in a law case connecting Commander Porte, R.N., with orders for Flying Boats given to the Curtis Company of America, I called upon the Third Sea Lord, and submitted to him that in common fairness to myself and those Airmen associated with me, could not the Admiralty publish their letter sent to Commodore Heneage at Taranto for my information, as it gave the credit for initiating the Tank to Squadron-Commander Briggs, Squadron-Commander Hetherington and myself.

The Third Sea Lord asked me why I was dissatisfied with the Admiralty letter. I said I was not, but it would be only fair if Their Lordships' letter could be made public, and it was against the Regulations for me to take it to the Press.

I informed the Third Sea Lord that his predecessor, Admiral Sir Frederick Tudor-Tudor, through the Director of Air Services, Admiral Vaughan Lee, had promised that my Airmen and myself would receive fair play for the Tank invention.

The Third Sea Lord said if the Admiralty letter was not satisfactory I could write officially my objections.

He did not think any useful purpose would be served by taking the matter any further.

My reply was that I had written a few days before and asked Their Lordships to issue a public statement, enclosing a rough draft embodying the chief points of the Admiralty letter giving credit to myself and my Airmen for initiating the Tank invention and showed the Third Sea Lord the draft. But he declined to take any further action in the matter. I told him it was most unfair to my Airmen and myself, and the interview ended.

At that time nobody knew better than I did that the pioneer Naval Airman's stocks were distinctly down at the Admiralty: they were then at their lowest ebb.

After leaving the Third Sea Lord, I took the advice of a very old Naval friend of mine, Admiral Sir Edmond Poë,[1] and told him I was thinking of appealing to High Authority over the "Tank" invention, as I had started the caterpillar experiments, and people were claiming the invention who had nothing whatsoever to do with it.

I told the Admiral that I had appealed to the Third Sea Lord, and he declined to do anything to put the matter right for the Naval Airmen. Sir Edmond then read with much interest the letter I had received from the Admiralty stating that my two Air Officers and myself had started the Tank idea, and said it seems quite clear from this letter you Airmen are responsible for the Tank invention, the Third Sea Lord should be pleased that you have helped the Army in such a practical manner. I do not understand the attitude he has taken up! "Most certainly write to High Authority, Commodore," Admiral Poë said, and he informed me that he knew for a fact that Admiral Lord Fisher, during many years of his Naval career, wrote to the Highest Authority, and in certain circumstances it was quite right and proper to do so.

The Admiral said if he had found himself in my position he would write to High Authority, and submit that recognition should be given to those Naval Airmen chiefly concerned in initiating such a valuable weapon that everybody in the Country was not only interested in, but distinctly proud of, and to judge from the accounts in the Press, seemed to be highly successful.

I thanked Sir Edmond Poë for his kind guidance, and in wishing me good-bye the Admiral said: "I feel quite sure the matter will be put right. But take my advice, do not give in to anybody. You have been doing great work for the Army, not the Navy. How you have managed to pull off such a success with a new weapon in such a short time I cannot imagine. In my gunnery days we would have taken

[1] Admiral Sir Edmond Poë, G.C.V.O., K.C.B.

years and years. If it was a Naval weapon there might be objections to you writing to High Authority, but as the weapon has been developed for use of the Army, and not the Navy, I am quite certain no right-minded person will object. Write the letter to-day. Make it quite short, and simply ask for public recognition. This will effectively stop everybody else claiming your work. The Admiralty letter you have shown me is quite clear and shows you were the first to initiate the Tank scheme. If you leave writing until tomorrow you may hesitate. After all, you have some responsibility in obtaining fair treatment for your two Airmen, quite apart from yourself. In fact, they will look to you, their Senior Officer, to put this matter right. All good luck to you, Commodore."

Fortified with this kindly advice from a very distinguished brother Officer and friend, I submitted a letter to High Authority, asking for public recognition for my two Airmen and myself for our Tank work.

Letters like this, when submitted to High Authority, are usually, as a matter of routine, referred to the Department concerned, and generally lead to action being taken about the subject in question.

The singular treatment meted out to me by the 1918 Board of Admiralty for submitting a letter on the advice of Admiral Sir Edmond Poë, asking for the public recognition that the Army Council's fine letter on page 235 shows was overdue, to the fountain-head of British justice throughout the Empire, is as follows:

After returning to Southern Italy, and whilst at Otranto in the Southern Adriatic preparing the Torpedo Seaplanes for my second attack on Cattaro—the Italian Commander-in-Chief, Vice-Admiral Vittorio Cerri, was again placing his destroyers under my command, as in our first effort on Cattaro which was frustrated through a storm rising on the eastern side of the Adriatic—I was sent for by Commodore Heneage, then British Senior Officer in command of H.M.S. *Queen* at Taranto.

On arrival on board the *Queen* he told me that for writing to High Authority asking for public recognition of my Airmen and myself for the Tank invention, I had incurred the severe displeasure of Their Lordships. I was ordered to haul down at once my Commodore 1st Class Broad Pennant, then flying in a "Drifter," and proceed home by the next train. My only reply was: "Very good, Sir. But I thought we were at war."

When he heard of this setback to my fortunes Vice-Admiral Cerri, the Italian Commander-in-Chief, was very much annoyed, as we had through his courtesy worked well together in establishing the British Air Bases at Taranto and Otranto in Southern Italy. This fine Admiral commanded all the Italian ships at Taranto and in the Lower Adriatic. He had been previously the Admiral Superintendent at Taranto, and was a very sound administrator and good thinker. He took practical steps against the Enemy's submarines by throwing a net across the Lower Adriatic, carefully planned air patrols in definite zones by Italian, British and French aircraft. These preventive measures gradually wore down the Austrian and German submarine menace in the Mediterranean until it became negligible. This great Italian Commander-in-Chief saved the Allies millions of money, as Admiral Mark Kerr in his interesting book[1] informs us that in 1915 the German and Austrian Submarines were sinking two million pounds sterling of the Allied shipping daily.

Whether Admiral Cerri was ever adequately rewarded by the Allies for his great services is not within my knowledge. But he deserved to be.

Admiral Cerri encouraged me to take out our formidable torpedo seaplanes with his destroyers in the Lower Adriatic, as he always hoped that one day we would bag an Austrian cruiser with a torpedo dropped from one of our Short seaplanes, and the Captains of the Italian destroyers were then full out for a scrap and only too glad to assist me in every way in their power in this new form of Naval warfare.

The Austrians feared these Whitehead torpedoes that could be dropped from the air, as after my Torpedo Seaplane Station was in full swing at Otranto they never appeared again in the Lower Adriatic. Previous to this station being established the Austrian cruisers damaged very heavily by gun-fire the British drifters guarding the nets.

[1] *Land, Sea and Air.*

When Admiral Cerri learnt that I was suddenly ordered home he sent for me to ascertain the reason. I told him, and the Admiral said it was disgraceful if other people in my absence on active service in Southern Italy were claiming the Tank invention, and added that Admiral Mark Kerr had told him the Tank invention was due to British Admiralty Officers, but he had never heard any names mentioned. In his opinion I was quite right to fight for what was my work and he would do the same if in my position.

In saying good-bye Admiral Cerri held my hand and told me "*to tell the Admiralty Sea Lords that it did not help the War by removing me just at the very time he needed my services most.*"

Commodore Heneage's instructions were to me that I was to leave without fuss and say good-bye to nobody. This order was carried out on my part, but quite unknown to me Admiral Cerri ordered out all the available Italian Officers in the Port of Taranto, and with his Admiral Superintendent came to the railway station to give me a final send-off, and said again that I was being treated unfairly.

As the train left the Commander-in-Chief and his Italian Officers cheered me over and over again. This was a great compliment and I have never seen before or since such a demonstration of goodwill towards any Foreign Officer.

To my surprise, running along the platform from the front end of the train, was the Commander-in-Chief's Secretary, and he thrust the following letter into my hand:

Naval Command,
  Taranto.
                                                     17th *January*, 1918.

Dear Commodore,
        On the occasion of your giving up, by order, the Command of the R.N.A.S. in the Adriatic, it affords me great pleasure to express to you my warmest thanks for all the zeal and interest which you have shown and for all that you have done to help the cause of the Allies.

You will regret your departure all the more since it takes place at a moment when the new methods to be tried by the British Admiralty and the more favourable weather conditions render likely the attainment of those military successes which formed the goal of your unwearied labours.

I also desire to convey to you my appreciation of the tact, friendliness and unvarying courtesy which characterized all your relations with the Chief Naval Command and with other Italian Authorities, and by the exercise of which you have still further strengthened the bond of union between the Allies, which will lead us to victory against the common foe.

I ask you to accept, dear Commodore, my heartfelt good wishes and the expression of my deep respect.

Vice-Admiral,
Commander-in-Chief,
(Sgd.) Cerri.

To Commodore M. Sueter,
Taranto.

This was a kind thought and I valued the Italian Commander-in-Chief's courteous act very much.

Strange to record, a year had almost elapsed since the warning that I was to be downed had come from one of our greatest Statesmen, who possessed the finest brain of any man it has been my good fortune to work with. The late Marquis Curzon was President of our first Air Board, and was always grateful to me for the small Air services I was able to render him when he was appointed to deal with Air matters—a subject which at that time he was not familiar with.

Lord Curzon's very kind letter speaks for itself:

1 Carlton House Terrace,
18th January, 1917.

Dear Commodore Sueter,

I do not quite know what is to be your fate, though I have done my best to save you from the vengeance of those who seek to destroy.

I am sure that quite the worst thing that could befall you would be the knowledge that I had written you this letter, and yet I cannot forbear, now my connection with the Air Board is over, writing you a line to say how much I have respected and admired your courage in difficult circumstances and how greatly the Air Service in my opinion has profited by your initiative, knowledge and ability. Wherever they place you, I wish you well.

Yours sincerely,
(Sgd.) Curzon.[1]

Am I wrong, then, in asking the Admiralty this question —why should I be destroyed? What harm had I done in creating the Royal Naval Air Service from nothing, and devoting with some little success nine years of my life to air development? Also creating the first Anti-Aircraft Corps for the Defence of London and the Armoured Car Force? In addition, as these pages show, I was largely responsible for giving the Nation the caterpillar landship which the Army Council in their letter express their gratitude and appreciative thanks for my "contribution towards the perfecting of a weapon which had so weighty an effect on the fortunes of the Great War."

Admiral Lord Fisher always appreciated my submarine and air work. He was instrumental in having me promoted to Commodore 2nd Class, and Mr. Balfour, when First Lord, would not let me be destroyed by the Noahs for my air and landship activities, but promoted me to Commodore 1st Class.

Maybe some person in high office at that time in the Admiralty was the unwitting tool of the Noahs or a Scrambler for Credit for the Tank invention who needed a not too enquiring agent for his underground methods.

Quite recently I was interested to read the following:

"Tumultuous petitioning"—and some of our present-day petitioning is little else—was made an offence in the days of Charles II, the penalty for repairing to the King and either or both of the Houses of Parliament accompanied by more than ten people being a penalty not exceeding £100 and three months' imprisonment.

However, it was provided that it is not an offence for

---

[1] The late Marquis Curzon, Secretary of State for Foreign Affairs, formerly Viceroy of India; President of the first Air Board.

persons not exceeding ten to present any public or private complaint to the King or any Member of Parliament.

One may ask what happened to the 140 Irish Officers who petitioned the King just before the War on the subject of Home Rule for Ireland. Were they placed on half-pay? Perhaps the Sea Lords at that time were not aware that it is not an offence to present a petition to High Authority after an approach through legitimate channels has failed, and the above Statute is, I am given to understand, still in force at the present time.

Many of the New Board of Admiralty did not know the hard struggle I had in building up the Royal Naval Air Service and for some eight years to receive much criticism and little help when pressing for air development. The efforts of the Noahs to retard Naval air progress were the last word in gross stupidity and showed they were men with microscopic vision. Anybody could see that the air was bound to become of great importance to the Fighting Services, and I was right to fight hard for air progress to assist Naval operations in War.

The habit of a longish life, during which much experimental work has been conducted, has led me to take a long view and not a short one on most questions that I have been privileged to deal with.

I would ask the Admiralty this simple question: Who has proved right over air development for the Navy and the value of caterpillar landships to the Army—the Noahs or myself?

As the Board of Admiralty would be unlikely to send me an answer to this question, can I do better than let our former Prime Minister answer the first part of it.

Mr. Stanley Baldwin at the end of the two days'[1] debate in connection with the £400,000,000 loan for Defence Services, in one of the most Statesmanlike speeches I have ever listened to, stated:

> That this Nation should possess an Air Force of immense power is the view of practically every soul in the Country.

[1] 17th and 18th February, 1937.

After having had a good deal of my Air work retarded by the Noahs, and being called the biggest damned fool in the Admiralty by a Sea Lord for ordering the first Handley-Page aeroplane of large dimensions, on the ground that this machine would not fly—but it did—my feelings on hearing the Prime Minister's historic statement can be imagined. Moreover, I have lived to see the British Mediterranean Fleet abandon Malta during the Italo-Abyssinian crisis for fear of what the former Sea Lords had so often scoffed at, and which I had so often warned them would come—the Air Menace.

Moreover, the bombing of the German battleship *Deutschland* at the end of May, 1937, by two Spanish Government aircraft shows that battleships can be hit by bombs dropped from the air. I do not share Mr. Winston Churchill's view that to hit a battleship by an air bomb is as difficult as putting salt on a sparrow's tail (Hansard, 22nd March, 1937).

In this unfortunate attack on the *Deutschland*, the loss of life was very large.[1] Much structural damage was not done to the battleship, but only light case bombs were used.

The second part of my question is answered by the International News Service, which estimates that Great Britain has 500 Tanks, and more in the 1937–8 Estimates are being provided.

Also in Command Paper No. 5374 we are informed that two more Army Tank Battalions are being raised.

Once more I repeat my other question to the Admiralty. What had I done that I should be destroyed one year after Lord Curzon's warning letter? I often have wondered what Nelson's opinion would have been of the Noahs or the Scramblers for Credit for their underhand work.

As I contemplate what our great Admiral would have thought I can imagine the smile of contempt on his face—because he was a "doer" and not an arm-chair destructive critic of all creative work.

May I recall that Lord Nelson wrote in a private letter on the 8th June, 1795, when he heard of Lord Hood's resignation.

---

[1] In reply to a question of mine the First Lord stated in the House of Commons that in this wanton air attack on the German Battleship "the casualties were 32 dead and 60 wounded". Hansards, 16th June, 1937.

"O miserable Board of Admiralty! They have forced the first Officer of our Service away from his command."

Again when some unlucky but gallant Captain ran his ship ashore, and was censured by a court-martial, Nelson wrote to the First Lord of the Admiralty:

> You must forgive the warmth I express, for he is in adversity, and therefore has more claim to my attention and regard. If I had been censured every time I have run my ship, or fleets under my command, into great danger, I should long ago have been *out* of the Service, and never in the House of Peers.

A little more of the Nelson touch and less churlish chidings in dealing with those who have creative minds, and who decline at any period of their careers to smother their new ideas to please Authority, and who absolutely refuse to be regarded as a sheep by their Senior Officers, would do no harm in the administration of the Naval Service.

One night we were having a very interesting dinner party in the House of Commons, and one of the guests was Admiral Mark Kerr, who served with much distinction in the War as Senior Officer at Taranto, and afterwards did fine pioneer work in helping to create the separate Air Service. He received no reward for his very good War services. I went up to greet my old Chief, and to my amazement Mark Kerr said: "Well, Sueter, you do not look as if you were crushed." I replied: "No, Admiral, I am not crushed. But what exactly do you mean?" "Oh," Mark Kerr said, "did I not tell you? When you came out to Taranto I had orders from one of the Sea Lords of the Admiralty that you were to be 'crushed'."

First, Lord Curzon tells me I am to be destroyed, in his letter, page 260. Then Admiral Mark Kerr informs me that I was sent out to Taranto to be crushed by him.

What a delightful game of cricket the Noahs occasionally play in Whitehall. The good willow becomes a corkscrew. Surely it is up to the political Chiefs at the head of our Fighting Services to see that those who are serving the State well with their novel ideas are not "done down" by the Noahs who have none.

No wonder when I had the audacity to write to High Authority in war-time, as advised by Admiral Sir Edmund Poë,[1] with the view of getting the Naval Airmen associated with me and myself the recognition the Army Council now give us for our Tank work, I was downed. But I have never been able to understand why the Sea Lords in 1918 did not follow early Air precedent and send orders to the Senior Officer, Commodore Heneage, at Taranto, to have their pioneer Naval Airman—myself—shot at dawn on the quarter-deck of H.M.S. *Queen* for producing the first caterpillar landship drawing. For were we not told some ten years ago[2] that documents were found in the Kremlin, according to an investigator who had just returned from Moscow to Strasbourg, showing that in 1560 a Russian named Nikichka made a gliding flight from the top of the tower of the Alexandroskaia Sloboda Cathedral in the presence of Czar Ivan the Terrible, and landed safely on the Cathedral square. Nikichka had fitted a pair of wings to his shoulders and held a parachute, which brought him gently to the ground. The crowd, which included an English mission, hailed the feat as a miracle, but the Czar fell into a violent temper and, ordering the inventor to be brought before him, said: "This man is a sorcerer, and his invention is an invention of the devil. Man is not a bird and wings are forbidden him." He immediately gave orders for the bird-man to be decapitated, and the head of the unfortunate Nikichka was struck off.

Recently serving at the Admiralty was an outstanding figure—the late Sir Oswyn Murray, Permanent Secretary. He was one of the really big men of our Civil Service, and stood unrivalled for his administrative abilities. Few know the fine work Sir Oswyn did in his high office during, and since, the War. Not the least of his good qualities was the detachment which he allowed himself when the silly intrigues that unfortunately from time to time arise, and which shake the very foundations of our great Naval Service, and do so much harm to all concerned.

To create three entirely new Services from nothing is no easy task. Many difficulties arose of a novel character. There was no precedent in the Admiralty Office to guide me

[1] Page 256.   [2] *Daily Mail*, 14th January, 1927.

in building up the Royal Naval Air Service, the first Anti-Aircraft Corps for London and the Armoured Car Force, all three from nothing. Consequently I had on many occasions to seek the good advice of Sir Oswyn Murray, and I fear my Airmen and myself troubled him much.

I can picture him now—surrounded during the War with a great pile of papers needing immediate attention. Everything was most urgent in those days. He would at once drop the matter in hand and with a kindly smile say: "Well, D.A.D.,[1] what can I do for you?" Both Sir Oswyn Murray and Mr. Evans were always most helpful. They impressed upon my Officers and myself that in these new Services we should work up to as high a standard of discipline as in the Navy. This was not an easy task. But the few Naval men attached to the Air Department to assist me at that time worked most hard in this direction. Our young Pilots had not the advantage of the Osborne or Dartmouth tradition behind them, but the records show we evolved a discipline of our own which was of a very high standard, and compared most favourably with that of the older Services.

When the decision was given that I was to receive no further active service employment, I had some correspondence with the Secretary of the Admiralty, and remarked in one of my letters that the future was looking black. This was natural after so many years of rather difficult work that took up so much of my time. I missed more than anything else experimental work that had been of such absorbing interest in so many directions.

In his reply Sir Oswyn Murray gave me most sound advice, and I have passed it on to dozens of my old brother Officers in the Navy, Submarine and Air Branch, who through the exigencies of the Service have been axed with their future looking none too bright, when they have appealed to me during the last sixteen years of my Parliamentary life for guidance. As it may be helpful to others similarly placed, may I repeat it?

Sir Oswyn Murray wrote:

> But in any case you must not talk of the future looking black, as for a man of your age, ability and energy, there is work to be done of a kind that I venture

[1] Director of Air Department.

to think is even more important in these changed times than the work of a Naval Officer. I shall expect to hear of you undertaking such work and coming to the top in it.

Needless to say, I took this very kindly advice. Turned a complete somersault as far as my Naval career was concerned, and sought a second career.

Pioneers like myself often hold convictions which are unpopular to Authority, particularly in a super-conservative service like the Navy. My submarine and air views were seldom popular. But when it came to armoured cars and caterpillar landships, it was a downright fight between the Fourth Sea Lord and myself. I refused to budge one inch, as I felt I was perfectly right in pressing my caterpillar landship ideas, and adhered to my air convictions, no matter what happened to myself.

Had I taken a different course and travelled the line of least resistance and said "Yes, Sir," "No, Sir," "Of course, Sir," "You are quite right, Sir," and similar piffle, no doubt much personal advantage with good posts would have come my way. But I took the long view over air development for the Navy, and the value of caterpillar landships to the British Army, and have proved right. So I can afford to laugh very loudly at the dear Noahs for their lack of vision.

I have mentioned these personal incidents that caused the Board of Admiralty over twenty years ago to censure first Flight-Commander Hetherington, then myself, the two Naval Airmen who were so largely responsible for initiating caterpillar landships, not out of any feeling of hostility to the Admiralty or of a personal grievance. I have none. No useful purpose is ever served by crying over spilt milk.

Pioneers like myself have always to take the good with the bad. It is only weak-kneed men who allow personal grievances to get the better of their good judgment. No sensible man should pander to such stupid sentiments or ever yield for one single moment to self-pity. That is a most disastrous course to take, and in my opinion shows a man is not master of himself. No petty outlook on life for me.

I am quite certain none of the pioneer Naval Airmen have the slightest grievance against the Admiralty because certain Noahs showed such open hostility to air development.

Their hostile actions indicated to the Naval Airmen that they were making good air progress and doing their jobs most efficiently and courageously. The hostility to armoured cars and caterpillar landships largely arose from a lack of vision and disinclination to study new ideas on the part of the Noahs —Noahs of the past have shown the same bad symptoms.

All responsible Authority will no doubt concur that the Tank, which was evolved from very small beginnings, was a determining factor in ending the War, and, moreover, saved thousands of the lives of our Army comrades.

It was merely stupid for the Fourth Sea Lord and some of the other Sea Lords after Mr. Churchill left the Admiralty to do all in their power to damn our armoured car and caterpillar landship work, as the official papers can show. Surely every Officer, even those called temporarily to high positions, should work in war-time with every fibre of his being to strengthen the bulwark of the State when it is in danger by the introduction of any new weapon of war that appears promising. In our novel experiments we were dogged by those amiable Noahs who circulated so freely round the Admiralty Office that caterpillar landships were useless, without being able to offer a single technical opinion on why those caterpillar experiments would fail.

Hostile criticism and crabbing every new effort, without having the ability to suggest something better, in war-time does not carry one very far and leads nowhere.

My point is that those who did so much to initiate caterpillar landships and create the confidence of Authority in these novel weapons, which was no easy task, should have received a little more considerate treatment. To do otherwise does not really hurt an Officer who has initiated a new and successful weapon of war such as the Tank, but it brings Authority into some contempt. All through the Admiralty neglected the interests of their Naval Airmen, who had the "guts" to advocate a new weapon of war for the Army. They were Admiralty Officers, and if the Admiralty cannot look after the interests of those who are serving them or the State, well, we come to a sorry state of affairs.

Serving Officers in the War had no leisure or opportunity when abroad to obtain advice on how to protect their personal interests. They are not allowed by the King's

Regulations to communicate with the Press and give a true presentation of the work they were engaged upon.

I fully recognize that during every war there will be friction. The great Prussian General and military writer, Clausewitz, refers in his writings to frictions of war. Recently the wonderful vindication of General Gough, one of our greatest fighters of outstanding merit, for his handling of the 5th Army in the Great War, by Mr. Lloyd George, is a courageous admission, and shows a bigness of mind that commends itself to his fellow-countrymen. This action is another feather in the cap of our War Prime Minister. There always have been these often regrettable incidents of removing very capable Officers from their posts, and I expect there always will be. But no one has written truer words or lifted to a higher plane what an Officer's feelings should be when the action of those in temporary authority have been grossly unfair, than the late Lord Esher, when he wrote these simple but only too true words:

Let those who are cavilled at, blamed, superseded, recalled, remain in good heart.

They have borne great responsibilities, run great chances, given all they had to give for England, and their critics are not worthy to unlace their field-boots.[1]

If "take off their sea-boots" is substituted for the last four words of Lord Esher's sound advice, they would apply equally to many a Naval Officer.

After reading Lord Curzon's letter warning me that I should be destroyed, no comment from me is necessary on the Admiralty's high-handed action in making me haul down my flag one year later because I submitted to High Authority that the recognition the Army Council now so generously have given to myself and those Naval Airmen associated with me for our Tank work should be made.

Anyhow, this chapter records with some amusement how I, the Admiralty's pioneer Airman, joined that great band of Naval Castaways, no doubt largely to please some Scrambler for Credit for the Tank invention, and because I refused to bend my knee to those very dear Naval Noahs who had forgotten how to think clearly.

[1] *Morning Post*, 10th April, 1918.

Where can I go for a better opinion on the value of those Officers who decline to bend their knee to High Authority to win promotion than our War Prime Minister? In his *War Memoirs* Mr. Lloyd George, in dealing with the attack on 8th August, 1918, states:

> The issue was one of the optime distribution of the man-power available. In the matter of Tanks, as well as in that of machine-guns and heavy guns, the common sense of the civilian, informed by the intelligent advice from Officers who were too independent to win high promotion, had saved the Allies from the narrowness and rigidity of Generals at the top.

May I ask who was the independent Officer who fought and beat the Fourth Sea Lord and some of the other Sea Lords when they tried to stop all caterpillar landship work? The answer is myself. Then I was supported most loyally by a little band of Naval Airmen, and we claim a share of Lord Haig's victories towards the end of the War that were made possible by the full use of Tanks.

These victories of our great General in no small way helped to the surrender of the German Fleet.

It is all very fine for the Admiralty during the War period to down some of their Naval Airmen, but I claim we did far more with the Tanks to help the Allies to victory than all the Admiralty Noahs put together, and may I submit that the evidence produced in these pages supports this claim.

After the War, when the irritation and strain inseparable from the conduct of gigantic operations were relaxed, a new Board of Admiralty were graciously pleased to review my position and recognize my former services with the view, I was informed, to mitigate to some extent the unfortunate severity of the action a former Board of Admiralty took in making me haul down my flag for appealing to the "Highest Authority" in our land in respect of the Tank invention. I was then sent an Admiralty letter in April, 1920, which stated:

> In view of the exceptional conditions under which you were retained in Shore Appointments and the valuable services then rendered, they have obtained the special

authority of an Order in Council (a copy of which is attached), to promote you to the rank of Rear-Admiral on the retired list when your turn for promotion arrives, without your having completed the necessary qualifying service as laid down in Order in Council of the 19th March, 1908.

For slaving at Air development during the best years of my life, from 1909 to 1918, during which time I created from nothing the Royal Naval Air Service, the first Anti-Aircraft Corps for London, the Armoured Car Force, initiated the caterpillar experiments that led to the Tank, a weapon unsurpassed in the Great War, the Admiralty did indeed show great generosity to a pioneer in promoting him to be a Rear-Admiral on the retired list! The ups and downs in a pioneer's life always strike me as being distinctly humorous. If my Colleagues ever see me in the House of Commons smiling as I walk through the Lobby for a division, they will know some reminiscences of first being flattened then elevated crosses my mind. To suffer the usual rebuffs and chagrins that a Pioneer has to put up with when carrying out original work, is in accordance with all precedent. Most Pioneers have a rocky time, for is it not true that the first man to take a moving picture on a celluloid film that started the cinema industry, died in poverty. And the inventor of the fly-shuttle which was appropriated without payment by the Lancashire cotton manufacturers, who made a fortune out of it, died in great want in a Paris garret.

Pioneers must always take the crumbs that fall from the rich man's table with due deference. An American[1] who had a good deal of contact with me during the War, when I was in one of the usual processes of being flattened for my air and landship efforts, which some of the Sea Lords of the early War period so cordially detested and which I forced and forced upon them in spite of their hostile attitude, as can be disclosed in many official papers, wrote: "Many have tried, but it is darned difficult to keep a cork under water. You will bob and bob well again." Maybe I have and this is how I bobbed again.

[1] Lieut.-Commander A. J. Stone, an Officer of outstanding merit in all questions of Air armaments, etc.

Shortly after becoming a Naval Castaway, as related in the previous pages, I became a candidate for that very fine constituency, the Hertford Division of Hertfordshire. In my first contest at a by-election I found my opponent to be a very able politician of much experience, Sir Hildred Carlile, Bart.—who had been a former Member of Parliament and was well skilled in political fights. We had an interesting contest. The High Sheriff declared the result on 16th June, 1921, outside the Shire Hall, Hertford, and it was a victory for me with a 6,776 majority. I am quite certain that out of all the hundreds of listeners when the figures were announced no one was more surprised than myself. To be elected a Member of Parliament at the first contest, and barely three weeks had elapsed since I made my first public speech, was following the same good fortune that came to me in my submarine and air pioneer work.

When I entered Parliament Lord Curzon had not forgotten me, and sent me the following letter, which I value, with many others of his, very much:

1 Carlton House Terrace,
S.W. 1,
21*st June*, 1922.

Dear Admiral Sueter,

I really do not know if you are an opponent or not of the Government of which I am a member.

But never mind. I remember the bold and courageous fight that you made for sound principles of Air Administration when we were associated in 1917, and also how you suffered for it.

Accordingly I welcome any success that comes your way.

Yours sincerely,
(Sgd.) Curzon.

It was indeed a thrill for a novice in political matters to find himself elected to the House of Commons in such a short time.

Shortly after this by-election I was approached by the Conservatives and asked to desist from being an Independent and join up with their Party. I agreed on one condition, and that was, a free hand was to be allowed me on all questions of Defence. On all other matters of importance I would consult the Chairman and Officers of the Association.

To find myself joined to the Conservative Party with my former opponent, Sir Hildred Carlile,[1] as Chairman of the local association, was a position that to many would have been awkward. But I found Sir Hildred Carlile, in the little friendship I afterwards formed with him, to be a great sportsman and a master of tact. He told me that I gave him the greatest thrashing of his political career. His guidance in those days was always most helpful and thanks to his generous character we never had any quarrels.

Since the first by-election we have had several elections.

The results may be of interest to those Service Castaways who could not do better than follow my example by taking up politics. They are:

1921. By-Election, 16 June:

Sueter	12,329
Carlile	5,553
	6,776

Poll declared at 2.15. 32,426 electors. 55 per cent polled.

1922. General Election, 15 November:

Sueter	11,406
Greenwood	6,534
	4,872

Poll declared at 1.30. 32,426 electors. 55 per cent polled.

1923. General Election, 6th December:

Sueter	10,660
Greenwood	9,763
	897

Poll declared at 1.18. 33,704 electors. 60 per cent polled.

---

[1] Sir Hildred Carlile was succeeded as Chairman by Sir Owen Wightman.

1924. General Election, 29th October:

Sueter	14,582
Davies	5,828
Selley	3,885

8,754

Poll declared at 1.25. 34,315 electors. 70 per cent polled.

1929. General Election, 30th May:

Sueter	13,525
Billing	10,149
Evans	6,419
Edwards	4,193

3,376

Poll declared 1.45. 45,795 electors. 74.5 per cent polled.

1931. General Election, 27th October:

Sueter	25,751
Edwards	7,092

18,659

Poll declared at 1.15. 49,023 electors. 68 per cent polled.

1935. General Election, 14th November:

Sueter	21,193
Edwards	11,492

9,701

Poll declared at 1.0. 50,975 electors. 64 per cent polled.

My good agent, Captain V. C. Roberts, tells me I should be proud of this record. I am. To win an election, I tell him, it is necessary first to have a good Chairman and then an up-to-date Agent.

Some of my contests have been, as the figures disclose, rather interesting. But my former Chairman, Sir Owen Wightman,[1] is a very astute politician of over thirty years

[1] Now Deputy President of the Hertford Division Conservative Association.

standing and he has always given me the soundest advice. For his courtesy and kindness that has extended over many years I am in his debt.

We have, thanks to all our supporters, managed to keep the Conservative flag flying in the Hertford Division for some fifteen years.

In that division we are fortunate in possessing an Agent in Captain V. C. Roberts who has worked extremely hard in raising our Association to a very high state of efficiency. His organization has stood many tests and has always come out victorious. Our victories have been largely due to his good work between the elections. Many elections have been lost by neglecting the outlying places in the division, but Captain Roberts has paid great attention to the villages and they have responded well.

Many of the electors in my fine constituency have been most considerate and kind to me in every possible way. They have done me a very high honour in permitting me to represent them for so many years at Westminister.

It is extremely difficult for any man to repay such confidence. All that can be said is: I am most grateful to my supporters: many of them are now my very good and much-valued friends. They are drawn from all Parties and are not confined to the Conservative Party.

During my thirty-five years in the Navy, the gunnery and torpedo Officers always seemed to me to be the salt of that Service and worked harder than any other men one generally came in contact with. Since then my views have altered and after sixteen years' experience in Parliament I can say the Members of the House of Commons put in a day's work that would be hard to beat.

Many of them carry great business responsibilities. They are always approachable by any constituent. Their letter bag is enormous. Committee work brings a large number of them to the House of Commons before 11 a.m., and very frequently it is the small hours before they get to bed.[1]

When controversial issues arise, the tact they have to use, not only with those supporters but opponents who may have extreme views, would alone entitle them to a crown in Heaven.

[1] On Wednesday, 22nd July, 1936, the sitting lasted over thirty-four hours.

Hundreds of people, and occasionally thousands, come to the Central Hall of the House of Commons to request their M.P. to put some grievance right or receive a deputation from some particular movement or receive a petition from the "antis" or the "isms."

Housing, transport, marriage laws, County Council Bills, reform of licensing laws, every crank with every sort of Bill, Officers about to be axed, and those already axed—all wanting jobs—borrowers of money, those who have reached a very ripe age, golden weddings, mothers with triplets, relations of those who have departed this planet, are problems or incidents in the day's work that generally need some attention from their M.P.

Then his advice is sought when family troubles often become acute. Heartrending cases have to be sifted and the best advice given or often action has to be taken immediately to prevent something worse happening.

Widows' pensions, naughty boys, accidents, careers for young men and women, British Legion cases, all have to be looked into with great care. Also bazaars and fêtes have to be opened and a good many dinners have to be attended.

Then there are the hundreds, that in the course of the year in some constituencies mount to thousands, who have to be shown round the Palaces of Westminster. All Members are ever willing to show the young people of the country where the laws are formed and made. Little time remains to prepare speeches for delivery, not only in the House of Commons but in the Member's own constituency, and his Friends' constituencies. Coming into politics rather late in life and looking at the devotion and self-sacrifice most Members of Parliament make in pursuance of their duty, I am of the opinion that their work is all too little appreciated by many of their countrymen and women.

Some people may consider that Parliament is slow of action. But it must be remembered many of their rules are based on experience running back some seven hundred years. When emergency arises, like it did in 1914, in 1934, and again in 1936, Parliament moved with immense rapidity. When the Members of the House of Commons feel that they have the support of the majority of their fellow-citizens they move quickly and decisively under the guidance of our gifted Speaker, Captain Fitzroy.[1] The tact and goodwill of Mr. Speaker to all Members of the House of Commons is well known.

As Chairman of the Lower Thames Tunnel Committee I have been assisted by my very able Colleague, Sir Irving Albery, M.C., the Member for Gravesend since 1924, who always gave me sound advice when taking many deputations to various Ministers in support of our Tunnel Scheme.

Mr. John Russell, who hailed from Gravesend, was a great tunnel enthusiast and raised a considerable sum of money for tunnel propaganda work. We were well served on this Committee by the pioneer of most of the schemes for a tunnel in the Lower Thames, Mr. Harry Towse, C.E. Our committee slaved for many years and pressed for a tunnel being constructed between Dartford and Purfleet. Eventually Parliament approved the construction of this tunnel, but work was stopped during the economic crisis. Lately it has been resumed, much to the satisfaction of my good Colleagues and myself.

But my main effort as a back-bencher has been to press for Air development, and that the Defence Forces of this Country should be placed upon a proper footing. Many Air Ministers have thanked me for my work on the Air Committee during the last fifteen years.

I was always fortunate when serving in the Navy in being somewhere about when the Admiralty required some new work to be undertaken, such as helping to introduce wireless telegraphy, gyroscope torpedoes, submarines and aircraft. This good fortune followed me in Parliament. Even as recently as February, 1936, I drew the first place in ballot for Private Members' Bills. In putting my name down on the list for the ballot 113 was the number if I had signed in order. But 13 being unlucky I skipped three lines and took 116. The Member standing behind me laughed and said sailors are superstitious! "I am not Admiral and will take 113." Immediately my good luck of taking first place in the ballot became known my letter-bag grew and grew. Everybody interested in a particular Bill begged my support to place it upon the Statute Book.

[1] Captain the Right Hon. E. A. Fitzroy, P.C., M.P., Speaker of House of Commons since 1928.

My able colleague, Sir Ernest Campbell, the Member for Bromley, a man with an extraordinary amount of common sense in his make-up, strongly advised me to stick to my Ministry of Defence Creation Bill.

This good advice I took.

When the day came for presenting my Bill (given in Appendix II), to my surprise a large number of Ministers, ex-Ministers and Members attended. I expected few, as it was a Private Member's Bill and the day was a Friday.

Having waited for this opportunity for some years and more than once balanced up in my mind certain of these defence matters, the task was not too difficult. Parliament is a good place for the test of nerves, and as I dislike speaking from notes it is not always easy for a sailor to find the right word at the right moment. But the report in Hansard of 14th February, 1936, shows I stated my case as fairly as I could and is given in Appendix I in full. Tanks were not overlooked in my speech. They are like submarines and have from time to time to be replaced by more up-to-date types. From the information in my possession a good many of our medium Tanks are becoming worn out. There is nothing more disastrous than for our very efficient Tank Brigade to have unreliable machines, and I submit to Authority that it is false economy to conduct training and manœuvres in Tanks that some experts state are not in a satisfactory condition.

Nobody could have seconded my Defence Bill with greater skill than Mr. Lambert. Having won the esteem and affection of the Naval men and Civil Servants at the Admiralty he has done exactly the same in the House of Commons, where every Member has a warm corner in his heart for this fine old Liberal statesman, who has done so much to help not only the Navy but our good friends the farmers of this country.

Mr. Lambert held office as Civil Lord of the Admiralty from 1905–14, so that when he speaks on the subject of the Navy he speaks with great authority. He is always most convincing in his advocacy of any Naval or Agricultural subject. His sentences are short and most impressive in their delivery. During our Defence debate he revealed that a struggle was constantly taking place between the heads of the Fighting Services and the Chancellor of the Exchequer. He argued that such should not be the case. There ought to be co-operation instead of competition—a linking up of the Services instead of a division and a weakening. Mr. Lambert's good speech made a great impression upon the House.

During the debate the late Sir Austen Chamberlain spoke with much force on the need for better co-ordination and co-operation in the administration of the Fighting Services, and stressed the point that Germany's Air power had been completely underestimated by Authority.

I thought it was a very courteous act for Sir Austen to come to the House of Commons on a private Member's day to support a back-bencher who was trying to obtain better co-ordination in the administration of our Fighting Services.

Both Sir Austen Chamberlain and Lord Eustace Percy, speaking for the Government, asked me to withdraw my Bill, otherwise, by the Rules of the House, we could have had no further debates on Defence that session. All I desired was that our Defence problems should receive greater and proper attention, and not wishing to embarrass the Government in any way, I withdrew my Bill. The Press throughout the Country were far more generous than my small effort deserved. I have ventured to give a few extracts from my Press cuttings to show the opinions then held on the value of this Defence Debate in Appendix III. In all some two thousand letters came from kindly persons in all parts of the World congratulating me on my speech.

Although the Prime Minister[1] did not travel the whole way with me in establishing a Ministry of Defence, on 27th May, 1936, he made the following important announcement:

> It has been decided that while the Prime Minister will retain, as he clearly must, the chairmanship of the Committee of Imperial Defence and of the Defence Policy and Requirements Committee, a Minister will be appointed as deputy-chairman of those committees, to whom the Prime Minister will delegate the following duties:
> The general day-to-day supervision and control, on

[1] The Right Honble. Stanley Baldwin.

the Prime Minister's behalf, of the whole organization and activity of the Committee of Imperial Defence.

The co-ordination of executive action and of monthly progress reports to the Cabinet, or any committee appointed by them, on the execution of the reconditioning plans.

Discernment of any points which either have not been taken up or are being pursued too slowly, and (in consultation with the Prime Minister or other Ministers or committees as required) of appropriate measures for their rectification.

In the Prime Minister's absence taking the chair at the Committee of Imperial Defence and the Defence Policy and Requirements Committee.

Personal consultation with the Chiefs of Staffs, including the right to convene under his chairmanship the Chiefs of Staffs Committee whenever he or they think desirable.

The chairmanship of the Principal Supply Officers' Committee.

It will be the duty of the deputy-chairman to make such recommendations as he thinks necessary for improving the organization of the Committee of Imperial Defence.

Confidential Reports

The positions of the Chief of Staffs Committee will be as follows:

The individuals composing it have a double function; each advises his own political chief, and, acting together, the Committee preserves unimpaired the right to submit confidential reports of their collective military view to the Chairman or Deputy-Chairman of the Committee of Imperial Defence.

It is not proposed that meetings of the Chiefs of Staffs Committee should normally take place under the presidency of the Deputy-Chairman.

He will supplement the present activities and initiative of the Chiefs of Staffs Committee by guidance and initiative of his own, his function being to ensure that every aspect is fully considered, and that difficulties and differences are frankly faced.

The Minister will be in a position to make recommendations as to any improvement that he thinks necessary in the organization of the Committee of Imperial Defence.

JOINT PLANNING

In any event, and for the purposes of co-ordinated planning, the existing Joint Planning Committee, which consists of the Directors of Plans in the three Service departments, will be supplemented by three Officers, drawn respectively from the Navy, Army and Air Force, who will be graduates of the Imperial Defence College.

The three new Officers will hold official positions on the staffs of their respective departments. Their work in their own departments will be chiefly that of obtaining the necessary material for the preparation of joint plans.

But the main work will be on collective plans prepared by the Joint Planning Committee for submission to the Chiefs of Staffs Committee.

In addition, steps have been approved for the strengthening of the secretariat of the Committee of Imperial Defence.

Shortly after this decision on Defence matters was given to the House of Commons, the appointment as Co-ordinating Minister of Defence of Sir Thomas Inskip was made. This is a very fine choice for a beginning because he can bring a legal mind to bear on the great problems of Defence, and I feel certain Sir Thomas being a hard worker and a very conscientious man will justify Mr. Baldwin's selection.

The appointment of a Defence Minister is a great step forward and one which in the natural evolution will, I hope, before long lead to a full-blown Defence Ministry being created.

After he has been in office for some time I am certain Sir Thomas Inskip will be the first to admit that better co-ordination and co-operation between the three fighting services was absolutely necessary for efficiency. But to be successful in his important office, Sir Thomas Inskip should not stand in awe of the Service Chiefs, and he must think more and more in terms of Air. All those interested or connected with Defence matters will be forced to do so.

We want not only good organization on the supply and personal side, but also the setting up of a "Thinking Machine" for working out the strategic problems connected with a modern war.

In giving these details in connection with my small efforts to obtain some improvement in the administration of our Defence Forces and the establishment of a "Thinking Machine" to deal with Empire Defence strategic problems,[1] I do so for the sole reason to show that a Naval Castaway may still be able to serve the State.

To give up hope and nurse grievances because one has been axed through one's own fault or because the exigencies of the Service demand it, always seems to me the very height of folly.

It should be part of the religion of every man and woman to see their Country efficiently governed.

Why should not ex-Service men take a greater share in this work is a natural question to ask?

Naval, Army and Air Officers gather much knowledge and experience in their travels in many parts of our great Empire and in distant lands.

They see how Foreign Nations run their internal and external affairs. Consequently, they are able to bring to bear the benefit of much experience on the problems of the day. Politics can offer to the Service Castaways a second and most interesting career, and I am certain it is always desirable to have a small number of Service Members in the House of Commons.

More than once we have been informed that Parliament is the embodiment of the coolness and good temper of Great Britain. This is true and never better shown than in the skilful handling of the delicate and critical situation that arose in this country towards the end of 1936, by our former Prime Minister, Mr. Stanley Baldwin. In that Monarchical crisis he showed a sterling character, combining firmness, patience, with much kindness of

---

[1] During the sittings of the very successful 1937 Imperial Conference it is gratifying to note in dealing with Defence matters, particular attention was paid to problems of technical co-ordination between the several parts of the Empire and the desirability of common arrangements for the production and supply of munitions in war-time.

heart, which raised the prestige of this Country throughout the whole world and earned for himself a high place in history that will be hard to beat. The Prime Minister was not only well supported by the back-benchers of the Conservative Party, but by Major Attlee, the Leader of the Opposition, who in a position which had for him many difficulties, so well played the game. Party differences were for the time buried by the Socialists to be replaced by sound Statesmanship of a very high order, which earned for Major Attlee and his supporters the gratitude, I am certain, of the majority of the men and women of our Country.

Although the work of a politician calls forth many home sacrifices, it is always most interesting, and from practical experience I can assure any ex-Officer placed in a similar position to myself, with no axe to grind, that not only our Country's and Empire's interests can be served, but also a good kick out of life can be obtained by becoming a back-bench Member of the House of Commons.

Ever since the Admiralty turned me down, then their senior Air pioneer, for appealing to the Highest Authority for public recognition for my Airmen and myself for our Tank work, which I thought was our just due, I have always had the feeling that one day all would come right.

Seventeen years after the termination of the War my long wait came to an end. The Army Council's magnificent letter[1] has given me the greatest possible pleasure in my later life, and is all the reward for initiating the caterpillar landship experiments that I ever wanted.

But why could not the Admiralty have seen that this was done before, is a natural question for me (a Flag Officer serving at the Admiralty at the time the Tank became a success at the Front) to ask, particularly when the great achievement of Commander Burney, in his successful development of the Paravane, received not only unstinted praise, but much financial reward, as shown in Chapter I,[2] came his way; whereas the only one of my little band of Naval Airmen, as previously shown, to receive any financial award for his share of the Tank invention was Lieutenant Macfie. Five hundred pounds—a maidservant's legacy—was awarded to him, which I am certain all fair-minded

[1] Page 235. [2] £300,000.

technical men in the Engineering profession will agree, was inadequate for his angularized track invention, which was a great feature of the successful Tank.

The Government, in securing the Tank invention for £18,000, plus one C.B.E. for Squadron-Commander Hetherington, did a deal which would make Shylock blush. Some of my Airmen were very badly off, and a small financial award that this rich Country could well afford would have been a godsend to them for educating their young children. They were strongly of the opinion that it was quite unfair for the Officers concerned in perfecting the Paravane to receive, from whatever source, so much money,[1] and the Naval Airmen who initiated the Tank practically nothing. Squadron-Commander Briggs always argued that the Tank did more to end the War than any number of Paravanes could have done with their very limited scope of utility.

None of my Officers wanted to make money out of the War, but they thought their claim should have received just a little more favourable consideration. The caterpillar landship—unlike the Paravane, an invention made by Naval Officers for Naval use—was initiated at the Admiralty for Army use by myself, as related in Chapter II.

The experiments carried out as shown in the many photographs in evolving the Tank, a novel weapon for trench warfare for the Army, was quite outside my Airman's or my legitimate air work.

We were, strictly speaking, misemployed. But to have our caterpillar landship taken up by the British Army, then used with some considerable success in the Great War, and have seven million pounds expended upon them, and finally to blossom into the Royal Tank Corps, and be the chief stepping-stone towards the mechanization of our fine Army, is an achievement Boothby, Briggs, Hetherington, Macfie and myself can be mighty proud of. No amount of Whitehall intrigues by the Noahs or Scramblers for Credit for the Tank invention can deprive us of this success in the Great War.

To have overcome the inertia not only of the Admiralty but the War Office in introducing a new weapon of war so novel as my caterpillar landship, which has influenced

[1] £304,800.

military thought towards mechanization in all great Countries of the World, gives me some personal pride that the Admiralty are quite powerless to deprive me of. Their Lordships could keel-haul me, have me shot in war-time, stop my promotion, wreck my Naval career (which they so kindly did), but they cannot take from me the feeling of good achievement which comes when one's creative work turns out so successful as it certainly did with the caterpillar landship.

John Morley once said: "Fidelity to conviction is the mainstay of human advancement." Those Airmen associated with me and myself certainly had conviction that the caterpillar landship could be made a good weapon of war. In spite of much opposition and open hostility, we stuck to our conviction and refused to budge one inch from the attitude we first took up. The Fourth Sea Lord did his utmost to break us, but we beat him. My only regret was that Admiral Sir John Durnford[1] did not live to see some of his good teachings come to fruition, not only with my torpedo-dropping aircraft, but with caterpillar landships.

We are often informed that Justice is the greatest interest of man on earth. I believe this to be true. It is the cement which holds Nations and individuals together. When fair dealing and justice are well established general happiness and security to humans prevail to a far greater extent than where these products of civilization loosely or scarcely exist. Fully believing in the sanctity of the spoken word, to obtain fair play, as promised me by the Third Sea Lord, Admiral Sir Frederick Tudor-Tudor, when he was Controller of the Navy, for myself and those Airmen who were associated with me in initiating the experiments that led to the construction of the first Royal Naval Air Service caterpillar landship, I sacrificed my whole Naval career.

I feel quite certain ninety-nine per cent of my Countrymen, placed in a similar position to myself, would have done the same. Like Neidpath I was called upon to hold the pass. Many precious things in these days are in danger. Not only justice but cherished beliefs in many Countries have been ruthlessly trampled underfoot.

[1] My Captain in Torpedo School *Vernon* and battleship *Jupiter*, one of our greatest Naval torpedoists.

All true men have to hold the pass to-day, and do their utmost to defend our liberties, the most important of which are justice, fair dealing and freedom. They are worth preserving and are the "Ark of the Covenant" which we must defend whatever the cost. Whilst travelling in many parts of the World I have found my Countrymen, whether they live within or without the British Empire, admired more than those of any other Nation for possessing a very true sense of justice and fair dealing, or what is and what is not good cricket in public life.

To fight for these liberties we need much faith. Faith has done most wondrous things in the past. It will work in an equally marvellous manner in the future. The great power of faith kept me going for some seventeen years, for did not Johnson write:

> "It is better to suffer wrong than to do it, and happier to be sometimes cheated than not to trust."

Also, did not the Rev. Burney, in my school-days, teach us boys at the Royal Naval Academy, Gosport, Hants, in our lessons in English history that:

> To none will we sell
> To none will we deny
> To none will we delay
> JUSTICE OR RIGHT.
> Magna Charta,
> 5*th June*, 1215.

Moreover, we have been told very often in this Country, that every human being, the civilized and uncivilized man is entitled to justice.

CHAPTER IV

TANKS OF THE FUTURE

"The key to the future is in the past."
AIR-COMMODORE CHAMIER.

THE Tank was accurately foretold in Holy Writ, for does not the Prophet Joel, Book II, verses 1–10, inform us that:

The appearance of them is as the appearance of horses, and as horsemen so shall they run. . . .

Before their face the people shall be much pained; all faces shall gather blackness.

They shall run like mighty men: they shall march everyone on his ways, and they shall not break their ranks.

The earth shall quake before them, the heavens shall tremble: the sun and the moon shall be dark, and the stars shall withdraw their shining.

In reading these verses we notice that a fair description of light Tanks, heavy Tanks and smoke-screens obscuring the sun and the moon is given.

In fact, modern warfare truly depicted. In discussing my first caterpillar landship proposals and going into the weight calculations with Squadron-Commander Briggs, I laid it down that we should start with caterpillar landships of small dimensions and then work up to larger types if they were required in exactly the same way as we developed the "A," "B" and "C" Class submarine from the small Holland boats.

During the War we did not develop in this country Tanks of large dimensions. The smaller Tanks were more in favour with our Military Authorities as they offered a less target to hostile gun-fire. Our heaviest Tank was the

Mark V, which weighed 27 tons when fully equipped, and at the present time the Medium "A" Tank weighs about 12 tons.

The French disliked the British rhomboidal Tank from the very first, chiefly on account of its ugly appearance. Many of my Airmen considered this was one of its great advantages, because the more ignorant German soldiers thought it such an uncanny weapon that the mere sight of a Tank, looking like some prehistoric beast, as it ambled along, caused some fear.

In addition to their light Tanks as described on page 157, the French constructed a heavy Tank of 65 tons, which was much on the lines of their Char-léger design, with the dimensions magnified ten times.

The Americans had a Tank under construction at Chateauroux of 40 tons. It was designed on similar lines to the British Mark IV Tank of rhomboidal form.

Towards the end of the War the Germans possessed a Tank of 45 tons, but for various reasons little use was made of this machine, and it was reported that they had one of 128 tons under construction.

If the War had continued for a longer period I am confident that Hetherington's dream of monster land battleships, carrying large-calibre guns, would have come true. During the last few years some experts do not seem to be able to agree whether Infantry Tanks should be seriously developed or whether the money would not be laid out to greater advantage in more high-speed Tanks.

There always will be controversies of this nature. We have plenty of them in the Navy over various types of surface ships. So far the Infantry Tank is largely in the experimental stage, but there is little doubt that its utility will be fully demonstrated in the Army annual manœuvres, to ascertain if this additional support is really helpful to the infantrymen or not. If I were an infantryman I am certain greater confidence would be within me when some supporting Tanks were nearby. The Army Council are, in my opinion, wise in developing Infantry Tanks.

There is every probability that Tanks with great speed will be developed that are proof against shrapnel, and the very latest machine-gun and rifle fire.

In addition modern Tanks will be capable of laying a smoke-screen in emergency. That is when they suddenly come upon a well-concealed anti-Tank gun. These guns will no doubt destroy some of the leading Tanks. But the provision of a large number of Tanks equipped with the latest smoke-producing device will screen the majority, and when located accurately, the anti-Tank gun can be knocked out by artillery fire (Plate LIII).

Perhaps the greatest difficulty the German Generals had to face in the late War was the transport of supplies to feed their men in the front-line trenches.[1]

For has not General Ludendorff stated in official papers that the 41st German Division let the British through the front line on 8th August, 1918, in the Battle of Amiens, but that it had suffered severely from influenza and had not received its ration of potatoes.

Road transport cannot carry all the supplies required by an Army. Railways must be used. These lines of supply are like our great sea arteries of food-carrying and trade ships. One objective in naval warfare is to sever as many of these arteries as possible.

Similarly it would seem that the greatest use the high-speed Tank can be put to is to cut the lines of supply of food and stores of an enemy to their Army. This would be a most suitable operation for Tanks to undertake, and in doing so, it would need the most efficient machines that engineering science of the day can produce. The greater the mobility the better.

Consequently it seems sound reasoning to press for very high speed Tanks to cut not only the enemy's rail arteries, but operate on the main roads carrying food and stores. These supply lines should be disorganized as much as possible.

Had I anything to do with Tank policy I would advocate the construction of every type of Tank the Army experts advocate. Large numbers are not necessary provided the nucleus is up to date. Quality counts far more than quantity. But every step should be taken by detailed factory organization to ensure that large numbers of any

---

[1] Small Caterpillar Tractors of high speed are not yet fully developed for the transport of Supplies and Ammunition to the front line. Germany's new Tractor when seen at recent manœuvres of mobile units near Hanover looked most efficient.

T

particular type can be produced with great rapidity. The type will naturally depend upon the war we have to embark upon.

Capacity for production is all-important, and our Military Authorities must consider this as the chief factor of Tank policy. Aircraft and Tanks, in my judgment, should have priority over all war material, and I submit this view to the new Defence Minister.

The other factor is training of personnel. All those who come in close contact with the Royal Tank Corps units are loud in praise of their high efficiency. This is borne out by Colonel James Dundas, who, in an interesting letter to *The Times*,[1] states:

> In respect of tactical training, my experience has been that under modern conditions greater speed both in appreciating a situation and in taking action thereon is necessary when either Tanks or armoured cars are in question than when the slower-moving horse is the medium of progression. I have found, too, that on the average this power of quick thinking and quick acting is more highly developed in Officers of the Royal Tank Corps (especially in the younger Officers, who have been brought up with the modern machines) than in Officers of mounted or other arms with whom I have come in contact.

In talking over the whole question of caterpillar traction recently with Dr. Emmet A. McCusker, a well-known medical man from Regina, Canada, he reminded me that agriculture was the World's oldest industry, and that thousands of Holt Caterpillars were used for agricultural work in Canada. These machines are often driven by old Airmen who served us so well in the Great War. I told the Doctor that many mechanical devices had been developed in this Country for farm work since the first motor plough was shown some twenty-three years ago at the Bristol Agricultural Show, and we were not exactly standing still.

The good Doctor then suggested mobilizing the men engaged in this mechanical work, not only in this Country but throughout the Empire, and form them into a Reserve Corps of skilled mechanics for manning the Tanks, should an emergency arise in the near future.

[1] *The Times*, 10th January, 1936.

I welcomed the idea, and if some more or less common form of caterpillar track could be used on the tractors with a standard type of engine to operate them, a complete corps of skilled mechanics could be built up at no great cost, and they would always be available for calling up for Tank work.

In further conversation I advised the Doctor to put forward his proposals to the Military Authorities on both sides of the Atlantic.

In the Autumn Military Manœuvres of 1935 we were informed that a large number of Tanks swam the River Avon, or crossed it when the water was up to the driver's neck. This would have interested my first caterpillar expert, Lieutenant Macfie, as he always advocated, when I gave him a free hand to build a caterpillar experimental landship at Mr. Nesfield's Works, that Tanks should be constructed so that they could swim a river.

If Lieutenant Macfie had not quarrelled so badly with Mr. Nesfield, we might have had some interesting experiments. After having dived the first Holland Submarines in the Barrow Docks and in the Irish Sea, it would have been a thrill to have steered the first Tank in swimming across the River Thames. Vickers 3 ton floating Tank is of considerable interest to those of us who considered this question of swimming Tanks across a canal during the War.

The whole question of the Army's requirements in regard to Tanks was laid down during the debate on their estimates for 1935, when Captain Douglas Hacking, then Financial Secretary to the War Office, in a very clear and Statesman-like speech, said:[1]

> The hon. Member for Central Bristol (Lord Apsley) asked me several questions. He asked whether the new machine-gun to replace the Lewis gun was a machine-gun or an automatic rifle. The answer is that the light machine-gun which is to replace the Lewis gun is definitely a machine-gun and not an automatic rifle. He spoke of the heavy cost of the Tank battalions and said the Japanese[2] were not placing great faith in this weapon.

[1] Army Estimates, 18th March, 1935.   [2] See footnote, page 169.

At the present time there are only five Tank battalions. Four of them, that is one light battalion and three medium battalions, constitute a Tank brigade, which must be regarded as part of the mobile troops of any field force. The remaining battalion, at Catterick, has been reorganized on a provisional basis as an Army Tank battalion intended for close co-operation with infantry divisions. In spite of the Japanese experience and after very careful consideration it has been decided by the Army Council that for modern warfare Army Tank battalions should be provided on the scale of one battalion per infantry division. He then spoke of the Tank battalions in India. I am informed that there are not eight light Tank battalions but eight armoured car companies, which will probably in due course be inverted on to a light Tank basis. I can only say that I have no doubt that the Government of India have thoroughly investigated the necessity for this number of armoured units, and it would be out of place for me to comment on that.

In mechanizing our small but splendid Army we must always recognize that wars of the future will largely depend upon the rapidity with which troops can be moved to points of strategic importance.

But care must be taken that in moving an Army that is largely dependent upon mechanical transport the whole force does not suffer in mobility by laying themselves open too much to hostile Air and Tank attack.

This traffic problem in moving a large number of troops must be exercising the minds of our Army Commanders. How to reduce the equipment and stores to a minimum to enable an Army to be transported without too much traffic congestion is a subject that needs the closest study by our Military brain-waves.

In view of the dangers that our railways are open to from aerial bombardment it would seem advisable to make more and more of our roads capable of bearing our heaviest Tanks, troop carrying trucks, heavily laden Army lorries, etc., as they cannot be put out of action like large sections of our railways might be in an aerial attack.

PLATE LIV

THE BRITISH MEDIUM 12-TON TANK

PLATE LV

(*Above*) SIX BRITISH MEDIUM TANKS
(*Below*) FIVE MEDIUM TANKS FIRING AT TARGET, LULWORTH, DORSET, 1936

The layman knows that the infantryman with his equipment cannot march many miles a day. Mechanical transport can assist him. But the multiplication of lorries for Army use in its turn brings forth many difficulties.

The great disadvantage of any armoured fighting landship is that they consume large quantities of petrol and lubricating oil. Consequently roads have to be kept open for transport. But in special cases it must always be remembered that Tanks can be fed with petrol and lubricating oil by aeroplanes.

This maintenance of oil supplies has now become a most important feature of modern warfare and presents a problem for the Army chiefs that is not too easy to solve.

When in the House of Commons Commander Kenworthy[1] always amused us by his very vigorous speeches. He was a hard-working Member and would tackle almost any subject, if he could score a point or two even against his own party when in office.

In a debate on Oil Supplies[2] he asked what would happen if our oil supplies were cut off? Not a warship could put to sea, not an aeroplane could leave the ground; our Army would be unmobilized. It is becoming more and more mechanized. Where it used to be said that an Army moved on its belly, now it moves on its petrol-tanks. The great Duke of Wellington was once asked what was the first requirement of an Army, and he replied: "Boots." He was then asked what was the second requirement, and again he replied: "Boots"; and, to still another question as to what was the third requirement, once more he answered "Boots." That was because boots on the feet of the soldiers were the motive power of Armies. To-day a modern Wellington, if asked the same question, would reply: "Petrol."

If the oil supply should fail, as Commander Kenworthy rightly said, the Army could not move.

The Russians offer a solution by carrying light Tanks, oil and their stores by air. This method of advancing Tank operations in certain isolated cases may be highly successful. We must all remember that one of the great successes the Italians obtained in their Abyssinian War was the large amount of stores carried day by day by aeroplane to supply their Army Corps in the field.

[1] Now Lord Strabolgi.   [2] Hansard, 11th March, 1931.

"Although the Country was in the main unsuitable for much Tank work, the Abyssinians were considerably embarrassed when they found Tanks, due to their great mobility, suddenly appearing in the rear of their Army during General Graziani's successful operations towards the Somalian border near Dolo.

High speed is necessary when Tanks are used to embarrass the flank of an opposing Army and difficulties will accrue to any Army passing through a Tank invested area. It is imperative that our Tanks must be developed to such a high pitch of efficiency that they can overtake and beat any opposing Tanks. Should an emergency arise again there is no other Country in the World in a more favourable position for developing landships than Great Britain.

Our industrial power for the mass production of Tanks is unrivalled. But we must have our factories organized with a reasonable number of tools, jigs, gauges, etc., arranged in peace-time for rapid production in war.

The new Minister of Defence will, I am confident, see that there is no slipping back in this Tank development in our Country.

It is welcome news to learn that Lord Nuffield, the great motor car manufacturer, is to take a leading part in the modernization and mechanization of the Army. He will, I understand, construct in his former aero-engine factory Tanks and motor tractors of a new and specially powerful type. Much research work in this connection will be necessary, and Lord Nuffield's good guidance will no doubt lead to many improvements in the heavier type of engines used in mechanical transport vehicles.

May I in this book suggest to Lord Nuffield that he might with advantage turn his attention to developing a very high-speed two-man Tank that could be transported by aeroplane wherever needed.

In quelling disturbances in India[1] or other parts of our Empire I am certain that the arrival of a few Tanks coming straight from Heaven would have an instant quieting effect, with a rapid restoration of normal conditions. The Government are well advised to make use of Lord Nuffield's

[1] In June, 1937, British Tanks made history when they were used in Waziristan operations, over the Sham Plain, towards the cave of the elusive Fakir of Ipi at Arsaikot—They were the first motor vehicles ever seen in this wild country.

wonderful organizing powers and great mechanical ability to assist in Tank development.

To those of us who were responsible for initiating caterpillar landships it is pleasing to learn that a splendid type of young man is joining the Royal Tank Corps. The Military Attachés representing United States of America, Japan, Austria, Sweden, Nepal and Siam were much impressed with the efficiency of the Tank crews and the way they manœuvred their machines when witnessing target practice at the gunnery school of the Tank Corps last year.[1] Targets representing different types of Tanks in various positions as end on, broadside on, then visible for a short time showed that the Tank gunners were being well trained at Lulworth (Plates LIV and LV).

During May, 1936, we learned from Canberra that the Minister of Defence, Sir Archdale Parkhill, has announced that six of the latest types of Tanks have been ordered in this country, as part of a new policy for mechanizing the military forces of Australia.

These Tanks would assist the field Army's front line to bear the brunt of an invader's first attack.

To strengthen the capacity for defence is an ever-increasing problem for Australia. If handled properly Tanks can play a very important part in a defence scheme for the Commonwealth. The right type of Tank must be provided for this purpose, and the crews must be thoroughly trained in handling these machines, so that they can become masters of any emergency that may arise.

Last year I read with great interest a book[2] written by a very able Officer and good thinker, Captain J. R. Kennedy, a gunner who has passed through the Staff College. In his pages he made some sweeping attacks on Britain's Military policy. Whether he is right or wrong in some of his criticisms is not within my knowledge. But I am certain Captain Kennedy is right when he is strongly critical of the support still being given to the cavalry.

Beyond all doubt, he declares, it must be adjudged obsolete. Yet over £1,000,000 a year is spent on cavalry, double the amount spent on Tank battalions.

[1] May, 1936.   [2] *This Our Army.*

Also a few thinking men can dispute that Captain Kennedy is right when he insists that:

> Armies of mass can never again take the field in the same way as in 1914. Air power has changed everything. Even if mobilization could be carried out as quickly as in 1914, which, he says, is impossible, the troops, when being transported, would be ideal targets for the air bomber, gunner and gasser.
>
> If they did succeed in arriving, "air observation has made Generalship of the old kind so obsolete that Armies will in future have as much chance of performing old tricks as would a mounted highwayman on an arterial road."
>
> It is the Air Officer, he contends, who will have to dictate to ground and sea units what he requires. Apart from this, "there will be only one fighting arm in the future—the Tank in one form or another."

Every visitor to the Continent[1] comes back with the information that all Continental Armies are adding yearly to their number of Tanks with the view of aiding their infantry in a future war. Tank Brigades are being organized to replace a good proportion of their cavalry brigades, which most military experts consider will play but a small part in modern warfare.

The question then arises, and it is one for the new Minister of Defence to consider seriously. Are we producing in this Country Tanks of sufficient gun power, speed and protection to enable them to knock out any Tank they may be called upon to meet on the Continent? If not, why not? The old contest of gun versus armour is always with us, whether on the sea, on land, or in the air.

It is for the military Tank expert—taking opinion from all those who have had practical experience in handling Tanks under war conditions to lay down how Tanks should be developed to meet any requirements that the Tank Corps may be called upon to undertake.

---

[1] The courtesy of the French Government and M. Deladier, Minister of War, in permitting many British Members of Parliament to witness some Tank Manœuvres at Versailles-Satory on 28th June, 1937, was highly appreciated. The Author was fascinated to see Light Tanks and Medium Tanks being operated with great skill at good speed over rough country.

Having been the first in this Country to carry out practical experiments for utilizing caterpillars in connection with developing a new weapon of war, it would seem to me that caterpillar landships will develop much on the same lines as Naval warships, and it will become necessary to provide:

High speed 2 or 3 men Tanks.
Tanks for working with infantry.
Medium Tanks.
Heavy Tanks of large dimensions for special service.

In a recent issue of the French *Revue d'Infanterie* there was a very interesting article comparing the casualties suffered in the late war by French and British Tank units. The conclusion arrived at was that on an average French Tanks went into action a greater number of times than the British. But the casualties to French machines were less, and the casualties to personnel substantially less, particularly fatal casualties.

This the writer attributes to the much heavier armour carried by French machines.

There is little doubt that our capable Tank designers in this Country will keep this point in mind when they are considering new designs of all types.

Most Nations have experienced much difficulty with their heavy Tanks, and have new designs embodying considerable improvements in hand.

The design of a modern Tank can only be considered good if thorough and skilled attention has been paid to every one of the many details which constitute an efficient machine. That is one which can carry out its duties with the minimum expenditure of power, and with the greatest margin of safety from breakdowns of the engines or tracks.

The Tank must possess an armament of the most up-to-date order for attack or defence. Well-placed position for the gunners must be found. They must not be too cramped, and the efficient ventilation of the Tank is of the greatest importance. A good look-out must be provided for manœuvring to enable the maximum gun-fire to be used when attacking and when fighting a rearguard action. The armour must afford protection from modern machine-gun and rifle fire.

The controls must be of the highest efficiency, and the crew operating them should have some measure of comfort to enable them to give their maximum efficiency.

High speed can only be obtained as the result of being able to operate the tracks efficiently without allowing them to cause unnecessary absorption of power. Power-weights must be kept as low as possible. Stability is needed in Tank design in order that the machine when going over rough terrain provides a steady gun platform, and to enable it to be manœuvred with assurance. The turning circle must be a minimum.

All these primary requirements must be dealt with by the technical experts, one by one, to determine which features of design must be considered in order to produce the most efficient machine.

Tanks must be designed to enable them to meet and engage a hostile Tank with every prospect of success.

The rapid production of smoke-screens is essential in a modern Tank. But speed is the most important factor of all, and those who are responsible for developing Tank tactics would do well if they studied the operations of surface ships in all phases of Naval war.

The Mechanization Board in this country is composed of a body of experts for advising on all questions in connection with Tank designs under the direction of Lieutenant-General Sir Hugh Elles, the Master-General of Ordnance. He was the great Tank leader in the War.

No doubt the speed of Tanks is ever on the mind of the experts, and the thickness of armour-plating is always a difficult problem for them.

Speed has to be sacrificed if armour is increased. In the balance climbing power, radius of action, space for crew, safety arrangements have to be weighed very carefully, as the margin of getting many requirements into a small tonnage is slender.

In the past four experimental 16-ton Tanks were constructed, but these turned out very costly when compared with our Medium 12-ton Vickers type. But these 12-ton Tanks are becoming worn out, and will have to be replaced by a newer design.

Many military Officers in all Countries hoped that the

Civil War of 1936–7 in Spain would afford a good opportunity for testing the value of Tanks and anti-Tank guns. But up to date no very definite lessons have been learned. In some cases the anti-Tank gun has been quite effective. This may lead to heavier armoured Tanks being constructed by the chief military Nations. One can only hope the mobility will not be sacrificed for too much armour.

On 18th May, 1937, our Empire Coronation contingents back in camp at Pirbright were shown some of the latest equipment of our modern Army.

Several new weapons were brought to the visitors' notice, including the Bren gun, our new light automatic, which is replacing the Lewis. Other new weapons are the anti-Tank rifles and the anti-Tank two-pounder gun.

The anti-Tank rifle, or "Boyes" gun, weighs about 35 lb., and fires a special bullet of half-inch diameter. It has effective range of something like 500 yards against modern armoured fighting vehicles, and can be fired at a rate of about six shots a minute. One is carried in each platoon truck of a rifle battalion. It is a good weapon.

The two-pounder anti-Tank gun—two pounds is the weight of the shell—is to be worked by the anti-Tank companies of the machine-gun battalions. There are sixteen of these guns to each A/T company, and the guns are drawn by the truck carrying the detachment and the ammunition.

An opinion on the value of anti-Tank guns is given by Colonel G. Le Q. Martel, the very able Assistant Director of Mechanization at the War Office, when recently[1] addressing the members of the Royal United Service Institution, said:

> The object of mechanization was to provide hard-hitting mobile troops—an Army with a punch.
> There were three types of troops. The armoured fighting vehicles which made up the Tank Brigade would, he thought, be employed in modern war in the first wave, since it would be required to break down stout resistance. The second wave would be composed of further and lighter armoured mobile troops in the shape of mechanized cavalry. The normal formations would follow.

[1] January, 1937.

There was a "school," Colonel Martel said, which thought that the development of anti-Tank weapons had caused the days of the Tank to be numbered. Those who saw the Russian manœuvres would not, he thought, cling to that view.

The Russians had some five Tank Brigades, and it was illuminating to see the movement of those armoured formations. Their manœuvring ground was ideal for the Tank. In an attack on a position the Russian machines moved at high speed and crashed through their objective.

They left little opportunity for anti-Tank weapons. There were casualties, but the effect of anti-Tank guns was like the firing of a single gun at a covey of partridges.

The Tank Brigade of our Army, he continued, wanted the best Tank that could be produced at a reasonable price.

Field-Marshal Sir Cyril Deverell, Chief of the Imperial General Staff, who presided, said they had to make every preparation against the possibility of another major war. Should such a disaster come they hoped, by their organization, to avert long, static warfare, and avoid casualties. Mechanization held out the only hope by which those results would be achieved.

The range of action of Tanks is considerable, and their mobility is far greater than any troops can possibly achieve. These two important qualities enable Tanks to attack positions often well in advance of their own Army on the flanks, and even at the supply services in rear of the enemy's first line. That is why very high-speed light Tanks should be developed.

I imagine that however high the efficiency of Tanks may become the expert Military opinion in all Countries still considers that the infantry will always remain the real decisive factor in war. But all real successes will be won by the co-operation of infantry, artillery, Tanks and aircraft, working in the closest possible combination.

Also it needs very little imagination to consider that our highly mechanized Army of the future will need "Tanks, Tanks, and more Tanks," and the infantryman should be the first to demand that these weapons of war are provided for his protection.

The Army Council are fully alive to the necessity of making provision for more Tanks.

In the statement[1] relative to Defence expenditure in connection with the £400,000,000 loan, we notice that two new Army Tank Battalions will be formed. This and other defence measures that will be taken shows the grim determination of the British Government to make good the deficiencies in our armaments. These have caused many Members of Parliament and others much anxiety during the last few years.

Some persons with a pacific leaning may ask: How long are we to go on building these chariots of iron?

The answer is given with great clearness in Psalm xlvi, 9, which runs:

> "He maketh wars to cease unto the end of the earth : He breaketh the bow and knappeth the spear in sunder : He burneth the chariot in the Fire."

[1] Command Paper No. 5374, 16th February, 1937.

CHAPTER V

CONCLUSION

"Don't look at your hill—climb it."

IN perusing my review of the evolution of the Tank from the armoured car of the Royal Naval Air Service and looking at the photographs showing the Officers and Ratings of our Armoured Car Force carrying out the necessary experiments with caterpillar machines, and remembering that the Tank, a product of evolution, was produced when things looked very black indeed at the Front, and His late Majesty King George V's Realm was in some danger; and remembering the words of the Army Council's gracious letter in sending their gratitude to myself and the Naval Airmen associated with me for our Tank work, and remembering that the great German Generals admit that the Tank was one of the deciding factors in the late War, may I leave it to posterity to judge whether our little band of Airmen, consisting of Boothby, Briggs, Hetherington, Macfie and myself, have had quite a square deal. I am convinced that the verdict of posterity will be in our favour, and that we have been none too well treated for having the "good guts" in spite of much opposition and many difficulties, as these pages disclose, in getting a completely novel weapon of war taken up by the Admiralty and developed for Army use.

The Sea Lords during the War period had great difficulties to surmount and many preoccupations that nobody was more fully aware of at the Admiralty than myself, as I had to be in many of their offices almost daily in 1914–16. To say that all the Sea Lords were stupid, conservative, or had unworthy motives, would be most unfair. But some of them certainly did lack vision, and were not helpful with Air development, armoured car and caterpillar landship work.

CONCLUSION

Undoubtedly a good many of the difficulties the Naval Airmen experienced in pressing their new ideas upon Authority was due to the fact that most of the Sea Lords during the War period had not time or the inclination to study Air matters, or the possibilities of caterpillar landships, and to hide their ignorance, and in some measure to salve their conscience, took the very easy line of hunting and bullying their Airmen.

The late Marquis Curzon, our first President of the Air Board, was amazed at the attitude certain Sea Lords took up over air development, and asked me how long this sort of opposition had gone on. The opposition reached its zenith in 1916, when several of the Naval Airmen were instructed to furnish no further information to the Air Board that had been appointed by the Government of the day to look into air matters.

Needless to say, this sort of Brahmanic outlook which tried to prevent opinion on air questions being fully and freely discussed received mighty little support from me, their pioneer Airman.

Many of the Airmen came from good and responsible positions in private life. They could not understand the repeated hostility that most of the Sea Lords, in the early War period, showed by the minutes they put on the various official papers dealing with Air matters, armoured cars, caterpillar landships, anti-aircraft Defence of London, etc., that were circulated in the course of business round the Admiralty Office.

It seemed to them that any informed opinion that aircraft, armoured cars or landships could be developed for any use except a "stunt" was non-existent. Because our experiments were conducted mainly on novel lines there was no need for Senior Officers to get so very peeved when they did not have the leisure to give them the close study in War that they could have given in peace-time.

It may be that on both sides of Whitehall the Noahs did not like to see the Airmen becoming almost daily more efficient and competing with no little success for public favour with their Navy and Army comrades, or was the reason for discouraging all new ideas that given by our great Admiral, Lord Fisher, in his book *Records*, when he wrote:

> It is an historical fact that the British Navy resists all change.

To support this view he tells us that in one set of manœuvres the young Officer commanding a submarine, having for the third time successfully torpedoed the hostile Admiral's Flagship, humbly said so to the Admiral by signal, and suggested the Flagship going out of action. The answer he got back by signal from the Admiral was: "You be damned."

The Army is in some respects less Conservative than the Navy, but they, too, have their Noahs, and the classic example of microscopic vision in recent years was the turning down by the Military Experts, in 1915, of all caterpillar experiments.

Even after the principle of caterpillar landships was established, it was a difficult task to obtain proper recognition for the Tank, as shown in one of General Fuller's latest books, when he states:

> While I was away visiting the Tank Corps Cadet Battalion at Hazeley Down, Foot nearly perpetuated murder. To quote his own words:[1]

> "Some of the Senior Officers at the War Office seemed almost demoniacal in the bitterness of their opposition to Tanks. Cavalry Officers were particularly fierce in their hostility to the new weapon, a very queer thing in view of the fact that many of the best Tank Corps Officers had come from the Cavalry. Possibly this was the reason and the defection of some of their numbers was responsible for the fury of the rest."

Again the Noahish tendencies of other military minds is well illustrated in a recent leading article in *The Times*, when the writer, who was dealing with new ideas in connection with Defence matters, observed:

> The obvious illustration is a pre-War episode when the adoption of the aeroplane was urged upon certain

[1] *Memoirs of an Unconventional Soldier*, page 361.

CONCLUSION 305

leading Soldiers after M. Bleriot's early success. A natural doubt of its practicability was expressed; but still more natural was the subsequent remark, in accents of repugnance, that if it were to fulfil the inventor's expectations it would ruin the cavalry's function, and thereby end a great tradition. The narrower the orbit the more strongly do such instinctive forces work, holding back a newer generation who, if less in subjection, would take a broader view.

Not one of my bitterest opponents, and I am happy in having had many, can accuse me of not taking a broad view with regard to Air development, landships and submarines: moreover, throughout my Naval career I have declined always to smother my views to please Authority.

Everyone knows that in all Countries the Fighting Services in a long peace tend to become more and more conservative, and those in Authority very often develop mental laziness.

In time of War, precedent plays no part. But in living up to precedent for a considerable period after hostilities commenced we saw thousands and thousands of our fine manhood sacrificed without a single finger being lifted to evolve a new weapon of war that could have helped them when ordered to take the offensive by their Military Leaders. Consequently, Mr. Churchill deserves everlasting credit for the way he urged his Naval Airmen to study the creation of a new weapon for trench warfare. These pages show that they did not fail him, and held the fort with some success after he left the Admiralty in May, 1915.

On the other hand they were damned for their new ideas:

> We Noahs smothered with gold lace must know more about war than these Airmen. Our importance must not be sacrificed to those who are so persistent with their new and awkward demands. . . .
>
> The War Office have not asked the Admiralty officially for caterpillar landships, therefore they cannot require them. It is only these stupid Airmen who will insist on wasting time and money upon idiotic caterpillar experiments that nobody wants or desires to have carried out, quoth the Noahs.

But I am convinced all fair-minded people will agree that the Naval Airmen were right to fight with all their might to get our novel ideas considered, and if they proved of any use to press that they should be developed by Authority. We had no use for Noahs, who seemed to be struck with pain at a new idea or those who so often argued to themselves:

> Why should our usual habit of thought be disturbed so frequently by these pushful Airmen who few people like.

The Airmen did not care two straws whether they were liked or disliked by Authority. They were full out to play their part, however small that part might be, in defeating our great Enemy and had an unswerving determination to succeed with all types of aircraft and caterpillar landships. In spite of much opposition on both sides of Whitehall, the official History of the War shows the value of their pioneer air and caterpillar landship work for the State.

The Airman's caterpillar landship alone is expressive of an age impatient of retaining, even to please Authority, old ideas and old theories when they lead to a dead end.

Happily a silver lining to a dark cloud appeared in 1936 on the Admiralty horizon in the shape of one of our finest and most courageous Statesmen—Sir Samuel Hoare, being appointed as First Lord. He has no use for Noahs, no matter how many stripes they may have on their arms. Besides being a sound administrator, Sir Samuel is a fearless Airman who has flown more mileage within and without the British Empire than all the Ministers and ex-Ministers put together. His wise handling of the India Bill in the House of Commons and other problems concerning India won the admiration of not only many of his Colleagues but a large number of his Countrymen. He did, I am certain, work in the closest harmony with our very able Air Minister, Lord Swinton, and there is little doubt that these two progressive Statesmen endeavoured to lay the seeds necessary to strengthen and not weaken the link between the Navy and the Air Service and, moreover, advocated that the old antagonism the pioneer Airmen had to encounter at the Admiralty is buried for ever.

We must remember that a modern Navy depends upon their aircraft for its sight, and sight is might. Whilst the Air Service depends on the Navy for the protection of the oil the aircraft require.

To have an Airman administrator like Sir Samuel Hoare to give good guidance in commencing to increase the strength of our Fleet Air Arm and make it more efficient was most valuable. His successor at the Admiralty is now Mr. Duff Cooper. He is a man after my own heart, with strong opinions and not afraid to state them. The new First Lord is not easily deflected by hostile criticism, and should do well in continuing Sir Samuel Hoare's policy of strengthening the Fleet on sound Navy-Air lines in the interests of not only National but Empire Defence.

There is no doubt that destruction faced the British Empire in 1914. But the superb efforts of our sailors, soldiers, airmen and munition workers, and the successful development of new weapons of war proved too much for those who sought to destroy.

Our gallant Tank crews under their most courageous leaders, Lieutenant-General Sir Hugh Elles and that singularly gifted man, Major-General Fuller, who was so largely responsible for the fine success of the Tanks at Cambrai, helped our Army to victory.

On looking back upon these great successes in the past and in visualizing future successes, I trust those that have benefited, or may benefit, by having the assistance of Tanks in military operations will sometimes remember that caterpillar landships were initiated by Naval Airmen serving at the British Admiralty. Pioneers are so often forgotten!

The Tank crews' achievement with a completely new weapon of war will appeal to all men-at-arms, and also to those militant pacifists who have been of recent years so vocal in advancing peace by the use of force, not only in this Country but throughout the World.

Some people one meets are over-enthusiastic about Tanks and say that the infantry soldier is likely to disappear. That is not my opinion. Every weapon takes its share in deciding the issue of a war. No final decision is likely to be made until ground forces, including Tanks, are in possession. The axiom of Napoleon's General Norand that "l'infanterie c'est l'Armée" is as true to-day as in the Napoleonic Wars, and does not Lord Haig conclude his Epic of December 17th, 1918, in these noble words:

> It would be impossible to devise a more eloquent testimony to the unequalled spirit and determination of the British soldier of all ranks and services. We have been accustomed to be proud of the great and noble traditions handed down to us by the soldiers of bygone days. The men who form the Armies of the Empire to-day have created new traditions which are a challenge to the highest records of the past, and will be an inspiration to the generations who come after us.

When Lord Haig penned the above inspiring sentences, that not only went throughout the British Empire but round the whole World, he no doubt had largely in mind our very gallant infantry men and the new traditions made by those courageous and skilful crews who manned for the first time in history caterpillar landships.

Many persons in this Country, including some of our leading Statesmen, have taken the greatest possible interest from the first in the development of the Tank, and in my introduction I quoted the last part of the following historic message that His Majesty the late King George V sent to Sir Douglas Haig in November, 1917:

> I congratulate you, General Byng, and the troops concerned on the successful operations in the neighbourhood of Cambrai. The complete surprise effected under such novel methods of warfare has been received with the utmost satisfaction throughout the Empire, while holding out great hopes for the future. It is especially gratifying that the Tanks, a purely British invention, should have played so important a part in your victory.

His late Majesty, from the days of the first experiments with a Tank in Hatfield Park, always took a very keen interest in their development and work.

The Special Order No. 18[1] issued by Major-General

---

[1] From the *Tank Corps*, by Williams-Ellis.

H. J. Elles, C.B., D.S.O., commanding Tank Corps in the field, is of great interest to myself and those Airmen associated with me in initiating caterpillar landships.

18th October, 1918.

1. His Majesty the King was graciously pleased to become COLONEL-IN-CHIEF of the Tank Corps on the 17th instant.

2. The following telegram was sent on behalf of the TANK CORPS:

To H.M. THE KING.

The news that your Majesty has graciously consented to become Colonel-in-Chief of the Tank Corps has just been received here. All ranks are deeply sensible of this signal honour conferred upon the Corps and are determined to continue worthy of it.

GENERAL ELLES.

Advanced H.Q. Tank Corps.
In the Field. 17*th October*.

3. The following reply has been received:

To Major-General H. J. ELLES,
H.Q. Tank Corps. In the Field.

I sincerely thank you for the message which you have conveyed to me in the name of all ranks of the Tank Corps.

I am indeed proud to be Colonel-in-Chief of this great British organisation invented by us which has played so prominent a part in our recent victories.

I wish you all every possible good luck.

GEORGE R.I.,
Colonel-in-Chief.

Buckingham Palace,
London. 18*th October*.

This thoughtful action of His late Majesty, due to his true vision of Service life, eased the situation and swept away a good many of the difficulties that the Senior Tank

Officers were experiencing from those who were so very hostile at that time to the further development of mechanical weapons for war purposes.

In the preservation and guarding His Majesty's Empire I have for many years held the opinion that caterpillar landships, perhaps of dimensions we can scarcely contemplate at the present time, will play a not unimportant part. More than likely there will be heavy battle Tanks, infantry Tanks, high-speed medium Tanks and light Tanks of very great speed. It is for our military experts to see that the proper number of personnel are trained and that we build the right type of Tank to meet and beat the latest pattern a possible Enemy may possess, and have sufficient numbers with reserves of all types for meeting any emergency that may arise.

Most students of the Great War, not only in this Country, but throughout the Empire, will not dispute that the Tanks which were so magnificently handled by their courageous French and British crews at the Front were one of the chief causes that brought hostilities to an end and also one of the chief means of smashing the mad dreams of Imperial Germany by helping so efficiently the infantrymen to knock out the German Armies on the Western Front. The caterpillar landship, commonly known as the Tank, that was evolved from the armoured car of the Royal Naval Air Service as these pages show, has made HISTORY for France and Britain.

Many Naval Airmen will remember with much gratitude how well our French opposite numbers worked with us during the War period in developing all types of aircraft and aero-engines. They will, I am certain, join me in an earnest desire to see our two great Countries stand together firmly and draw nearer to one another in doing their utmost to bring a lasting peace to distressed Europe and continue to be the great mainstay of democratic principles and practice. Some Politicians and others consider that the internal affairs of a Nation are of no consequence to neighbouring States. The unfortunate civil war of 1936-37 in Spain provides evidence to the contrary.

Without wishing to interfere in any way with the internal affairs of other Countries, we must see that no Country interferes with our business by propaganda or any acts of aggression. Also, we must remember that no truer words have been uttered than those of His Royal Highness, now the Duke of Windsor, when he said:[1]

> This Country will always have to take a leading part in the affairs of the World.

It is quite impossible for us to keep out of the International arena and always separate our own internal affairs from a general survey of World affairs.

A new spirit of responsibility is discernible amongst the youth of this Country in connection with promoting our own interests whilst doing our very best for other Nations.

Such a spirit might be encouraged and we should see that the majority of our Countrymen and Women have a clear conception of the needs of the Fighting Services in connection with the maintenance of the security of the British Empire and to carry out our World responsibilities.

When our People are considering the measures we are taking for our Defence not only for these Islands, but the whole Empire, it is profitable to recall that the late Joseph Chamberlain's conception of this country's Imperial mission has been summed up in these few words:

> Great is the task,
> Great is the responsibility,
> But great is the honour.

To discharge our duty effectively as a great Empire and great World Power, it is imperative that Britain should be strong.

Our Sea, Land and Air Forces must be kept always in the very highest state of efficiency to enable us to conduct any operations we may be called upon to undertake in the Empire's interests and to do our level best to help to keep peace amongst the other Nations. There are, however, limits to our peace efforts.

In these very difficult days we are now passing through in Europe, it is often stated there is justified fear that this Country may become entangled in the net of international pacts and covenants and be dragged into a European war

[1] At Windsor Castle, 18th April, 1936.

against the will of the majority of our people. With advantage we can in this connection recall the words of Disraeli, who at the Guildhall, London, on 3rd November, 1876, declared:

> England is the Country of all others whose policy is peace. We have nothing to gain by war; we are essentially a non-aggressive power. There are no cities and no provinces that we desire to appropriate. We have built up an Empire of which we are proud, and our proudest boast is this—that this Empire subsists as much upon sympathy as upon force.
>
> But if the struggle comes it should also be recollected that there is no Country whose resources are so great in a righteous cause; and I trust that England will never embark in war, except in a righteous cause—a cause that concerns her liberty, her independence, or her Empire.

Many people consider we must always be prepared to fulfil what they call our historic mission as peace-maker and peace-keeper in Europe. But this should not be overdone.

I imagine the majority of my Countrymen feel as I do and that is—we should use our arms mainly to protect British interests. Let us keep out of war for old blood-feuds and other old religious causes. Whilst holding these views, they should not prevent us from being prepared at all times to protect this Country from invasion, safeguard our Empire and overseas interests, and see that our Nationals are well treated in all parts of the World. Also we must be prepared to play our part in carrying out our Treaty obligations. Because we do not pledge ourselves too much in advance it does not follow that this Nation will not take forceful action if required. I am convinced that in the strong arm of Britain lies the greatest hope for peace in the World, and upon the Navy, the Army and the Air Force depends the safety and prosperity of all the Peoples of our Empire. Even in peace-time calls may at any time be made upon the Fighting Services, as instanced by the recent very fine work of the British Navy off the coast of Spain in guarding our food-carrying ships and ships laden with raw material for our factories and those carrying our manufactured goods to all parts of the World.

CONCLUSION 313

Then they have had to collect and carry to safety not only our Nationals, but those of many Foreign Countries in the Spanish Civil War,[1] thus proving themselves, as the former First Lord of the Admiralty, Sir Samuel Hoare, has said only too truly—a great humanitarian force.

Britain's recent decision to re-arm has not only the approval of the majority of the people of the Empire, but most other Nations. Many repercussions are likely to occur as a result of this Policy. Some will argue that rearmament is only justified if it is used as a means to obtain some measure of disarmament and eventually peace. Maybe this will come in due course. Our rearmament is being welcomed not only by all Nations who desire peace, but the majority of our Countrymen and Women who feel it will do much to tranquillise a troubled World and make our Empire safe.

We have tried unilateral disarmament; it has failed dismally. No other Nation has followed us, and while the World presents its great Navies, huge Armies and formidable Air Squadrons, with its industries capable of war-mobilization in a few hours for the production of munitions, Britain can never be too strong or too vigilant. Within the next few years the decision for Peace or War in Europe will have to be taken.[2] The Statesmen of the great Nations will have to use every artifice that Statecraft possesses to maintain peace. All questions of Defence turn upon Foreign Policy. It is the vital issue. But there are other difficulties, so in my last pages let me fix the most earnest attention of the Reader upon the dangers from within and without which are now confronting us.

The Spanish developments[3] that have proved so disastrous to that distressed Country give an example to the whole World of the complete breakdown of sound administration and responsible Government, and show in that tragic struggle the danger of allowing the subservient element too much freedom of action. Events are moving fast in many Countries. As Commander King Hall rightly points out,

[1] 1936–1937.
[2] M. Blum, ex-Prime Minister of France, stated in a speech on 12th July, 1937: "People will realize how narrowly they escaped war when the archives of the period are made public." He added: "I realize we are entering a still more dangerous zone in International Politics."   [3] In 1937.

it would be well for some other Countries nearer Spain to see that moderation and democratic practice does not also break down. If it does, the fight between the principles of Democracy and Dictatorship will be a hard and bitter one, and it may be that we alone will stand amongst the great Nations of Europe as the one that is maintaining the principles of Democracy and all the toleration those principles stand for. Every possible step to defend Democracy and our liberties within the British Empire is the obvious duty of our Government. In considering our Empire, as long as the British people continue to hold this great heritage that our Forefathers have handed down to us and which our generation has successfully retained and improved, we must always be an object of envy to those people who would like our place in the sun and only await a favourable opportunity to capture coveted vineyards. This applies more particularly to those Nations who have in recent years developed power politics to a fine art and who have hitched most things of importance on to their War Chariot. They have sacrificed Civil to Military needs, as shown by the complete militarization of the active Forces of the Nation. In fact, force only is respected and there is nothing more glorious than a conquest. These Countries have developed an entirely new nationality with a different outlook on World affairs and they prefer the rule of force to that of law.

With these new dangers that confront us, which may tend to increase rather than decrease, it is clear we will require a new mentality in dealing with all questions that concern Defence.

I hope and pray most earnestly that this Country will never again make the mistake of allowing our Defence Services to fall so low as they were two years ago. This lack of vision by those in Authority is the main cause of it becoming necessary for the Chancellor of the Exchequer to come to Parliament in February, 1937, and seek power to enable him to raise a loan for Britain's defences up to a maximum of four hundred million pounds over a period of five years. Mr. Neville Chamberlain in doing so stated that: "The general experience of the last twelve months has in no way relieved the urgency of our heavy task nor

CONCLUSION

lightened the cost of raising our Forces to a proper standard of defensive strength."

The futility of overdoing peaceful diplomacy is now recognized. But in my humble opinion there can be no real peace in Europe unless this Country makes it quite plain we are not only prepared for war, but prepared to show our strength when necessary and back our words by deeds.

Our Foreign Minister with a powerful Britain to support him in all negotiations and at the Conference table is in a better position to bring peace than when supported by a weak Britain. In Europe there will be a trial of true Statesmanship and I am convinced the Statesmen of our country will not fail us. Recent World events have shown that the strong arm must maintain what the strong arm has won, otherwise we will be like China and the prosperity, freedom and liberties we now enjoy within the Empire will soon vanish.

England without an Empire would be a poor Counrty. If a powerful Nation wrested our heritage from us, in all probability the inhabitants of these Islands would become munition workers for that conquering Nation, and their Military leaders would soon see that they got a good pound of flesh out of our people. Having inherited the Empire with World resources built up by the initiative, energy and courage of generations of British subjects and with freedom unknown in the majority of other Countries, it is our clear duty to see that the torch of liberty and progress is kept alive and take care that those with hostile intent do not break up the Empire and deprive us of our freedom, our high standard of living, our fine social services or our industrial supremacy. Wars of the future will not be so much won by courage, but by the Nation with the most modern and powerful material. The factories of Britain are our one great asset. In the advancement of new and improved weapons of war by knowledge and good experience of experimental work, to ensure the proper protection of our far-flung possessions, there is no limit but the stubborn habit of antagonism and prejudice of those with Noahish tendencies.

The keys of our Defence measures lie in Whitehall. In my pages there is evidence of an enfeeblement, a want of grip in handling by Authority Naval Air development and the Tank idea, that proved when developed during the Great War most helpful to the State at the time most needed. This must be put right. It is imperative that Noahs and not progressive men should find their right place, which is obscurity.

Perhaps the most ominous of all symptoms is the misguided habit of popularity hunting. It is the favourite pastime of chocolate or place-men with little real ability. They are those who agree with everything Authority wishes or says or desires to be said. They owe their advancement to these tactics and, moreover, climb to high places and become Noahs; a murrain on these Noahs, they are no good servants of the State. We have far too many Noahs of this type in our Country.

These Noahs rigorously oppose innovation of any form. When not thwarted or contradicted they are the most amiable Officers the Services can produce. To maintain themselves in high office they take care to be surrounded by "Yes men" as the Americans would say. The honest "Yes Officer" who, regardless of the real truth, tells Senior Officers what they want to hear, obtains much praise for himself, but leaves the still more honest "No Officer," who is not afraid to form his own opinion, give his judgment freely and tell the truth, to incur the displeasure of Authority, is guilty of a crime against the State.

The handling of some of the incidents in connection with our Fighting Services that have taken place during the last few years has clearly indicated that the "Eye on the Upper Bridge" type of Officer has been selected for posts that he is ill chosen to fill. The Political heads of our Fighting Services would do well if they discouraged this line of advancement and selected for promotion younger Officers who are not afraid to express their opinion freely before Authority.

Some drastic reforms are necessary not only in the promotion of younger Officers,[1] but in several branches of the Fighting Services, and none more so than in the way new ideas are handled.

Vice-Admiral Alfred F. B. Carpenter[2] confirms my

[1] For example, zones of promotion in the Navy are struck far too high—Commanders and Lieutenant-Commanders run too long in their respective ranks before promotion.
[2] Admiral Carpenter, V.C., the hero of Zeebrugge.

CONCLUSION

opinion in a letter to *The Times*, dated 3rd March, 1937, in connection with Naval Officers' Training when he states:

"There is now less initiative and more discouragement of ideas than ever before. This must be heartrending to all Officers who are really ambitious to achieve and deserve the higher commands, but who are aghast at the prevalent belief that the royal road to promotion in peace-time is that of doing what they are told while, in the name of discipline, suppressing any progressive ideas that they may possess. When Officers, after years of such training, do eventually reach the higher ranks it is only natural that they, in their turn, should tend to regard their juniors as mere automatons. It is within the bounds of possibility that this mental attitude is the primary cause of the apparent lack of brains in both the older Fighting ervices.

To get a man who will break away from the commonplace and work at problems on entirely new lines is surely an asset and should not be discarded, even by the Admiralty.

The new co-ordinating Minister of Defence, Sir Thomas Inskip, has a golden opportunity and should press that the Committee of Imperial Defence be fed frequently with the frankest, freshest and most alert minds that can be found in the Services who can do a little new thinking in connection with the fresh factors brought in by the introduction of air and mechanical weapons of war, and see that the man with the first idea gets a square deal. Also one of the most important duties of his high office is to see that the right weapons of war are forged. We are pledged to our people at the last General Election[1] to re-organise the Defence Forces. Parliament has voted large sums of money for this purpose. More will be needed. This money will be wasted if the Noahs are allowed to have the chief voice in our Defence needs and progressive men are kept in the background.

Future wars will be fought with new weapons. It is the responsibility of the younger men of our Country to

[1] 1935.

demand that new ideas be encouraged, out-of-date weapons are scrapped and the very latest types are provided for their use whether they be for service on the Sea, under the surface of the Sea, on Land or in the Air. If this demand is satisfied and the provision of supplies[1] and personnel is properly organised and trained in technical efficiency to meet all requirements, there will be no great difficulty in preventing hostile forces in any attempt they may make to break up the British Empire.

Should we ever have this misfortune of having another war forced upon our Country and international emergency again arise, I know my Countrymen well enough to believe with confidence that, in spite of the record of difficulty disclosed in these pages, there will be no lack of eager Pioneers ready to overcome all obstacles and defeat the Noahs in true British bull-dog style.

Moreover, I am sufficiently optimistic to think that the established Noahs in high places have had their day, but should that view prove incorrect I trust most sincerely that the future Pioneer will earn the right to laugh at the Noahs of his day as I have earned the right to laugh very loudly, and do so daily, at the Noahs of my day.

If I have helped to torpedo some of these opposers to every novel idea or new scheme and have exposed them to some ridicule in my books, *The Evolution of the Submarine Boat, Mine and Torpedo; Airmen or Noahs*, or in these pages with the view to ease the path of the future Pioneer, I shall be amply gratified and, maybe, gleaning some encouragement from this book, written by one who has not shirked in fighting the Noahs for progress in the development of submarines, all types of aircraft and land-ships, he will not fail our Country, the Empire or the World in producing a new weapon that will be as successful as

"THE TANK IN OUR WAR."

The eyes, brain and will of the Pioneer must be set forward and never backward—with firm resolve to over-

---

[1] Not only munitions but food, raw materials, oil reserves and general supplies must be kept efficiently organised to meet any likely emergency. Also, all planning should be co-related to obtain the best results.

CONCLUSION 319

come every difficulty—no matter how great it may be—and with fearless courage to win through and to fight with all his might the Noahs who persist in blocking the path of progress. Duty and high purpose are his watchwords. The Nation's resources include many men of this type. They are those who have the capability of seizing upon a new idea: see what the discovery might lead to, then swiftly follow up thought with action by seizing the right moment for setting the new idea in motion, and then see it brought to fruition for the good of the State. Such men would seem to be of incalculable value to this Country.

In my humble opinion it should be an axiom in all Government Departments in Whitehall that such men should have very great care taken of them and they should not be discarded because they hold strong views in connection with introducing new weapons of war that may be antagonistic to those held by Senior Officers who may be in temporary Authority. It is common knowledge the only sin Noahs never forget or forgive is difference of opinion. The duty of the Pioneer is to stand up squarely to the Noahs and damn the personal consequences. For doing this over air development and the introduction of caterpillar landships, the Admiralty in their very great wisdom discarded me, then their senior submarine Pioneer (except Admiral Sir Reginald Bacon), and their Air and Tank Pioneer.

But no matter, and if I smile few will take exception to my doing so. For did not I commence this book by quoting Field-Marshal von Hindenburg's nephew, who is of the opinion that *Tanks proved the turning point of the War*, and being a Naval man I am naturally very proud to have received, in a letter[1] dealing with Tank development, not only the gratitude but the appreciative thanks of the British Army Council for

My contributions towards the perfecting of a weapon, which had so weighty an effect on the fortunes of the Great War and the modern type of which now forms so valuable a part of the armament of the British Army.

[1] Army Council's full letter, page 235.

List of books from which information has been gathered:

Memoirs of an Unconventional Soldier, by General Fuller.
Tanks, 1914–18, by Sir Albert Stern.
War Memoirs, by David Lloyd George.
The Tank Corps, by Williams-Ellis.
The Way of the Guns, by Wade.
My War Memoirs, 1914–18, by General Ludendorff.
Tanks in the Great War, by General Fuller.
The World Crisis, by Winston Churchill.
Land, Sea and Air, by Admiral Mark Kerr.
With Lawrence in Arabia.
Hindenburg, 1847–1934.
This Our Army, by Captain J. R. Kennedy.
Airman Friday, by William Courtenay.
Sous L'armure, by Lieutenant Pierre Lestringuez.

List of papers, etc., from which extracts and illustrations have been taken:

The *Times*.
The *Morning Post*.
The *Daily Telegraph*.
The *Daily Mail*.
The *Daily Express*.
The *Evening Standard*.
The *Evening News*.
The *Illustrated London News*
The *Observer*.
The *Sunday Times*.
The *Sunday Express*.
Strand Magazine.
Aeroplane.
Commander King Hall's publications.
R.U.S.I. Journal.
Army and Navy Gazette.
United Services Review.
Reports of Royal Commission on Awards to Inventors.
Hansard.
The *Royal Tank Corps' Journal*.
Army Ordnance Journal, United States Army.
Völkerbund, the journal of the German Association for League of Nations questions.
Revue d'Infanterie
Le Matin.

APPENDIX I

SPEECHES WHEN INTRODUCING MINISTRY OF DEFENCE CREATION BILL, FEBRUARY 14, 1936

THE NEED FOR FORGING THE RIGHT WEAPONS OF WAR—TANKS FOR WORKING WITH ARTILLERY—HEAVY TANKS AND LIGHT TANKS.

MINISTRY OF DEFENCE (CREATION) BILL.

Order for Second Reading read.

11.6 a.m.

REAR-ADMIRAL SIR MURRAY SUETER : I beg to move, "That the Bill be now read a Second time."

Some 14 years ago Mr. Speaker gave me permission to bring in my first Ministry of Defence (Creation) Bill under the Ten Minutes Rule. I brought in that Bill because from personal experience in the War I was not satisfied that the administration of our three fighting services was as efficient as it might be when it was largely administered by the Committee of Imperial Defence. There always were difficulties in the administration when we had only an Army and a Navy. There was a good deal of friction in the old days, but fortunately the line of demarcation was the high-water mark where the sea water touched the shore. That was a very good line of demarcation then, but there was a good deal of friction over coast fortifications as to where the Royal Engineers should drop their observation mines and their electro-contact mines, and where the Army should put their cordon of search-lights for the defence of our ports. There was a good deal of friction and many difficulties at times to settle. Sometimes there were even dog fights. The late Lord Randolph Churchill suggested that a Minister of Defence should be created to be over those two services and settle differences.

Since that time the air development has come upon us and all nations are creating very large and efficient air forces, and are depending largely on the bomb. The Navy could not help in any way in an aerial bombardment of London, and neither the Army nor the Navy could help in an aerial bombardment of our chief cities, our great factories, our royal dockyards, our shipyards or our homes. That has to be left to the Air Force. The Air Force has to-day that duty, and many duties in different parts of the world. It has also to assist the Navy and the Army with their air requirements. New and very difficult problems have been created by the introduction of this third service, but I submit that it is no solution of the problem for some people to advocate the breaking up of the Royal Air Force into a central force, a smaller and weaker Naval air force, and an Army air force. During and since the War in manœuvres the air has become a connecting link between the two services, and we should strengthen that link and not weaken it; we should consolidate it and make it as strong as possible. I submit that the way to do that is to put a Minister of Defence over the three fighting services to whom he could give wise guidance.

Can we learn anything from the past? Before the War, under the Committee of Imperial Defence, we were badly handicapped. The Navy was deprived of Zeppelins in the North Sea. The Germans had a monopoly of aerial reconnaissance in the North Sea before the War. The Committee of Imperial Defence advocated that we should build Zeppelins, but after the *Mayfly* accident the Admiralty tore their recommendation up and refused to build Zeppelins. Towards the end of the War Zeppelins were asked for by Admiral Beatty, and a few were supplied, but they arrived too late to be of any use in the War. It was exactly the same with the torpedo-dropping seaplanes and aeroplanes. Before the War they were shown to the right hon. Gentleman the Member for Epping (Mr. Churchill), when he was First Lord, and to Lord Fisher. We sent three torpedo-dropping aeroplanes to the Dardanelles, and the gallant pilots got three hits out of three shots on enemy shipping, but the Admiralty refused to develop the torpedo-dropping machines. They were asked nine months before Jutland for that development, and it was turned down. Towards the end of the War Admiral Beatty asked for these machines, but they were delivered too late. I submit that under a Minister of Defence that would have been impossible. In the case of aircraft-carriers, before the War one of the Directors of Beardmores submitted plans to the Admiralty for aircraft-carriers. That was turned down by the Admiralty, and when War broke out we had to convert cross-Channel steamers into aircraft-carriers because we had nothing else. That would have been impossible under a Minister of Defence. Take the case of the submarines. Before the War all the submarine experts warned the Admiralty of the danger of enemy submarines. The Admiralty took little or no notice of their submarine experts, with the result that during the War we lost 6,750,000 tons of British shipping because of the action of enemy submarines. I submit that a good deal of that would not have been lost if we had only studied the submarine menace a little more before the War. Under a Minister of Defence

APPENDIX I 323

that would have been looked into, I am certain. These are a few of the Naval errors.

As to Army errors, when war started we found that the Army had only three 1-inch pom-poms for the anti-aircraft defence of this country—one over the Treasury, one over the Admiralty Arch, and another one. Would that have been possible under a Minister of Defence? Would he not have inquired, and said, "Surely you have more than three 1-inch pom-poms to defend a great city like London from Zeppelins and hostile aircraft?" We have only to look at General Sir William Robertson's book. He said that before the War there was no Army policy got out for a war. He said he could not make any plans or orders because nothing was ready. Then there was the case—and it is on record—of General Sir Ian Hamilton, who was sent to the Dardanelles with no plans from the War Staff. Would that have been possible under a Minister of Defence? I think not. Then there was Lord Kitchener who, when he sent the last man in the Expeditionary Force across the Channel, said: "If I had any more men, I have got no munitions for them." Would not a Minister of Defence have looked into that? I submit he would. But it is not good to dwell too much on the errors of the past, except to draw lessons from them. Otherwise, it is not too profitable.

Towards the end of the War the right hon. Member for Carnarvon Boroughs (Mr. Lloyd George) set up his War Cabinet. It was composed of the Ministers who did not have departmental responsibilities, and it functioned very well. There was an authority giving executive orders over the three fighting services, and they accepted those orders and the system worked uncommonly well. Since the War that has been allowed to drift away, and there is no authority over the three fighting services. We have got back to the Committee of Imperial Defence, with its innumerable sub-committees and sub-sub-committees guiding the three fighting services.

I submit that we should look for a moment into the Committee of Imperial Defence and its organisation. It has many sub-committees, the chief of which are the Chiefs of the Staffs Committee and the Supply Committee. We were told in this House when the Chiefs of the Staffs Committee was set up that everything would be all right, that the Chiefs of the Staffs Committee would look into everything. I have raised certain questions with Ministers and ex-Ministers and other people in authority, and they have always said, "It is perfectly all right; the Chiefs of the Staff Committee will look into it. They are the people." I read my *Times* of 14th December last and I saw a letter from Viscount Trenchard. He says the Chiefs of the Staffs Committee have done nothing about looking into the great problems of defence, much less to solving them. The Chiefs of the Staffs Committee have been torpedoed by a member who was six years on it, and Chairman of it for two and a half years. I ask the House, "Have the Chiefs of the Staffs Committee given us any guidance on some of the vexed questions of the day, any guidance on the question of the battleship versus the bomb?"

There is so much confused thinking over this battleship versus bomb question that I really think the Chiefs of the Staffs Committee might have looked into it and given the nation guidance. In one of our leading papers, the *Morning Post*, there was a letter last Monday from a Naval Officer dealing with this question of defence, and he stated that if an aerial bomb dropped alongside a surface ship it could do little or no damage. I ask this House, "If you drop a 1000-lb. bomb under the quarter of any ship in existence would it not damage her propellers, her propeller shafting and her rudder, and make her leak aft?" That is an instance of the wrong guidance which has been given to this country by certain people who want to minimise the effect of the aerial bomb.

I ask the Prime Minister whether he could not have an experiment made. Take an old battleship, build her up inside to make her as unsinkable as naval constructors can, and then send up the airmen with bombs to attack her—but not with bombs manufactured or ordered by the Admiralty. Let the airmen choose their own type of bomb, with an armour-piercing point, and have their own explosive in the bomb. Then send them up and see whether they will do a little more damage, perhaps, than was done to the *Centurion*. Try the 1000-lb. bomb for a start. The whole world wants these experiments. We have America talking about 40,000-ton battleships. The sooner large experiments are carried out and the world knows of them the better. The Chiefs of the Staffs Committee have never given any guidance about putting ships under smoke screens—small smoke bomb or phosphorous bomb screens. Have any experiments been carried out? If not, I submit they should be. It is not the slightest use for the First Lord of the Admiralty to come down to another place and make a wonderful speech saying that the whole Navy, practically, has been turned into an anti-aircraft platform. We cannot prevent the bombing of ships by anti-aircraft guns. It is impossible. The guns may do a certain amount of damage, but look at what happened at the front during the War. In spite of those great barrages, with every gun that could be aimed at aircraft firing, the airmen got through. Certainly a few were "downed," just as men going over the top were "downed," but mostly the aircraft got through. People who say that anti-aircraft can stop aerial bombardment have not the vaguest idea of what they are talking about.

I should like to dip for a moment into the future. We have only to look at the Mediterranean and see what happened when the Italo-Abyssinian crisis came to a head. Our Fleet was moved from Malta to

Alexandria. I do not know whether it was moved because of the Savoia bombing machine of the Italians, which was fairly near by. That machine can carry 2 tons of bombs, can fly 1250 miles at a top speed of 266 miles an hour, and has a cruising speed of 236. A pretty formidable weapon. I, personally, think the Admiralty were wise in taking every precaution and in moving the Fleet away from Malta. But let anybody imagine the grand harbour of Malta with the Fleet there, and the nearest nation hostile and able to fly over and drop these large bombs, as they can now. The Fleet could not stay there for a minute.

The aerial bomb is becoming a very formidable weapon. I can give an example of the moral effect of the aerial bomb in the Mediterranean. A short time ago, during the Greek rebellion—the last one, the Venizelos rebellion—some of the rebel cruisers put to sea. The Greek Government were not quite satisfied with their naval air pilots, they did not think they were loyal, so they had to call up any pilots they could find to man the machines and send them to search for the rebel cruisers. Those Army pilots were not very efficient, but, however, two of the machines located one rebel cruiser and dropped a 250-lb. bomb 500 yards off. I do not think the pilots wanted to sink their own national ship or injure their own nationals, only to shake them up. The next bomb they dropped 100 feet off the beam of the rebel cruiser. What happened? The whole of the crew—all the engine staff and everybody else—came on deck and refused to steam the ship any more. They refused to go on. They said to the officers, "If you do not take us back to port we will do nothing, the ship will stay here"—they were so alarmed, they had had a pretty good shake up from that 250-lb. bomb. That will give an idea of the moral effect of bombing. [*Laughter.*] I said "moral effect."

If what I have said of Malta is true—and I do not think any Member can deny that the battleships could not stay in Malta if there were a hostile, near nation, on account of the aircraft—it is also true of Gibraltar. A short time ago an article appeared in one of our leading papers with a great picture of the Rock of Gibraltar. The article had been written by a former Governor of Gibraltar, who had not long given up that position, and it was headed "Gibraltar is safe." Well, the great rock may be safe, but it certainly would not be safe for the British Fleet to lie behind the breakwaters there if a near nation was hostile and there was an aerial attack. The ships cannot lie in the dockyards now because of the bombs. The sooner we in this country understand that the better.

If what I have said is true of Malta and Gibraltar, it is surely true of Devonport, Portsmouth, Chatham and Sheerness. Have the Chiefs of Staffs given us any guidance about those? Have they done anything about having a war port up as far as they can in the north-west of our islands? Rosyth is too near Germany. What have the Chiefs of Staffs done about that? Have they given us any guidance? I submit that they have not. These southern ports are all open to an aerial bombardment, and it is high time we considered it. When anybody says, "Shift Portsmouth, or Chatham or Devonport," the answer always is, "That is where the wives and the children of the seamen live." That is not war thinking. The sooner we look into the whole question of our war ports the better.

If we set up a Ministry of Defence with a Minister over it all, I can imagine him sending for the Chief of the Naval Department and saying, "You want a large battle-fleet. Tell me how you are going to use a battle-fleet when oceans separate you from a hostile nation?" I put that question the other day to a well-known admiral of very high scientific attainments. I said, "How would you use a battle-fleet 3000 miles from its base?" He said, "It would be impossible." To be effective with your Navy you must work on to the enemy shore with your battle-fleet, and there you would be met by fast craft carrying torpedoes, mine-layers and submarines dropping mines and firing the Whitehead torpedo, aircraft dropping bombs and the Whitehead torpedo. It would be impossible for the fleet to operate on an enemy coast. A Ministry of Defence would look into that, and I think he would rather question that provision. He would ask his chief naval officer: "Would the security of this Empire suffer if you did not have battleships?" and the Chief of Staff would say, "Well, Sir, we want the battle-fleet so that light craft, if they are being chased or are in difficulties, can come and shelter behind the fleet." If light craft were being chased by hostile cruisers they would soon flick up an aircraft with their catapults and see where the fleet were, and they would not be likely to go into the jaws of death. The argument that the battle-fleet is required as a screen for lighter craft to shelter behind does not cut much ice with me. If the raiding cruisers came within sight of the battleships, they could alter their course 16 points, and the battleships would not overtake them, as they would not have the speed. The whole of the battleship question needs to be threshed out. Take Admiral Richmond and bring him into the councils of high authority. Ask what he thinks about it, and ask what the other Admirals think about it. Let us have the benefit of their experience before we are asked to spend something like £120,000,000 upon a replacement programme for our battleships.

The Minister of Defence would also talk about cruisers. He would say: "How many cruisers have you? You have only 50? Surely it would be better to have more cruisers and fewer battleships." Then he would say to the Chief of the Navy: "How does it come about that foreign countries have destroyers of larger displacement than we have?"—and faster, as a right hon. Gentleman reminds me.

Then he would turn to the question of submarines, and he would say: "How is it that we are the fifth Power in submarines? Surely that cannot be quite right." Some hon. Members and some Members of the Government say that we should do away with submarines. I am an old submarine man. From the day the French had success with the submarines *Goubet, Gustave Zede* and *Narval*, they forced us to build submarines in this country, and the French will never give up submarines. It is no good Ministers going to these conferences and starting off by saying: "We will give up submarines," because all that the French do is to say: "The islanders have got the wind up."

My Minister of Defence would send for the head of the Army and he would say to him, "What are your war plans? Have you got your war plans out? Have you asked the Navy and the Air Force about it?" "No, we have not done that," the answer would be. "Oh, you have all got your separate war plans," the Minister would say. Then he would say, "What about Tanks? Have you Tanks for working with artillery, heavy Tanks and light Tanks in sufficient quantities, and is your mechanization following on right lines? Have you an anti-Tank rifle?"—and so on. Then would send for the Minister of Air or the head of the Air Service and he would say, "You have an expansion programme of 1500 first line machines by 1937. I understand that other nations also have an expansion programme. Are you following that out? How is that going?" Then he would say, "Where is your research done? At Farnborough? Farnborough gets about £500,000 a year, and in the last 10 years it has had some £4,000,000 or £5,000,000. What have they to show for that?" I think you could get some value out of criticism from above.

After those preliminary remarks, I submit that the House now turn to my Bill. My Bill seeks to set up a Minister of Defence. I should choose as Minister in charge of the defence forces one who is airminded, who has had some experience of the air and who values the air bomb. The air bomb is gradually becoming the master weapon. I would set up a council to advise the Minister that would consist of Service Officers who had passed through the Imperial Defence College. That College has been in existence for nine years and has trained Officers very efficiently. They would give advice on defence problems. I would attach Civil Members who have great experience of industry. In a future war it will not be only a matter of the Navy, the Army and the Air, but you will have to bring in the whole of industry. You should have some of the ablest brains in your country to advise on these matters. I attach very great importance to that.

I would have representatives of the Dominions, and when they were sitting in council that body would form in effect an Empire Defence Council. The problem is not only our own defence, but that of the whole of the Dominions, and we ought to have Dominion representatives to go into the whole question. We have a very good example in Australia where there is a scout and cadet movement. That ought to be extended throughout the whole of the Empire. It is not necessary for me to go through all the Clauses of my Bill, but I would like to refer to one, which proposes to place the representatives of the Admiralty, Army and Air Ministries on an equal footing. I would call them the First Members of the Navy, the Army and the Air Board. Somebody said to me that we ought to call them air lords, because we have sea lords already and we might want Army lords, but I think we ought to have them all on the same footing.

That brings me to the second point. No Service man would ever say a word against the very able Secretary of the Committee of Imperial Defence, Sir Maurice Hankey; but he has a very difficult task. He is Cabinet Secretary; I am not sure that he is not the Secretary of the Privy Council; and he is Secretary of the Committee of Imperial Defence as well. It is an impossible position when one man has to be divided up like that, and cannot give his whole time and thought to these great problems of defence. I hope we shall have a full-time Secretary studying these problems of defence. All the intelligence services I would get together—I think that that is very important; and also, as regards research and scientific work, I should like to have all new ideas looked into very carefully. Lord Fisher in his book says that the Admiralty are the past masters of blocking new ideas, and I have found that to be the case in my own experience when serving under that great Department. Hospitals and medical services also I would bring together. A Colleague of ours in this House, who used to sit in the place from which I am now speaking, and who was a doctor, went out to Malta and was making some inquiries at the military hospital. He asked, "How do you treat this sort of malady?" and they told him. He said, "I am not quite satisfied about that; how do they do it at the Naval Hospital?" "Oh," was the reply, "we know nothing about what they do at the Naval Hospital." That is the actual experience of a Doctor who went out there; the Army Doctors did not know or confer with their Colleagues of the Navy.

I would like now to say a word about the criticisms of my Bill. It is said that, if a Ministry were placed over these departments of defence, it would only add to their dead weight. But they have the Committee of Imperial Defence over them now, and, as the right hon. Gentleman the Member for Carnarvon Boroughs (Mr. Lloyd George) has said, they have a warren of committees and sub-committees. I submit that it would be no greater weight to have a Ministry of Defence over them. Then it is said that you would have to have a super-man as Minister of Defence. I do not think people would say that the present Prime Minister, the late Prime

Minister, or the right hon. Gentleman the Member for Carnarvon Boroughs, are super-men. They are Statesmen of great ability, but they are not quite super-men, and I do not think there is much in that argument. It is said, too, that the Minister of Defence would be a greater man than the Prime Minister, but that is a ridiculous argument. The Prime Minister surely would choose a colleague who would work with him.

I would make an appeal to the Prime Minister. The Prime Minister may not go the whole way with me over this question of a Ministry of Defence and the putting of a Minister of Defence over the three Fighting Services, but I would ask him to create the machinery to start it, to see whether we are forging the right weapons of war. Many people are disturbed about this question, and I think the Prime Minister should look into it. The taxpayers of my constituency say, "We do not want our money wasted on the wrong weapons." They say to me, "Admiral, do try and see that they get the right weapons of war, and that nothing is wasted on obsolete weapons." I make that appeal to the Prime Minister in the interests of the taxpayers in my constituency and throughout the country; and I would ask him also to forge the right weapons of war in the interests of the young Service people, the young men who have to use these weapons of war, and not to place them in the position in which General Henderson and myself were placed at the beginning of the War. We were asked for aircraft, pilots and bombs from all theatres of the War, and we could not provide them. We did our best with the help of our great aircraft industry, but we could not do it at first, because this House had made no provision for it, nor any provision for reserves, and we were handicapped in that way. I am one of those who believe that a strong Britain means more for peace among the nations than a weak Britain; I believe that a strong Britain is necessary in order that we may carry out our obligations under the League of Nations; and I believe that a strong Britain is the rock of hope on which the collective security of the whole world rests. I ask the Prime Minister not to fail Britain by the faulty high-level-bridge administration of the three Fighting Services.

When I drew the first place in the Ballot, I had Bills sent to me by kindly people all over England—Bills dealing with licensed houses, the export of horses, matrimonial causes, electricity, all sorts of Bills; but I thought the matter over and chose this Bill. I present it to the House with great deference. I know that all those Bills to which I have referred ought to be on the Statute Book, but I thought it was more important to defend our home-land and the homes in it. I bring forward this Bill with great diffidence, as I have said, but I really have felt that the Service men in this House should give guidance wherever they possibly can in these difficult matters of defence.

I apologize to Members of the Opposition for not having any of their names on the Bill, for I know that some of them are very interested in it. I did ask the former Under-Secretary of State for Air, the hon. Member for West Islington (Mr. Montague), but I did not get an answer from him, and, as I had a very important engagement in my constituency on that evening, I had not time to get the name of the right hon. Gentleman the Member for Newcastle-under-Lyme (Colonel Wedgwood), who always backs these Bills so well. But I have among the supporters of the Bill my right hon. Friend the Member for South Molton (Mr. Lambert), who is a Statesman of wide experience. He was for many years Civil Lord of the Admiralty. The late Lord Fisher had the greatest admiration for the ability of my right hon. Friend the Member for South Molton. I was at the Admiralty at the time, and whenever Lord Fisher had a difficult problem to solve he would always send for my right hon. Friend. My right hon. Friend earned the esteem and affection of all naval men and civil men who worked with him at the Admiralty, and I am quite certain that from his wide experience he will give us good guidance to-day.

MR. LAMBERT: I beg to second the Motion.

My hon. and gallant Friend made me blush with his compliments. I was going to say of him that he rendered notable service at the Admiralty, but I really must refrain from expressing the sentiments that I feel for him. At any rate, he has rendered notable service to the country in bringing this question before the House to-day. He speaks from a technical point of view; I speak from a civilian point of view; and I would say this, that spending is not defence. We want wise expenditure. I have taken the trouble to look up the expenditure for the past 10 years. The Government say, rightly, that our defences are inadequate. In the 10 years from 1925–6 to 1934–5 we have spent on the average £112,000,000 a year. The total is something like £1,120,000,000, yet our defences are inadequate. There must be something wrong. These are astronomical sums. This year the expenditure is £124,000,000. Before the War it was £80,000,000 and, when I went to the Naval Review last year, I saw a very large number of ships which were built in the days when I was at the Admiralty. I cannot help thinking that our expenditure has not been wise. All the services had the advantage of the War stores and to-day we are told we are to have a new expenditure of something like £250,000,000 to £300,000,000. If that is so, I should like it to be more wisely spent than it has been in the past for, after all, finance is not an unimportant matter in the question of defence. We have a war debt of £7,000,000. I do not know whether the Chancellor proposes to have a loan. We shall find that out later. But finance is all-important.

Taking my hon. and gallant Friend's illustration about the lessons of the late War, in a time of emergency all exports cease. We have to pay for imported food. I should like the House to consider what would have happened in 1917 if we had not had the American loans to assist us in providing us with food. In this question, though it may seem remote to naval and military experts, the question of food is all-important. In the last War we were never in danger of invasion, but we were perilously near starvation. You may have a fortress with the finest armaments and the most gallant defenders, but you must have provisions, and in 1917 we had six weeks' supply of corn only in the country, and we were saved then by the heroism of our mercantile marine. Never once did they falter, although our coast was like a cemetery for merchant ships. We do not want these things to happen again. Again, great industries are coming South. The population round London is increasing. Something like 11,000,000 people have to be fed from the Port of London. Is the Port of London safe to rely on for the feeding of this enormous population? Is the Channel safe? Can you bring ships up the Channel? We had then difficulties enough, but to-day the difficulties are enhanced by the advent of aircraft. The Government, wisely, in their first year said, "We will grow more wheat." British agriculturists grew wheat, but what happened? They said, "You must grow only 6,000,000 quarters. If you grow more, we shall stop giving you extra support." This question of food may not appeal to the naval and military experts, but in my judgment you must have first things first, and we must remember that Britain is the heart of the Empire and, if the heart fails, the extremities will wither.

I think sometimes of those Napoleonic strategists who spend something like £20,000,000 on a base at Singapore and leave the food supply of London the same as it was in the last War. They leave Woolwich, the great military arsenal on the east coast, most vulnerable to air attack. My hon. and gallant Friend has instanced Chatham and Portsmouth. According to the First Lord of the Admiralty everything in the garden is lovely. All is perfect. I should like my hon. and gallant Friend's Minister of Defence to make an enquiry as to whether there is waste in the Admiralty. I am certain that there is enormous waste there. Look at your shore establishments. Look at the large proportion of men on the land compared with the fighting Services. You will find an enormous disproportion. It has been brought to my attention quite recently that in the repairing and designing of ships in the dockyards the designers in my hon. and gallant Friend's time and mine were under the capable guidance of Sir James Marshall, who was a practical shipbuilder. To-day I understand it is in charge of an Admiral. An Admiral knows little about the practical construction of ships. These are questions that require elucidation, because we do not want waste.

I am sure that one reason that has influenced my hon. and gallant Friend is the state of Europe. Europe to-day is one vast arsenal. Armaments are growing. They are in the charge of Dictators. There is more loot in London than in Addis Ababa. I should prefer that London should not be at the mercy of any dictator. We must recognise, however much we rely on the League of Nations, that it has failed to arrest armaments and has failed to avert war, and British security cannot rely upon collective security. It can only rely upon its own strong right arm. A little imagination is required. My hon. and gallant Friend has shown how difficult it is to get the older Services to adopt new craft. We are to-day at the parting of the ways. Are we going on building large battleships? Are we going on with the mechanization of the Army and leaving out of account this new weapon which has absolutely transformed the whole of future warfare? I remember that before the War the submarine was regarded as a toy. It was a very terrible toy in the War and very nearly brought us down. I shudder to think what would have happened if Germany had won. Probably England would have been discovered to be a spiritual home for the Jews. In my younger days we had a two-Power naval standard to protect us against invasion. To-day we should have a two-Power air standard, because, though we might not be able to prevent invasion, we certainly should be able to put up a good defence and make it pretty hot for those who might attempt to invade us. In this question the Air Force must come first, the Navy second, and the Army third. An Air Force can bomb our cities, they can close the Channel which is very important indeed—to food ships, and they can make our naval bases very insecure.

My hon. and gallant Friend rightly asked the Government to go into the question of battleships. A battleship costs £7,000,000, and is all in one restricted area. The battleship requires a convoy. The Great Fleet could not leave Scapa Flow without a hundred destroyers. Then there is the Army. It is to be mechanized, and for what purpose? Is it to go abroad. Do not make any mistake, the embarkation at Southampton will not be carried out with as little friction, with aircraft swarming in the air, as it was during the last war. Let us look at the proportion of expenditure. The expenditure this year is £124,000,000, of which the Navy absorbs £60,000,000, the Army £43,500,000 and the Air Force £20,600,000. That is to say, that on the most important force there is only one-sixth of the expenditure. That is wrong. We require more co-ordination. What has been the co-ordination? When I was at the Admiralty the co-ordination was really a fight between the Departments and the Treasury. When we had a forceful personality like the right hon. Gentleman the Member for Epping (Mr. Churchill) at the Admiralty we got all we wanted. That was the co-ordination, and I suspect that that is the co-ordination to-day, and that it is a fight between the heads of the Departments and the right hon. Gentleman the Chancellor of the Exchequer. Therefore, it is necessary to change this system and to have a co-ordinating Minister. The Committee of Imperial Defence on whom my hon. and gallant Friend poured contumely—he could not pour too much—have had a thousand meetings, I understand, according to the First Lord of the Admiralty, in the last four years. They must have been like squirrels running round a cage for all that has been done. We have had this huge expenditure and still inadequate defence.

My hon. and gallant Friend spoke of the Prime Minister who comes down here with an air of the most engaging innocence. [An HON. MEMBER: "It serves him well."] I sometimes think that there is a good deal behind that innocence when I know how he has handled the Conservative Party and the attacks of the Press peers. I do not think that there is a Simple Simon behind our Prime Minister to-day, but he has his other work to perform. He is the Chairman of the Committee of Imperial Defence, but he has all these other duties. He has to keep his erring colleagues in order. I wonder if the Prime Minister would be able to pass an examination on the deluge of Bills which is now almost drowning the House of Commons. I do not think that he would be able to pass a real examination upon all those Bills. We ought to co-ordinate the question of defence; it is a full-time job for any Minister. These are days of real emergency. The country has trusted the Government, and I ask the Government not to fail the country.

APPENDIX II

MINISTRY OF DEFENCE CREATION BILL

MINISTRY OF DEFENCE (CREATION)

A BILL

To subordinate the three fighting services to a Ministry of Defence; and for purposes connected therewith.

Presented by Rear-Admiral Sir Murray Sueter.

Supported by

*Mr. Lambert, Sir Ian Fraser,
Colonel Moore-Brabazon, Captain Balfour,
Mr. Simmonds, Mr. Wells, Mr. Chorlton,
Colonel Cruddas, Mr. Perkins and Mr. Patrick.*

Ordered, by The House of Commons, *to be Printed,*
7 February 1936.

MINISTRY OF DEFENCE (CREATION) BILL

MEMORANDUM

(1) This Bill is to establish a Ministry of Defence consisting of a Principal Secretary of State, who shall be President of the Defence Council, and a Secretary of State or an Under Secretary of State for each

of the three departments: Admiralty, War Office, and Air Ministry respectively, for purposes connected with the development and maintenance of the three fighting services, viz., the Navy, Army and Air Force, in an up-to-date and efficient condition, with the utmost economy, consonant with the increased efficiency which this Bill is designed to effect, and for other purposes in connection therewith.

(2) It empowers His Majesty's Government to appoint such service and civil members to form, under the Presidency of the Minister of Defence, the Defence Council as may be necessary. The service members to be drawn from those officers who have passed through the Imperial Defence College.

(3) It empowers His Majesty, by Order in Council, to appoint such representatives of the Dominions as the Prime Ministers of those Dominions may select, to sit upon the Council—thereby creating, in effect, an Empire Defence Board.

(4) The Minister of Defence is responsible to His Majesty's Government for the proper consideration of all strategical and tactical questions bearing on the defence of the realm, i.e., on the surface of the water, under the water, on land and in the air; for the proper equipment and maintenance of all arms of the three fighting services in a state of readiness and efficiency according to the principles of strategy and tactics adopted; to arrange for the provision and regulation of an adequate supply of personnel to all three fighting services; to examine the estimates which may be prepared by each of the services with a view to the co-ordination and reduction of unnecessary services and to maintain a balance as between one service and another in the expenditure required to carry out the general scheme of defence; and will be responsible to His Majesty's Government that the actual expenditure is the minimum that can attain this object.

(5) Provision is made for a committee to be appointed to consider and report as to what Acts or portions of Acts it will be necessary to repeal.

(6) His Majesty may, by Order in Council, transfer such rights and powers from the three existing services to the Minister of Defence, or establish such new powers as may be necessary to carry out the duties of Minister of Defence.

[26 GEO. 5 & 1 EDW. 8.]

A

BILL

TO

A.D. 1936. Subordinate the three fighting services to a Ministry of Defence; and for purposes connected therewith.

BE it enacted by the King's most Excellent Majesty, by and with the advice and consent of the Lords Spiritual and Temporal, and Commons, in this present Parliament assembled, and by the authority of the same, as follows:

Constitution of Ministry of Defence.
1.—(1) There shall be established a Ministry of Defence for the purposes laid down in this Act.

(2) The Minister of Defence shall be one of His Majesty's Principal Secretaries of State who shall be President of the Defence Council.

(3) There shall be three Secretaries of State or Under Secretaries of State—one in charge of the Admiralty, War Office and Air Ministry respectively; and they will be directly responsible to the Minister of Defence for the efficient working of their respective departments.

(4) There shall be appointed by His Majesty's Government such service and civil members to form, under the Presidency of the Minister of Defence, the Defence Council as His Majesty's Government may consider necessary.

Provided that the service members shall be drawn from those officers who have passed through the Imperial Defence College.

(5) His Majesty may, by Order in Council, appoint such members of his Dominions as the Prime Ministers of those Dominions may select to represent them as members of the Defence Council when that body deals with matters that concern those Dominions.

(6) The Defence Council shall form the nucleus for an Imperial General Staff; it shall absorb the advisory duties now performed by the Committee of Imperial Defence; and it shall have power to co-opt representatives from other government departments.

(7) Subject to the provision of this Act it shall be lawful for His Majesty, by order signified under the hand of the Minister of Defence, to make orders with respect to the higher administration of the Navy, Army and Air Force and with respect to all other matters and things relating to any matter by this Act authorized to be prescribed or expressed to be subject to orders or regulations.

(8) Subject to the provisions of any such order the Minister of Defence may make general or special regulations with respect to any matter with respect to which His Majesty may make orders under this Act.

(9) All orders and general regulations made under this Act shall be laid before Parliament as soon as may be after they are made.

(10) In order to place the members who serve at the Admiralty, War Office and Air Ministry on a footing of equality, the members of the various boards shall be generally known as First Member of Naval Board, First Member of Army Board, First Member of Air Board, Second Member of Naval Board, &c., &c.

(11) The Defence Council may appoint such secretaries, officers, and servants as the Council may, with the sanction of the Treasury, determine.

(12) *The salaries of the Ministry of Defence including the salaries of the Defence Council shall be such as the Treasury may determine and shall be paid out of moneys provided by Parliament.*

(13) *The expenses of the Ministry of Defence including any expenses of the Defence Council, to such an amount as may be sanctioned by the Treasury, shall be paid out of moneys provided by Parliament.*

2.—(1) The Minister shall make such provisions as may be necessary to constitute a department to consider and co-ordinate the planning of future operations of all three fighting services, viz.: Navy, Army and Air Force. A.D. 1936.
Duties and powers.

(2) The Minister shall co-ordinate the operations of the three branches so that these operations may be executed in the most efficient and economical manner. Provided, however, that after operational programmes have been approved by the Defence Council they shall be carried out by the Admiralty, War Office and Air Ministry themselves and, except in special circumstances, the Minister shall only issue executive orders to active units and commanders-in-chief through the operations departments of the Admiralty, War Office and Air Ministry, as the case may be.

(3) All intelligence services shall be centred in the Ministry of Defence where the departments of Director of Naval Intelligence, Director of Military Intelligence, and Director of Air Intelligence shall be very closely associated together with certain other branches of the Secret Service now directed by other departments.

(4) Except for the co-ordination of principles and system, training shall be administered by the respective departments.

3.—(1) The construction, inspection and testing of new matériel shall be carried out by a department of the Ministry of Defence, so as to provide a nucleus which shall be capable of expansion into a Provisions as to matériel.

Ministry of Munitions in time of war should His Majesty's Government consider it desirable. Detailed designs shall be elaborated in the respective departments.

(2) Advisory bodies for research, scientific work, examination of inventions, new ideas, &c., shall be formed under the Defence Council.

(3) The Minister of Defence shall take steps to co-ordinate and centralise with a view to efficiency and economy the supply of all armament and other equipment, stores and provisions to the three services. He shall be responsible that each of the fighting services is equipped with the most up-to-date weapons that modern science dictates.

Personnel. 4.—(1) The Minister of Defence shall be responsible for centralizing and administering all branches of recruiting for the three fighting services; and for making arrangement that this section can in time of war expand to a Ministry of National Service. He shall also arrange that as far as possible, the same system of giving orders, drills, drawing rations, stores, &c., shall be adopted for the three fighting services.

(2) The Minister of Defence shall centralize and administer all common subsidiary services such as staff colleges, medical branch hospitals, dental, chaplains departments, meteorology, transport, works and lands, &c.

(3) The Minister of Defence shall be responsible for the appointment of officers to certain higher posts and commands which he shall specify in orders later.

Finance and accounting. 5.—(1) The Minister of Defence shall regulate the rates of pay, pensions, gratuities, and allowances in all three services.

(2) The Minister of Defence shall take steps to amalgamate and administer all accounting and audit departments, and shall institute as soon as possible a uniform system of accounting and auditing for all services.

(3) The Minister of Defence shall be responsible for the preparation and placing of all contract work.

Civil aviation. 6. The Minister of Defence shall be responsible that civil aviation is developed and maintained, having due regard to the defensive requirements within the Empire, comparable with the development and maintenance of civil aviation by other leading powers and that subsidies as necessary are provided similar to those arrangements that have previously existed with armament firms, mercantile marine and cable companies, and that air enterprise within the Empire shall be encouraged to allow a nucleus being ready for immediate expansion should the necessity of doing so arise.

APPENDIX II 339

7. The Defence Council shall have an official seal which shall be *Official* officially and judicially noticed and that seal shall be authenticated by *seal.* the signature of the president or of a secretary or of some person authorized by the Council to act on behalf of a secretary. Every document purporting to be an instrument issued by the Defence Council and to be sealed with the seal of the Council authenticated in manner provided by the Act, or to be signed by a secretary, or any person authorized by the Council to act on behalf of a secretary, shall be received in evidence and be deemed to be such an instrument without further proof unless the contrary is shown.

8. A committee shall be appointed by His Majesty's Government *Provisions* to consider and report as to what Acts or portions of Acts it will be *as to* necessary to repeal. *repeals.*

9.—(1) This Act may be cited for all purposes as the Ministry *Short title,* of Defence (Creation) Act, 1936. *commence-*
(2) This Act shall come into operation on the first day of October *ment and* nineteen hundred and thirty-six. *duration.*

(3) This Act shall continue in force so long as the Naval Discipline Act, the Army Act, and the Air Force Act continue in force.

APPENDIX III

SOME PRESS OPINIONS ON DEFENCE DEBATE

THE following are some opinions on the value of this Defence Debate:

"*The Times,*" 15th February, 1936.
The Defence Debate.

Sir Murray Sueter is to be congratulated on the best use made of a Private Member's day for a long time past.

Call for better co-ordination.

The House of Commons has not been so full on a Friday for a long time as it was to-day, for the first of a long series of debates on defence. Sir Murray Sueter's Bill to establish a Ministry of Defence was made the text for expressions of views over a wide field, and the debate must have proved very informative to the Government.

Sir Murray Sueter himself used his chance to deliver a breezy and forceful attack upon stereotyped ideas. He recounted at length the alleged sins of the Admiralty before 1914 in pooh-poohing Zeppelins, aircraft carriers and submarines, and seemed to think the Service Departments were little brighter to-day.

He declared that all our Naval ports were vulnerable to air attack, that battleships might well be useless, that each Department had separate war plans, and there was little co-ordination.

"*Morning Post,*" 15th February, 1936.

Although Friday is a private Member's day and although to-day's debate was on a private Member's bill, the House was never seen more in earnest, and the Session is unlikely to provide an experience more significant and even sensational.

The occasion was the second reading debate on Rear-Admiral Sir Murray Sueter's Bill for the creation of a Ministry of Defence, and there was revealed an impressive unanimity in all parts of the House—opposition as well as Ministerial—on the necessity for the re-ordering of the National defences.

We are all getting back to the idea that the country must be defended although there is still a good deal of doubt as to how it is to be done.

Rear-Admiral Sir Murray Sueter, who did a public service by raising the issue in the House of Commons yesterday, proposed a Ministry of Defence.... It seems also evident that if the Government reject a Ministry of Defence as impracticable, they must at least be able to show that they have unified executive machinery to supply its place. May we add it is impossible any longer to postpone this vital matter, which has already been delayed far beyond the point of danger.

"*Daily Telegraph*," 11th February, 1936.

Rules of procedure prevent M.P.s discussing the creation of a new Ministry except on special occasions like the Appropriation Bill. Sir Murray Sueter, however, has used his few opportunities well.

At various times he has had the support of speeches from Mr. Lloyd George, Colonel Moore-Brabazon, Mr. Amery and Sir Roger Keyes, who is a recent convert.

"*Daily Telegraph*," 15th February, 1936.

Yesterday's debate on Admiral Sueter's proposal for the creation of a new Ministry of Defence was the most hopeful sign for more than a decade that at last we have a House of Commons fully alive to the real problems of National Defence.

"*Daily Mail*," 15th February, 1936.

In the House of Commons yesterday the question of national defence was considered in a debate of first-class importance, which showed *how abundantly justified have been the efforts of the "Daily Mail*," and how grave is the necessity of making Britain safe against air attack.

"*Observer*," 16th February, 1936.

With last Friday's remarkable debate the real awakening has begun and the next few weeks will make it complete. The thanks of the country are due to Rear-Admiral Sir Murray Sueter for his motion and its consequences. He moved formally for the creation of a Ministry of Defence, but his real purpose admirably attained was to arouse strong discussion on the matter of absolute necessity.

"*Sunday Times*," 16th February, 1936.

The very important debate in the Commons on Friday has made it practically certain that the Government will deal at once with the vexed question of unity of direction and the co-ordination of the three services.

For years past there has been demand for a Ministry of Defence with jurisdiction over Navy, Army and Air Force. The question had been raised under Conservative, Labour and National Governments, and they have all turned the proposal down. Sir Murray Sueter put the case for it with great force on Friday. The significance of the debate, however, was not so much the support given to his Bill as in the insistence from all parts of the House that something effective must be done to secure unity of direction and the development of the three services in due proportion and relation to one another.

"The Evening News," 15th February, 1936.

Admiral Sir Murray Sueter's Bill provided the House of Commons with an impressive excursion into the grim realities of Defence. If one fact only emerges from the present international confusion and uneasiness, it is that the world has moved from a post-war to a pre-war era. And there is one certain way to war: for Britain to remain disarmed and defenceless in the face of a re-armed world.

"Yorkshire Post," 15th February, 1936.

Rarely are so many Cabinet Ministers in the Commons on Friday as there were to-day. Normally Friday is a short Parliamentary day, when the Chamber is sparsely filled and debates excite comparatively little interest.

To-day, however, the spectacle was changed and at times the Treasury Bench was uncomfortably crowded with Members of the Government. Rear-Admiral Sir Murray Sueter, whose Private Members' Bill proposing the establishment of a Ministry of Defence had brought this Ministerial array into the Chamber, scored a personal triumph in attracting such influential attention, and he largely achieved his purpose by stimulating a good discussion on his suggestions.

Defence and Foreign Affairs are two subjects which nowadays arouse special concern among Members of all parties, and to-day's debate was a useful preliminary to the pending debates on the Service Estimates.

"Referee," 16th February, 1936.

In the House of Commons on Friday Admiral Sir Murray Sueter, war-time Director of the Admiralty Air Department, withdrew his Bill for the establishment of a Ministry of Defence. But that does not mean that his efforts to expose Britain's peril in war-fevered Europe have been in vain.

Having focussed attention on the subject, he has been able to obtain from the Government what was tantamount to a promise that the points which had been debated would at least receive consideration.

"*Daily Mirror*," 12th February, 1936.

The point is that Sir Murray Sueter has done us a public service in calling the attention of the Government and of the House of Commons to the need for the reorganization and co-ordination of the Fighting Services.

"*News of the World*," 16th February, 1936.

The proposal to create a Ministry of Defence was made by Admiral Sir Murray Sueter who moved the Second Reading of the Bill to set up such an organization.

Much in the same way as Lord "Bobs" and Lord Charles Beresford and others used to do before the War, he pointed out the dangers with which the country is confronted and tried to make the House of Commons realize the full gravity of the air menace, the vulnerability of our cities and towns, and the need of unified control and strategy of all our defences.

"*Leeds Mercury*," 15th February, 1936.

Yesterday's debate on Rear-Admiral Sueter's Bill for the creation of a Ministry of Defence served the very useful purpose of bringing home to the House of Commons and to the public the extreme complexity and difficulty of the problem that has to be solved.

"*Western Mail*," 15th February, 1936.

It was inevitable that the Debate, which took place on the subject of the proposed establishment of a Ministry of Defence, should have covered not only the need for a co-ordination between the services, but the present inadequate state of our National Defences. Admiral Sir Murray Sueter based his case for a new Ministry on the need for greater preparedness.

In one of the most remarkable speeches the House has heard for a long time, he gave startling facts about our present unpreparedness, showed the dangers of depending upon collective security and emphasized the vital need for Britain to be ready to defend herself. One noticed that the problem was approached by the House with unaccustomed gravity. . . . The Government could not accept the Ministry of Defence proposal and the Bill was withdrawn after five hours of most profitable discussion.

The Government gave an assurance that they were fully alive to

"Scotsman," 15th *February,* 1936.

Sir Murray Sueter's Bill was useful in another respect. It gave Members an opportunity to show their doubt whether the present arrangements for meeting an emergency are adequate on the administrative side, especially having regard to the fact that the country is about to be asked for heavy sacrifices necessary for its defence.

"Daily Despatch," 15th *February,* 1936.

The debate in the House of Commons yesterday on Rear-Admiral Sir Murray Sueter's Bill to establish a Ministry of Defence was of great importance if only because it cleared the air.

"Glasgow Evening News," 15th *February,* 1936.

For the second time in his Parliamentary career Rear-Admiral Sir Murray Sueter, who is a Conservative representative for Hertford, submitted such a Bill (Defence).

He had the satisfaction of seeing one of the best attended of Friday debates, Ministers and ex-Ministers came in full force.

Very briefly, what Sir Murray wants is the establishment of a Ministry of Defence, whereby one man, working in conjunction with an advisory body, would have charge of the three fighting services, and thus by this means create a policy for a modern war so that we would not be taken by surprise as we were on the last occasion.

"Bournemouth Daily Echo," 15th *February,* 1936.

Admiral Sueter deserves general thanks for sounding so effectively the note of alarm in connection with the subject of National and Imperial Defence.

Although he withdrew his motion in order not to embarrass the Government, the air has been cleared for rapid and definite action in this most vital matter of defence planning.

"Northern Daily Mail," 17th *February,* 1936.

If Sir Murray Sueter's real object on Friday was to arouse interest in defence he has succeeded admirably.

Although it is probable that the House of Commons will not have another opportunity of discussing the subject until the Government's plans are published, defence is the principal topic of discussion in Parliamentary circles. There is practical unanimity on the desirability of co-ordination.

Sir Roger Keyes, for instance, says the Committee of the Chief of Staff could do this work and it would be greatly helped if a Minister was put in charge of it, a Minister with vision, courage and experience, such as the Socialist Government had when Lord Haldane presided over the Committee of Imperial Defence, and gave up his whole time to the work.

"*Dundee Advertiser,*" 15th February, 1936.

Although Admiral Sueter's Bill dealing with the Ministry of Defence was withdrawn in the House of Commons to-day, his purpose had been achieved. The question has been debated. Members of all parties agreed that the discussion has been one of the most fruitful of recent years.

The attack of the Admiral in his attempt to secure a Ministry of Defence was startling, and in some respects sensational, but it has thought behind it and obviously it could not be ignored.

INDEX

"A 1" submarine, 20
Abyssinia, 163, 164, 165, 166
Addis Ababa, 164
Admiralty, 8, 27, 86, 94, 108, 181, 182, 207, 208, 214, 238, 239, 259, 261; 262, 269, 283, 285, 302, 305, 306, 307, 319
Aeroplane, the, 106, 110, 320
Airman Friday, 132
Aisne, 139
Albery, Sir Irving, 277
Allday's, 108, 110
America, 144, 158, 159
Amery, The Right Hon. Leopold, 341
Amiens, 128, 140, 143, 289
Anti-Tank guns, 289, 299
Ardenne, General von, 144
Ark of the Covenant, 286
Army Council, 22, 94, 174, 194, 213, 235, 236, 269, 283, 288, 292, 300, 302
Army Ordnance Journal, 162
Army Tank Battalions, 301
Arras, 120
Arthur, Lieutenant, 109
Artillerie d'Assaut, 138
Asquith, the Right Hon. H. H., 48, 49, 227, 253, 254
Attlee, Major the Right Hon.C., 283
Austin, Lord, 61
Australia, 207, 295, 328
Australians, 143
Austria, 172
Austrians, 258

Bacon, Francis, 21
Bacon, Admiral Sir Reginald, 20, 62, 187, 188, 189, 249, 250, 319
Baddeley, Sir Vincent, 238
Badoglio, Marshal, 165
Bagehot, Walter, 241

Baldwin, The Right Hon. Stanley, 262, 279, 282
Balfour, the Right Hon. Arthur, 78, 79, 91, 94, 95, 104, 182, 245, 246, 247, 251, 254, 261
Balfour, Captain Harold, 334
Bapaume, 129, 145
Barry, Lieutenant, 54, 56, 57, 62, 90, 108, 109, 184, 229
Bartolomé, Commodore de, 91, 95, 248, 249, 251
Beatty, Admiral Lord, 240, 322
Beaverbrook, Lord, 159, 160
Belgium, 167
Bentley, Captain Bede, 177, 178
Beresford, Lord Charles, 250, 343
Bethell, Admiral, 249
Berwick Castle, S.S., 20
Bleriot, Louis, 83, 155, 305
Boadicea, Queen, 13, 14
Booth, Mr. Harris, 50, 211, 220, 224
Boothby, Commander, 46, 47, 71, 74, 75, 76, 78, 79, 81, 82, 88, 96, 101, 106, 108, 148, 154, 174, 203, 204, 215, 221, 226, 233, 284, 302
Bournemouth Daily Echo, 344
Boyes gun, 299
Brackenbury, Mr., 65, 69, 85, 190
Bren gun, 16, 299
Breton, M., 157
Briggs, Squadron-Commander W., 31, 33, 34, 35, 45, 50, 57, 62, 65, 68, 98, 154, 174, 204, 209, 215, 219, 220, 229, 255, 284, 302
Briggs, Mrs., 98
Brille, M.. 157
Britain, 310
British Museum, 13
Brownrigg, Admiral Sir Douglas, 178, 179
Buchanan, Sir George, 40

348 INDEX

Buckham, Sir George, 15, 45, 64
Bulgarian, 41
Bullock Caterpillars, 72, 80, 81, 84, 87, 104, 112, 113, 213
Bumpus, Major, 212
Burgoyne, Sir Alan, 208
Burney, Commander, 92, 110, 216
Burney, the Rev., 286
Burns, Robert, 177
Bussell, Mr. Dale, 67, 90, 186, 221
Byng, General, 308

Cambrai, 123, 133, 150, 307
Campbell, Sir Ernest, 278
Canadian Pacific Railway, 18
Canadians, 128
Capron, Mrs., 194, 235
Carlile, Sir Hildred, 273
Carpenter, Admiral Alfred, 316
Cerri, Vice-Admiral Vittorio, 257, 258, 259, 260
Chamberlain, the Right Hon. Sir Austen, 279
Chamberlain, the Right Hon. Neville, 314
Chamier, Air Commodore, 287
Charles II, King, 261
Chatham, 325
Chauteurs de France, 30, 31, 218
Chief of Staff Committee, 280, 281, 323, 324
Chorlton, Mr. A. E. L., 334
Churchill, Lord Randolph, 321
Churchill, the Right Hon. Winston, 20, 27, 28, 29, 38, 45, 46, 47, 48, 49, 51, 52, 53, 56, 57, 58, 59, 60, 62, 64, 65, 66, 67, 68, 75, 77, 78, 87, 92, 95, 99, 100, 111, 118, 149, 155, 179, 181, 183, 184, 186, 187, 189, 190, 191, 192, 193, 202, 209, 212, 221, 225, 226, 229, 230, 231, 233, 237, 239, 240, 241, 242, 243, 244, 245, 246, 263, 268, 305, 322, 323
Civil Servants, 19, 185, 195
Civil Service, 18, 185, 195, 265
Clausewitz, 269
Cologne, 29
Cooper, The Right Hon. A. Duff, 153, 307

Courtenay, Mr. William, 132
Cowan, James, 15
Creedy, Sir H. J., 235
Crompton, Colonel, 67, 69, 70, 71, 72, 73, 74, 75, 76, 77, 78, 80, 81, 86, 87, 90, 98, 99, 100, 101, 102, 103, 104, 105, 108, 148, 204, 213, 221, 226, 229, 247
Crompton, Major J. E., 155
Cruddas, Colonel B., 334
Cull, Squadron-Commander, 43
Currey, Admiral Bernard, 249
Curtis and Co., 71
Curzon, the Marquis, 182, 254, 260, 261, 263, 264, 269, 303
Czechoslovakia, 170

Daily Despatch, 344
Daily Express, 165, 182, 206
Daily Mail, 29, 30, 47, 122, 265, 341
Daily Mirror, 343
Daily Telegraph, 127, 341
Daimler, 83
Dawes, General, 159
Debeney, General, 131
Defence, Co-ordinating Minister of, 281, 317
D'Eyncourt, Sir Tennyson, 67, 73, 79, 80, 81, 82, 83, 86, 90, 92, 94, 96, 107, 113, 118, 119, 191, 204, 206, 209, 212, 224, 247
Delauny, Belville, 34
De Lisle, General, 37
Delville Wood, 119
Deraa, 43
Deutschland, battleship, 263
Deverell, Field-Marshal Sir Cyril, 300
Devonport, 325
Diplock, 15, 45, 65, 68, 69, 80, 89, 95, 96, 99, 101, 111, 112, 114, 148, 149, 185, 190, 195, 202, 212, 213, 215, 230, 231, 233, 237
Disraeli, 312
Döberitz, 166
Dobrodya, 41
Docker, Mr. Dudley, 161
Dolo, 164
Dominion Troops, 135
Donop, General von, 49, 188, 229
Dreyer, General, 44

INDEX

Dumas, Admiral, 75, 77
Dumbell, Colonel, 67, 221
Dundas, Colonel James, 290
Dundee Advertiser, 345
Dunkirk, 28, 29, 30, 32, 43, 240
Durnford, Admiral Sir John, 35, 191, 249, 285
Dusseldorf, 29

Edinburgh, Duke of, 41
Edwards, E. and A. E., 211, 214
Elles, Major-General Sir Hugh, 116, 124, 133, 135, 149, 298, 307, 309
Ellis, Major Clough Williams-, 134
Ellis, Mr. A. Williams-, 134
Esher, Lord, 269
Estienne, Colonel, 137, 155, 156
Evans, Mr., 111, 185, 186, 187
Evening News, 149, 320, 342
Evening Standard, 141, 162, 320
Evere, 241
Excellent, 204

Farnborough, 327
Field, Lieutenant, 72, 73, 90, 100, 104, 204
Fifth Army, 125, 269
Fisher, Admiral Lord, 52, 239, 256, 261, 304, 322, 330
Fitzgerald, Colonel, 34, 35
Fitzroy, the Right Hon. E. A., 277
Flame-throwers, 121
Flers, 119, 120, 180
Flers-Courcelette, 93
Foch, Marshal, 17
Fontes, 68, 101
Foot, 304
Foreign Office, 28
Fosters, Messrs., 83, 84, 86, 88, 93
Fourth Army, 128
France, 154, 174, 310
Fraser, Sir Ian, 334
French, General Sir John, 38, 111
Friedrichshafen, 241
Führer, 167
Fuller, Major-General, 116, 117, 133, 135, 304, 307

Gaedke, Colonel, 146

Gatling, 16
Gaza, 132
Germany, 166, 174
George, the Right Hon David Lloyd, 46, 75, 76, 77, 86, 88, 96, 100, 126, 127, 132, 135, 148, 154, 158, 159, 181, 190, 203, 213, 217, 221, 226, 227, 228, 254, 269, 270, 323, 328, 341
Gerrard, Major, 28
Gibbons, John Murray, 18
Gibraltar, 325
Glasgow Evening News, 344
Gordon, Mr., 225
Gort, Lieutenant-Colonel Viscount, 130, 131
Gough, General, 125, 269
Gould, Lieutenant C. Muirhead, 243
Graziani, General, 294
Greece, Queen of, 41
Gregory, Squadron-Commander, 73
Grey, Mr. G. C., 106, 107, 110
Guendecourt, 119
Guthrie-Smith, General, 49

Hacking, The Right Hon. Douglas, 16, 291
Haig, General, 117, 119, 134, 137, 179, 184, 308
Hamilton, General Sir Ian, 323
Hankey, Captain Maurice, 15, 44, 45, 47, 48, 49, 90, 91, 112, 202, 222, 228, 328
Hatfield Park, 90, 91, 92, 124, 222, 308
Havrincourt, 124
Hazeley Down, 304
Henderson, Admiral Sir W. H., 79
Heneage, Commodore, 232, 255, 257, 259, 265
Hetherington, Flight-Commander, 31, 33, 34, 35, 45, 47, 87, 100, 112, 154, 174, 190, 204, 209, 215, 219, 220, 221, 222, 224, 225, 229, 233, 252, 253, 255, 267, 284, 288, 302
Hetherington, Mrs., 193
Hill, Brigadier-General, 90
Hindenburg, Field-Marshal von, 17, 18, 319

INDEX

Hindenburg Line, 120, 121, 122, 123, 124, 125, 129, 150
Historius, 239
Hitler, Herr, 166
Hoare, the Right Hon. Sir Samuel, 306, 307, 313
Holden, Colonel, 49
Holland Submarine, 60, 83, 113
Home, Lieutenant-Colonel, 37
Holt Caterpillar Tractors, 49, 54, 62, 188
Hood, Admiral Horace, 32
Hood, Admiral Lord, 263
Hornsby-Akroyd Caterpillar, 49
Horse Guards Parade, 65, 149, 233

Illustrated London News, 158, 172, 320
Imperial Conference, 282
Inskip, the Right Hon. Sir Thomas, 281, 317
Italy, 163, 174

Jackson, Colonel, 75, 90
Jaffer Pasha, 43
Janin, General, 157
Japan, 169
Jehol, 163
Joel, prophet, 287
Johnson 286
Joyce, Colonel, 43
Juggernaut, 56, 70, 218, 222

Kabisch, 140
Kashi, General, 169, 170
Kavanagh, Major-General C. M., 36
Kennedy, Captain J. R., 295, 296
Kenworthy, Commander, 293
Kerr, Admiral Mark, 258, 259, 264
Keyes, Admiral of the Fleet Sir Roger, 341, 344
Killen Strait Caterpillar machine, 72, 75, 76, 112
King George V, His late Majesty, 16, 92, 127, 150, 184, 216, 302, 308, 309
King Hall, Commander, 313
Kitchener, Lord, 35, 48, 91, 92, 177, 178, 323
Kitson, Clarke and Co., 93
Kremlin, 265

Lake, 68
Lambert, the Right Hon. G., 278, 279, 330, 331, 332, 333, 334
Lanchester, 34
Landship Committee, 67, 69, 81, 107, 112
Lee, Vaughan, 205, 255
Leeds Mercury, 343
Le Gros, Mr., 67, 98, 99, 101, 103, 104, 105
Leningrad, 167
Lestringuez, Lieutenant Pierre, 156
Lewes, 16
Littlejohns, Commander A. S., 243
Locker-Lampson, Commander Oliver, 38, 39, 40, 41, 42, 43
Longcroft, Wing-Commander, 193
Loringhoven, General von Freytag, 145, 146
Louchier, M., 137
Lowe, Mr., 68, 69, 99
Ludendorff, General, 17, 128, 137, 145, 289
Lupuis, Captain, 191

MacDonald, the Right Hon. Ramsay, 195, 196
Macfie, Lieutenant, 46, 47, 62, 73, 81, 105, 106, 107, 108, 109, 110, 111, 154, 163, 174, 206, 215, 229, 283, 284, 302
Macnamara, Mr., 32
Macnamara, the Right Hon. T. J., 32, 208
Maitland, Colonel, 193
Malta, 325
Mansergh, Lieutenant, 20
Mark V Light Tank, 153
Mark V Tank, 288
Marshall and Co., 93
Marshall, Sir James, 331
Martel, Colonel, 299
Marne, 139
Masefield, Mr. John, 59
Mauser, 31, 59
Maxim, 16
Mayfly, 64, 322
Mbuynia, 43
McCardie, Mr. Justice, 178
McCusker, Dr. E. A., 290

INDEX 351

McGrath, Lieutenant-Commander, 82, 90, 97, 98, 204
Mechanized Cavalry, 151
Melbourne, 207
Medium "A" Tank, 288
Members of the House of Commons, 275, 276, 277
Metropolitan Carriage Works, 93
Michell, Flight-Commander, 68, 96
Minister of Defence, 290, 296, 322
Ministry of Defence, 278, 279, Appendices I and II
Ministry of Munitions, 110, 112, 181, 187, 207
Moncrieff, General Sir Scott, 49, 50, 75, 111, 183, 188, 212, 222, 229
Mons Meg, 14, 15
Montagu, Lord, 151
Moore-Brabazon, Colonel, 334, 341
Morning Post, 129, 166, 172, 180, 269, 320, 324, 340
Murray, Sir Oswyn, 186, 224, 265, 266

Nanton, General, 90
Napoleon, 91
Nelson, Lord, 263, 264
Nesfield, 73, 81, 89, 105, 109, 110, 111, 163, 206
Nesfield and Mackenzie, 108
News of the World, 343
Nicholas, Grand Duke, 39, 40
Nicholson, Admiral Stuart, 249
Nickerson, Captain, 32, 33
Noahs, 21, 22, 74, 254, 269, 303, 304, 306, 318, 319
Norand, General, 307
Normandie, 155
North British Locomotive Co., 93
Northcliffe, Lord, 30
Northern Daily Mail, 344
Nuffield, Lord, 294
Nyren, Richard, 195

Observer, 320, 341
Okada, Admiral, 169
Ostend, 27, 28

Palestine, 132
Palmerston, Lord, 15

Parkill, Sir Archdale, 295
Patrick, Mr. C. M., 334
Pedrail Transport Co., 64
Percy, Lord Eustace, 279
Perkins, Mr. W. R., 334
Perrin, Lieutenant-Commander J. T., 247
Pershing, General, 129
Phillips, General, 75
Pioneer Naval Net Cutter, 75, 77
Pisani, Captain, 44
Press opinions on Defence Debate, Appendix III
Prince of Wales, 127
Pöe, Admiral Sir Edmond, 256, 257, 265
Poland, 170
Porte, Commander, 255
Portholme, 84
Portsmouth, 325

Ramleh, 43
Ras Desta, 164, 166
Rawlinson, General H., 35
Rees, Mr. Caradoc, 203
Referee, 342
Renault Tank, 137
Repington, Colonel, 27
Rhomboidal Tank, 84, 89, 148, 234
Roberts, Captain, V.C., 274, 275
Robinson, General Rowan, 165
Rolls-Royce, 31, 33, 34, 68
Roumania, Queen of, 41
Royal Commission on Awards to Inventors, 196, 197, 198, 199, 200, 201
Royal Naval Air Service, 18, 22, 88, 108, 174, 310
Royal Tank Corps, 116, 133, 290
Runciman, the Right Hon. W., 215
Russell, Mr. John, 277
Russia, 167, 174

Samson, Squadron-Commander, 27, 28, 30, 31, 36, 218
Sarell, Mr., 28
Scientific American, 65
Scotsman, 344
Scott, Admiral Sir Percy, 52, 53, 57, 64, 70, 87, 220, 229

INDEX

Scott, Captain Robert, 45, 61, 62, 189
Seabrooke, 34
Seely, Colonel Jack, 134, 136
Service, Mr., 30
Sheerness, 325
Sheppard, Canon Dick, 217
Siberia, 167
Simmonds, Mr. Oliver, 236, 334
Simmonds, Mrs., 236
Sinclair, Sir Archibald, 153
Singer, Vice-Admiral Morgan, 30, 90
Somme, 93, 120, 180
Soviet, 168
Spain, 170
Starace, General, 165
Stern, Lieutenant, 70, 74, 81, 83, 84, 88, 89, 90, 95, 96, 97, 112, 118, 119, 143, 204
St. Michel Salient, 129
St. Quentin, 140
Stone, Lieutenant-Commander A. J., 271
Strand Magazine, 15, 88, 320
Submarine " A 1," 20
Sueter, Lady, 193
Sueter, Tom, 195
Sunday Times, 341
Sweden, 170
Swinton, Lord, 306
Swinton, Major-General Sir Ernest, 49, 90, 111, 112, 113, 114, 115, 116, 150, 180, 181, 182, 188, 197, 202, 206, 229
Switzerland, 171
Sydenham, Lord, 254
Symes, Lieutenant, 31, 46, 90

Tangye, Nigel, 171
Tank Board, 97
Tank Dominion, 128
Thetford 115
Thomas, Sir William Beach, 122
Thomas, Lowell, 43
Thomson, Lieutenant-Commander Hyde, 209, 212, 239
Threshing machine, 141
Thucydides, 22
Tiergarten, 166
Times, The, 126, 142, 164, 167, 290, 304, 316, 320

Tollemache, Lord, 226
Towse, Mr. Harry, 277
Tritton, Sir William, 69, 70, 84, 85, 88, 89, 90, 92, 94, 104, 148, 174, 206, 228, 229, 230, 237
Tudor-Tudor, Admiral Sir Frederick, 46, 54, 76, 90, 95, 202, 222, 223, 255, 285
Tulloch, Major, 49, 111, 188, 202, 228, 229, 251
Turkey, 41

Usborne, Captain, 110, 205

Vernon, 19, 20, 74, 81, 204
Vickers, Messrs., 15, 16, 34, 45, 64, 92, 110, 205, 206, 216, 231, 236
Villers-Cotterets, 17, 18
Voroshilov, Marshal, 168

Wal Wal, 165
War Office, 8, 22, 30, 34, 44, 50, 87, 88, 94, 112, 183, 208, 218, 235
Wavell, Major-General, 168
Waziristan, 294
Wedgwood, the Right Hon. Josiah, 43, 330
Wells, H. G., 15, 27, 182
Wells, Mr. Sydney, 334
Western Mail, 343
Westminster, the Duke of, 38
Whippet Tank, 126, 234
Whitehead, Mr. James, 149, 202, 209, 210
Wightman, Sir Owen, 273, 274
Wilson, Lieutenant 70, 72, 82, 84, 87, 88, 89, 90, 92, 94, 100, 112, 148, 174, 204, 206, 228, 230, 237
Wimborne, Lord, 32, 219
Windsor, Duke of, 317
Wolseley, 34, 61
Woods, Colonel, 132
Wormwood Scrubs, 29, 31, 45, 46, 56, 64, 65, 74
Wrisberg, General von, 140

Yorkshire Post, 342
Ypres-Menin, 37

Zeppelin airship, 28
Zwehl, General von, 147

www.ingramcontent.com/pod-product-compliance
Lightning Source LLC
Chambersburg PA
CBHW070958160426
43193CB00012B/1824